T0231196

The Effective

CIO

How to Achieve Outstanding Success through Strategic Alignment, Financial Management, and IT Governance

The Effective

CIO

How to Achieve Outstanding Success through Strategic Alignment, Financial Management, and IT Governance

Eric J. Brown | William A. Yarberry, Jr.

CRC Press
Taylor & Francis Group
Boca Raton London New York

CRC Press is an imprint of the
Taylor & Francis Group, an **informa** business

AN AUERBACH BOOK

Auerbach Publications
Taylor & Francis Group
6000 Broken Sound Parkway NW, Suite 300
Boca Raton, FL 33487-2742

Library of Congress Cataloging-in-Publication Data

Brown, Eric J.
    The effective CIO: how to achieve outstanding success through strategic alignment, financial management, and IT governance / Eric J. Brown, William A. Yarberry, Jr.
      p. cm.
    Includes bibliographical references and index.
    ISBN 978-1-4200-6460-5 (alk. paper)
    1. Chief information officers. 2. Information technology--Management. 3. Information resources management. I. Yarberry, William. II. Title.

HD30.2.B79 2009
658.4'038--dc22
                                              2008044335

Visit the Taylor & Francis Web site at
http://www.taylorandfrancis.com

and the Auerbach Web site at
http://www.auerbach-publications.com

Dedication

To my lovely wife Anne, son Remington, daughter Kira-Nariese, brothers Mark and Tate, and for my parents, Ko`u mau makua i ola mau i ko makou pu`uwai. Mahalo no kou aloha me kou kako`o.

—EJB

To Carol, Will, Libby, and my parents.
Thank you for your love and support.

—WAY

Contents

Preface..xiii

Acknowledgments xv

The Authors...xix

1   Core Skills and Career Development 1
CIO Roles — A Sampler..2
No One Is Planning Your Career..3
Strategic Planning...6
Technical Expertise...8
The Generations..8
What Affects Compensation? 9
CIO Viruses..11
The Magic "AND"...12
References...13

2   Information Technology Governance 15
CIO Success Pills — For Best Results, Take with Governance 15
Alignment — How to Avoid Growing Weeds...16
First Step — Make Sure a *Business* Strategy Exists.................................16
Prioritization..19
Alignment Tools 19
  Value Delivery...22
  IT Risk Management..23
Compliance 24
  Ten Steps to Sarbanes-Oxley Compliance 25
Resource Management...31
Performance Management 31
The Nut-and-Bolt Stuff — Managing Your Own Department with
Governance...32
References...34

3 **Information Technology Finance** **37**

Budgeting 38

Constructing the Budget 40

Rational Buying...43

Managing the IT Investment 46

SOP No. 98-1 50

Cost Management 52

Gray Areas and the Tilt 54

Chargeback..56

Looking Financially Smart 57

Managing Contracts 59

Summary 61

References 62

4 **Project Management**...**63**

Project Organization...64

Systems Development Methodologies 65

    Model #1: Informal Approach — Code First, Fix Later.................65

    Model #2: Traditional Approach — Waterfall 67

    Model #3: Rapid Prototyping/Rapid Application Development
    (RAD) 68

    Model #4: Agile Methodologies..68

    Model #5: Rational Unified Process (RUP) 71

    Model #6: Out of Scope/Embedded Project 73

Project Dynamics 73

    Why Do Projects Fail? 73

    Planning the Work 75

    Project Risk Assessment..76

Scope of the Job — The Program Management Office's (PMO)
Dilemma..81

A Practitioner's Perspective 83

The Future of Project Management..86

References 86

5 **Creating Good Enough Code**...**89**

How Do You Do Good Code?...89

How Important Are Coding Standards? 90

Toolboxes Are Useful 91

Some Example Guidelines 91

Release Philosophy...91

Porting...92

The Ultimate Answer — Hire Good Developers and Keep Them Happy ...93

References 93

6   Enterprise Architecture **95**
    Develop the Business Model 98
    Business Drivers and Selling the Enterprise Architecture (EA) 100
    Information Architecture and Process Modeling Perspective 101
    Technology Architecture Perspective 105
    Road Map to an Effective Architecture..107
        Business Architecture...107
        IT Architecture...108
    Pushing Out the EA — Communicating with Management and
    Employees...109
        The Outsourcing Alternative...110
        Tools...111
        Enforcement and Governance of the EA..111
    Architectural Maturity...114
    Putting It All Together 116
    References...118

7   Mergers and Acquisitions **119**
    The CIO's Golden Opportunity..120
    The CIO's Two Responsibilities 120
        Responsibility #1: Due Diligence..120
            Staff Due Diligence 123
        Responsibility #2: IT Integration..124
            One Approach to Integration..126
    Success Factors...128
    References...128

8   Sourcing **129**
    The Pendulum of Opinion 129
    The Traditional Pros and Cons 130
        Pro — From the Provider's Perspective 130
        Con — From the Customer's Perspective 131
    To Outsource or Not to Outsource? 133
    Xshoring...134
        The Proximity Factor...135
        Keeping Xshoring and Sourcing in Perspective..............................136
        Sourcing Is More Than IT Services...137
    References...137

9   Business Intelligence and Analytics **139**
    Getting Started — Selling Business Intelligence (BI)...........................140
        Value Proposition..141
        Core Components..145

Data Warehouse..145
    A Data Warehouse Alternative.......................................147
Predictive Analytics and Data Mining....................................148
    The Nuts and Bolts of Predictive Analytics....................150
    Data Mining...151
Survey of Business Uses 151
    Security and Data Quality..151
Effective Implementation 153
    Distributing the Intelligence..155
    Organizational Structure 156
    Roadblocks 156
    What Elephant? 158
The Bottom Line...158
References..159

10 Security 161
The Sources of Risk 162
It's about the Money — Script Kiddies Persona Non Grata 162
Defense in Depth..162
Tools and Defense Automation 163
    Frameworks 165
Telephone Security..166
A Checklist for Building Security 167
Some Comments from Security Practitioners.........................168
References..176

11 Training...179
Tools...180
User Needs Vary 181
How Much Training Is Needed?..181
Seminars or Vendor-Specific Training for IT 182
The Harsh Punishment of Silo Knowledge 182
Knowledge Management 183

12 Effective Use of Consultants...185
Becoming a Skilled Buyer of Professional Services 185
    On One Side of the Table: The Consultant's Objective...186
    On the Other Side of the Table: The CIO's Objective....186
Matching Interests 187
Some Miscellaneous Defense Tactics 189
Knowledge Transfer 191
A Few Closing Comments about Consultants 191
Reference 191

13   Operations **193**
      Tree Houses Are Great for Kids 193
      Management Frameworks... 193
      Change, Configuration, and Release Management 194
      Help Desk, Incident and Problem Management 195
      Capacity Management, Service Levels, Availability, Job Scheduling........ 195
      Day-to-Day Management 197
      Some Common-Sense Approaches to Good Operations 197
      Cloud Computing 198
      The Bottom Line — Discipline... 199
      References.. 199

14   Futures..**201**
      Society and Demographics... 202
      Technology 203
      References... 206

15   CIO Interviews **207**

Appendices

A   Examples of Key IT General Controls................................**225**

B   Examples of Key IT Application Controls.........................**231**

C   Project Management Artifact Examples............................**237**

D   IT Risk Assessment Checklist **247**

E   Due Diligence Checklist for Mergers and Acquisitions (Business) **257**

F   Due Diligence Checklist for Mergers and Acquisitions — IT...........**281**

G   Example IT Policies and Direction for "XYZ Corp".........**285**

H   Recommended Reading..**315**

Index **317**

Preface

Many books treat the chief information officer (CIO) as some remote, purely rational decision machine rather than as a fully realized human being. CIOs, like other executives, want excitement, visible success, challenge, job satisfaction, and, of course, high compensation. To make our points more relevant to day-to-day information technology (IT) management life, we interviewed successful CIOs and others performing the real work of running an organization's information factory. In our opinion, too much of the IT literature is excessively abstract; the practitioner may wonder "This is all great but how do I get started in *my* shop?" We have included governance checklists, sample IT controls, merger and acquisition recommendations, a framework for IT policies, and other practical materials. Though it is a bit overworked, the phrase "news you can use" seems to aptly summarize our approach.

As Yogi Berra observed "The future ain't what it used to be." It is both better and worse than the Jetsons™ portrayed in their cartoons. Energy shortages, health care costs, security breakdowns, an aging workforce, relentless competition — all challenge the CIO of the early 21st century. Offsetting these threats are massive technology improvements, easier flow of people and ideas across national boundaries, advances in IT management theory and its alignment with the business, and a positive shift in the attitude of senior management toward the potential uses of technology.

The philosopher Bertrand Russell said that "no matter how eloquently a dog may bark, he cannot tell you that his parents were poor but honest." We view IT governance in the same light. An IT organization that tries to prosper or scale without governance is like the dog that tries to communicate complex thoughts — it is just not going to happen. In Chapter 2 we outline the core elements that need to be in place for effective governance. Chapter 3, almost a corollary to governance, is a highly practical discussion on managing your department's money. Knowing about money and the basics of finance is a good way to gain acceptance by senior businesspeople; cash is the universal language. We asked our trusty legal advisor, Alison Meyer Van, to give us some tips on her specialty, IT and telecom contracts.

To advance in any company, you need a good "sound bite." Implementing a project that everyone wants, and doing it on time and within budget, is a primo sound bite that will stick with you for a long time. Chapter 4 includes the pros and cons of various approaches, some best practices, and a practical perspective by Chris Chambliss, Vice President (VP) of the Program Management Office (PMO) at NCI Building Systems. Chapter 5 is a short, follow-up chapter focusing on nut-and-bolt code development and how you can improve quality and throughput.

In Chapter 6 we discuss the value of a strong architecture and how it needs to be built from the bottom up, based on the requirements of the business. Questions of architecture have to be addressed during mergers and acquisitions, which is covered in Chapter 7. Depending on your firm's philosophy of acquisition, you could absorb the acquired or merged firm's IT functions into a central group, build interfaces, and let them remain as a silo group, or choose some other configuration. Whatever the end result, it is easier if the process and strategy is formal and conscious rather than reactive.

By the time this book goes to print, the United States may or may not be in a recession. Either way, outsourcing will continue to be a way of life as baby boomers retire and the dearth of skilled IT talent becomes more obvious. As pointed out in Chapter 8, sourcing is not about some massive job loss in the United States; by 2015 there will be many more skilled jobs than people, so the trend will continue. The CIO's job is to do it well.

The mathematicians and logical analysis enthusiasts among our readers will enjoy Chapter 9 on business intelligence and analytics. We could have written an entire book on this topic alone. Proactive CIOs will create the data standards, tools, and educational structures that enable this growing function.

The dour New England Puritans were fond of quoting the lines, "we are pilgrims going to and fro, in this world of earthly woe." Things have gotten a bit better since then, but there are hackers and terrorists who would take us back centuries and destroy or destabilize capitalist organizations and governments. In addition, online thieves are going after financial assets. Governments and regulatory bodies, in response, are developing demanding regulations and standards (think PCI for credit cards). In Chapter 10 we talk about the contents of a security plan and also present a couple of interviews from practitioners.

We wrap up the book with chapters on training, tips on the proper and effective use of consultants, IT operations, and some stargazing into the future of IT. Chapter 15 is the final and perhaps the most important chapter — interviews with highly successful CIOs provide practical, no-fluff lessons on how to manage large IT departments. So many times we hear individual perspectives that are thinly veiled agendas to get us to buy something or move in a certain direction. In contrast, these are, as Detective Joe Friday would say, "just the facts…."

Consistent with our philosophy of including "news you can use," we developed appendices that can be used as templates for IT governance, acquisitions, control checklists, and other purposes.

Reader corrections, comments, praise, or chastisements are always welcome. Please send e-mails to Eric J. Brown at ebrown@ncilp.com or to both of us at TheEffectiveCIO@iccmconsulting.net.

Acknowledgments

Many individuals contributed both directly and indirectly to this book. Joel Garmon, Director of Information Security for Florida Power & Light, provided real-world insights into current security trends as well as an introduction to his boss, Dennis Klinger, Vice President and Chief Information Officer, who contributed a broad-based perspective on IT management. David Finn, CIO at Texas Children's Hospital, gave us confidence that previous background is no impediment to the top IT job, even if that includes a stint in the theater arts.

Chris Chambliss, VP of the PMO at NCI Building Systems, contributed a refreshingly candid perspective of project management. Clare Cooper, owner of Aircoop Technologies, gave us a solid understanding of the implications of SOP98 as well as some insights into the *real politic* of systems development.

Sometimes, we in the information technology business really enjoy hearing from those who consume our services. Brad Robeson, Executive Vice President and Chief Operating Officer of NCI Building Systems, impressed us with his daily use of business analytics to find both financial and operational efficiency opportunities. We included his comments in a sidebar in Chapter 9 on business intelligence and analytics. Tracy Forrest, IT manager at NCI, supplied details of the day-to-day support and development requirements that enable Robeson and others to see useful summaries on their business intelligence dashboard.

We need to include two more valuable contributors from NCI: Marge Muniz, Director of Information Security and Sarbanes-Oxley Compliance, contributed a wealth of information on IT segregation of duties and good security practices; and Quintin Prior, Vice President of Operations, outlined a vision of an effective operations infrastructure, along with some examples of his favorite do's and don'ts; the words "nonstandard and unmanageable" are not within his lexicon of acceptable practice.

If there are authors who do not get into a time crunch as the book manuscript submission deadline grows near, we would certainly like to meet them. Late in our schedule, we asked Mark Radulovich, President of Process Advisors, to help with research and ideas for the book. He dug into operations, security, code development, training, and effective use of outside resources, providing us with a number of useful insights. Thanks Mark — we will take you to a restaurant nicer than the 59 Diner one of these days.

Mark Collier, Vice President of Technology at Secure Logix, supplied a vendor's perspective on IT security for both data and voice. Unlike some others on the provider's side of the table, Collier tells it like it is and does not promote his or other technologies beyond what they can practically do. Speaking of someone who tells it like it is — we are grateful to Alison Meyer Van, a Houston, Texas-based attorney specializing in IT contracts and negotiations, for the practical tips on managing contracts. Pat Graham, CIO of Centerpoint Energy, gave us informal tips on motivating employees, handling acquisitions, and proactively suggesting innovative uses of existing IT capabilities to business executives.

We thoroughly enjoyed talking with the CIOs who agreed to be interviewed for the book. We already mentioned David Finn and Dennis Klinger. George Conklin, Senior Vice President and CIO, CHRISTUS Health, provided a fascinating view of how IT and health care are moving toward better, more targeted, and ultimately less-costly services to people in the United States and other nations. Harold D. Bates, Certified Public Accountant (CPA), Executive Vice President and Chief Information Officer (EVP/CIO), Community Resource Credit Union, shows us again the importance of core business knowledge to a successful CIO.

And let us not forget to recognize our friends at Auerbach/Taylor & Francis: John Wyzalek, Stephanie Morkert, Linda Leggio, and Vice President Rich O'Hanley. This is Yarberry's third book through this publisher, and each time it has been a pleasure to work with the helpful and mercifully tolerant staff.

We conclude our acknowledgments with some individual thanks.

Brown: I thank all those who have provided informal but important support — my wife for tolerating the distractions of writing a book during my "off" hours; Norman Chambers, CEO, President and Chairman of the Board; all the executives and employees at NCI Building Systems for allowing me the opportunity to work for such a great company and support one of my lifelong goals; and Dr. James Scott, President; Ron Higgins, Trustee; Wendy Takemoto, Director of IT; and all of the trustees, administrators, students, and alumni at Punahou School for entrusting me in implementing a vision for Punahou School that has set the mark for all other educational institutions across the globe to follow.

Yarberry: I too thank NCI Building Systems, which has provided me with encouragement, material, and a congenial atmosphere for writing this book. As these words are being written, my patient wife Carol is anxious for me to resume life, including working down my heavy "household chores" debt, accumulated over weekends of writing. Robert A. Sandifer, former VP of MIS for Malone & Hyde, gave me an early education in the challenging art of managing skilled developers on a "low fat" budget; fairness, respect, and encouragement were his primary tools of motivation. I owe much to my high school science teacher, Mrs. Coralee Jones, who showed vision and respect for an awkward high school student, many years ago. Finally, I appreciate the support of my professional clients, whose faith in my company gives me exposure to new ideas and the freedom to use them.

Eric J. Brown
The Woodlands, Texas

William A. Yarberry, Jr.
Houston, Texas

The Authors

Eric J. Brown, RCDD, is a senior technology executive with more than 20 years experience implementing global IT solutions throughout Asia Pacific, the European Union, and Middle Eastern regions. He is currently the Executive Vice President and Chief Information Officer (CIO) of NCI Building Systems, Inc., the largest manufacturer and marketer of metal building components and preengineered metal building systems in North America. With a workforce of 5,000 employees, NCI Building Systems provides extensive metal product lines under well-recognized brand names.

After joining NCI in June 2004, Brown developed an IT vision and strategy designed to strongly link information technology with NCI's key business objectives. The Information Technology Department has operational, strategic, and fiscal responsibility for the innovation, implementation, and advancement of technical solutions for all NCI divisions.

Prior to his position with NCI, Brown has been CIO of Punahou School in Honolulu, Hawaii; Senior Vice President and CIO for a global travel industry software development company; Vice President and CIO for a Chevron/Texaco company; and an executive with KPMG Consulting. In addition, he founded a professional services firm, cofounded two software consulting firms, and held a key position in two international start-ups. Past publications include "Lessons Learned in Telecom Negotiations" in *CIO Decisions*; "Create an MA&D Ready IS Organization" in *Gartner CIO Signature Report*; and "Achieving Success as a CIO" in *Aspatore Books*.

William A. Yarberry, Jr., CPA, CISA, is President, ICCM Consulting LLC, based in Houston, Texas. His practice is focused on IT governance, Sarbanes-Oxley compliance, security consulting, and business analytics for cost management. He was previously a senior manager with Pricewaterhouse-Coopers, responsible for telecom and network services in the Southwest region. Yarberry has more than 30 years experience in a variety of IT-related services including application development, internal audit management, outsourcing negotiations and administration, and Sarbanes-Oxley consulting.

He is the author of the first and second editions of *Computer Telephony Integration* and the coauthor of *Telecommunications Cost Management*. In addition, he has written over 20 professional articles on topics ranging from wireless security to change management. One of his articles, "Audit Rights in an Outsource Environment," received the Institute of Internal Auditor's Outstanding Contributor Award.

Prior to joining PricewaterhouseCoopers, Yarberry was director of Telephony Services for Enron Corporation. He was responsible for operations, planning, and architectural design for voice communications servers and related systems for more than 7,000 employees. Yarberry is a University of Tennessee Phi Beta Kappa graduate in Chemistry. He earned an MBA at the University of Memphis. He enjoys reading, swimming, occasional scuba diving, and spending time with his family.

Chapter 1

Core Skills and Career Development

For to win one hundred victories in one hundred battles is not the acme of skill. To subdue the enemy without fighting is the acme of skill.

Sun Tzu

A leader gets people to do things on their own, through inspiration, respect, and trust. A boss can order you to do things, sure, but you do them because it's part of the contract.

Craig Newmark, Founder of Craigslist

However beautiful the strategy, you should occasionally look at the results.

Winston Churchill

Chief information officers (CIOs) vary in appearance, age, gender, educational background, hobbies, and personality. There is no average CIO. However, successful CIOs have a core set of skills which allows them to succeed in an age of complexity and constantly shifting business requirements. In the same way that a "new" dictionary cannot have all new words (it would be practically useless), we do not present in *The Effective CIO* a large number of absolutely new ideas and concepts. Our intent is to outline the skills, challenges, and important management and information technology subject matter to help you with your own career and

1

long-term strategic planning. Every successful person acknowledges the need for discipline — going beyond the "order-taking" mindset and deliberately working toward increased personal productivity, satisfaction, and contribution to the business. The following sections are a high-level road map to becoming an effective CIO.

CIO Roles — A Sampler

In the 1960s, information technology (IT) was a back-room, low-prestige operation. The "electronic data processing (EDP) manager" would typically not be on the same social, educational, or organizational level as, for example, the vice president (VP) of finance or the head of manufacturing. Roll forward to the 21st century and the CIO is now blessed with acceptance into the "senior leadership club" but challenged by responsibilities never imagined in the past. Following are some of the roles the new CIO is expected to play:

- Providing technical strategy that seamlessly segues into the corporate business strategy — even in the absence of a well-defined business plan and implementation road map. As Sun Tzu said, "Strategy without tactics is the slowest route to victory. Tactics without strategy is the noise before defeat."
- Maintaining a computing and communications (people, data, phone, cell, etc.) infrastructure that is always available.
- Having knowledge and foresight enough to develop an architecture that, after implementation, enables the business to provide many new services, reduce costs, and streamline operations *with existing infrastructure and systems*. In other words, you can avoid the scenario where the chief executive officer (CEO) says "I want to do X" and your response is usually "Great, we'll need to install Y to make it happen and it will cost $Z."
- Ensuring that the IT portfolio fund is utilized and managed properly. Dollars go toward high-value return-on-investment (ROI) projects that support the business strategy.
- Hiring the right people, having a tier one Rolodex, chock-a-block full of trusted contractors, and retaining high performers.
- Developing and maintaining a spot-on IT governance structure that does all the things governance is supposed to do — ensure alignment with business goals, ensure proper controls (e.g., change management, security), provide communications up and down the management chain, monitor progress, and manage risk.
- Proactively develop strategic project ideas and suggestions for the business — "the art of the possible." This is the opposite of the order-taker perspective of your muscle car era predecessors.

- Working to seamlessly integrate acquisitions into the IT/business fabric of the organization, or inversely, help to divest subsidiaries without undue disruption.
- Keeping the lid on expenses. Not only do the high-profile new projects need to be managed, but the day-to-day operating expenses and budget must be scrutinized as well (see Chapter 3 for cost-management tips).
- Translate, communicate, and educate. To paraphrase former President George H.W. Bush, you need to promote the "vision thing." Short-term thinking is the enemy of effective IT, and the CIO must constantly translate (from "geek speak" to English) and communicate (two way) with the business — here is the plan, here are the benefits, and here is what will happen if we take a short-term, expedient approach. Assume, for example, that your users have always used bicycles to get to work. You suggest an automobile. "Good idea," they say, "but we're used to handlebars and this steering wheel feels awkward; let's install handlebars in the automobiles." At that point, you and the user's management need to communicate so that the message to the users is clear — we are going to have a little short-term pain for some long-term benefit.

No One Is Planning Your Career

There has never been a recorded instance of an overgrown backyard spontaneously rearranging itself into a neat English garden. Careers work the same way. Here is the etiology of promotions: Some event happens — perhaps someone leaves, a new business line is started, a new office is opened up in a foreign country, or some group is consolidated. The decision maker looks around and thinks "who can do this job? Who has shown initiative, energy, gets along with people, is not afraid of different cultures and has the ability to learn?" X, Y, and Z are considered, and Y gets the job. In essence, Y had the job beforehand but neither Y nor the decision maker knew it — the event simply caused Y's accumulated skill set and achievements to be *recognized*. The point is that advancement is almost completely a function of steady accomplishments, skill, and relationship building, all of which need to be consciously planned. Again, we quote Sun Tzu: "Can you imagine what I would do if I could do all I can?"

The big career jumps may sometimes happen by chance, but they are usually just recognition, like medals pinned on a hero after the battle is over. Following are some suggestions for planning and enhancing your career:

- Get educated. If your intellectual interests are in the realm of computer science or systems, an IT degree may be appropriate. But we emphatically suggest that majoring in IT is unnecessary. Anthropology, geology, math, business, political science, and even theater majors have become CIOs. As you move up the ladder, general knowledge becomes increasingly important. Particularly in larger organizations, narrowly educated managers may bump up against a glass ceiling. Unfair as it may be, there is a "club," and those who know only bits-and-bytes may never be admitted, as those skills, in the bigger scheme of things, are as useful as a chocolate teapot.

■ Diversify your business experience. Take every opportunity to work on projects outside IT so you can get exposure to the core business. Charity and community service projects, where you meet executives from the rest of the organization and other companies, can also be helpful.

■ Learn the business. We will say this dozens of times. If, for example, you are in publishing, you need to understand the terms "back list," "galley proofs," and "over the transom," even if the IT group never gets involved in that part of the business.

■ Learn IT finance. If you are a CTO (chief technology officer) and want to be a CIO, here is one piece of advice that may push you over the top — learn budgets, basic accounting, and a few specialized concepts such as SOP-98. (We will discuss this topic in Chapter 3.) If you can stand up in a senior management meeting and say, "If this project is implemented it will improve earnings by 2 cents per share, our operating margin will increase by 200 basis points, and our operating costs will reduce by $10 million annually," then you have gone a long way toward membership in the club. Money is the *lingua franca* of the boardroom.

■ Show enthusiasm for analytics. Whether you or your staff does business analytics or you merely provide the tools, showing support for this approach shows you "get it." Businesses are becoming almost mind-numbingly complex, with global supply chains, constant product innovations, and changing customer demands. Analytics identifies critical bottlenecks, inefficiencies, customer preferences, and other vital information.

■ Publish your performance. IT usually gets projects funded from the business units (corporate being one of those business units). To show you are a responsible steward of your organization resources, use dashboards, benchmarks, six sigma presentations, and other governance-type reporting tools. This accomplishes two things: it tells management how their money is being spent, and it shows you have a grasp of your own department and how it performs.

■ Be proactive. Suppose you are provided a budget of $25 million. You divvy up the pie into operations, ongoing software/hardware maintenance, new internal projects, personnel costs, and a few other categories. Then you start hammering away at each line item on the budget, hoping to stay within the $25 million by the end of the year. That is the way to perhaps keep your job, not the way to advance. You have to be — in a polite way — in the face of the business executives, coming up with ideas on how IT can help with marketing, operational efficiencies, process changes, development of new products, and so forth. Sometimes it does not even need to be anything related to IT. Michael Hites, CIO for New Mexico State University, got frustrated with the university's lack of strategic planning and bugged people for several years to fix it. In the end he got the magic "and" added to his title. He is now Vice President of Planning *and* Technology.[1]

■ Limit the time you spend on mechanical, repetitive activities. Those need to be handled by your direct reports or lower in your organizational structure. Trust whom you hire and whom your hires hire. You need time to focus on higher-order activities.

■ Do not mistreat vendors and consultants. You may not have time to talk to them, but do not take advantage of their subordinate position. There are many hidden relationships within cities, industries, and associations. Unfairness is like a hidden iceberg just waiting for its career-titanic to come along. You never know when you may need that one person whom you previously had taken advantage of and who will no longer work with you or your organization. Think of how many people you may have in your Linkedin community and how many of your contacts have contacts in their Linkedin community. One bad reference or working relationship will permeate the Internet faster than a Bugatti Veyron EB 16.4.

■ Read and comprehend constantly. Find good Web sites and follow current trends. Read books of all kinds. If your commute is long, consider listening to recorded books. Communication skills (nongeek speak) are built on words and concepts, so consider reading as part of your job.

■ Be aware of the unwritten rules and foreign culture differences. There are lots of them. People sometimes say one thing but mean something else. The nuances of body language, clothes, stride, voice tone, and even pupil dilation[2] hold clues to the hidden social fabric. In some cultures, nodding yes may mean they understand what you said but that does not mean they agree with what you said. When do you shake a hand and when do you not? Other nuances of behavior include when and how to sip your tea and how to hold the cup, in what order do you place the business cards you receive on the table in front of you, how do you hand a business card over to another executive, and why do you never ever put your business cards in your front shirt pocket? What is most important to your career is simply the awareness that a hidden world of innuendo exists in the organization and that it can help or hinder your career dramatically (and sometimes unfairly). Following are just a few of the "unposted" rules:

  – Stay positive. Even if it is not directed at them, your management peers will be uncomfortable if your world perspective is consistently negative.

  – Dress as a member of the upper class. You should not overdress for your organization, but dressing cheaply suggests a "paper bag lunch" mentality. You want to look like what you are striving to become. Copy the next level up.

  – Be careful with e-mail. Studies have shown that the higher up on the chain of command, the less text is included in the e-mails of the sender. This does not mean rudeness but merely that complexity at the management level is best handled via face-to-face conversation. And, of course, avoid negative emotion, even if you are ready to send someone a fan, because you are sure he or she will soon be in hell.

– Respect the time of senior people. One of the interesting traits of the most seasoned executives is that they have the ability to project an image of calm and availability when in fact they are nearly always pressed for time. Do not be fooled. Chit chat works for about 10 seconds; get on with your business and then leave. Occasionally senior executives are not skilled at closing a conversation, so you need to gracefully do it for them.

– Do not go into critical meetings without an agenda.

– Strenuously avoid topics that cause dissention between people — politics, religion, pros and cons of various groups, sex, and even history if it brings up sensitive subjects. A corporation or nonprofit organization is a place where people come together to earn a living and work; it is not a platform for zealotry.

– Positive extremes will help your career. For whatever reason, we are attracted to and retain memories of events, places, and people out of the ordinary. For example, consider the following unusual life events or personal characteristics. Your "interesting personality profile" is above average if you have:

  • Gone night diving in a cave and only surfaced when your flashlight is on the blink, your glow sticks have run out, and your air pressure gauge is below 200 psi
  • Mastered four languages, including medieval Occitan
  • Written to Thorstein Veblen as "Uncle Thor"
  • Been bitten by a shark and rescued by the Coast Guard

– Help everyone you can. All the world's religions recognize the core principle that "Giving = Power." In one sense, it is a selection process; those who can give to others have extra power (money, time, or merely energy). Practically, it means you are constantly building a pool of people who are rooting for you. Success comes from the support of superiors, peers, and subordinates.

Strategic Planning

Think. Talk. Plan. Now you are ready to write. Unfortunately, some CIOs believe that 50 cent words, Power Point slides with heavy graphics, and a ream of bond paper are *de rigueur*. In fact, simple is best. Following are some guidelines:

■ Start with business needs. Consider sales projections, markets, changing technology, cost factors, and other service/production factors.

■ Develop a high-level timeline.

- Show how IT can influence and support business plans.
- Break down the plan into sections that relate to the enterprise, specific business units, and anything IT specific, such as infrastructure.
- Create an executive summary in short direct sentences: "By first quarter 2002, we will provide a portal for online ordering and configuration of small- to medium-sized metal buildings."
- Lay out any major technologies or business events that must occur in order for the strategy to be accomplished: "In order to complete our supply chain management system implementation, all business units must be on a common enterprise resource planning (ERP) platform."
- Include a plan B and plan C if funding or other uncertainties may affect the outcome.
- Provide a framework for tracking progress.
- Provide a framework for change management and communication.

Many CIOs avoid a written strategic plan because of the perception that it must be a polished presentation with stratospheric abstractions straight from a high-power consulting firm. "Heck, we just make widgets over here in Midland. I'd be laughed at if I came in with something fancy like this." Here is a dirty little secret: You are not in high school anymore! No English teacher is going to take a red pen and mark it up.[3] The strategic plan need be no more complex than is needed to do the job.

Along similar lines, Stephanie Overby, in a CIO magazine article, debunks four strategic planning myths[4]:

- Technology changes so fast that planning is no longer necessary. Planning is only partially connected to specific technologies. You are trying to execute business goals; if it turns out that your current system will not do the job, maybe some software-as-a-service package will suffice. What matters is that the business is properly supported.
- A strategic plan should be good for 5 years. This might have been true in 1960 but is ridiculous now. You should do a plan because planning gives your current efforts direction. Sticking to a 5-year plan sounds suspiciously like the central committee planning done in former communist countries.
- Small budgets do not need a strategic plan. In this case, size really does not matter. Planning scales both up and down. You still need to plan the outcome, even if smaller dollars are involved.
- You cannot have a strategic plan in IT because your business does not have a strategic plan. The business plan might exist in the CEO's head or in two or three other executives' heads. You can articulate an IT strategy based on conversations and shrewd guesses. You may be able to help the organization by demonstrating how it is done.

Technical Expertise

We will repeat many times in this book the need for business expertise. But you still need to maintain basic technical knowledge. Here is a list of mainline technologies that should be part of your CIO repertoire, at least at a high level:

■ Web development technologies
■ Security
■ Software as a service (SaaS)
■ Cloud computing
■ Business analytics tools
■ Wireless technologies
■ Mobile devices and their options
■ Remote and mobile user support alternatives
■ Virtualization
■ Communications, including IPv6
■ Project management tools/Knowledge sharing tools

The Generations

Regardless of your age, you will be managing and interacting with a variety of generations. The exact labels for the generations are not quite set in stone, but they are roughly as follows:

■ Matures: born 1925–1945
■ Baby Boomers: born 1946–1964
■ Generation X: born 1965–1979
■ Generation Y (also called Millennials and Echo Boomers): born 1980–2000
■ Generation Z (also called Trophy Kids): born 2000 to date

According to futurist James Canton, by 2015 there may be 14 million more jobs than workers to fill them in the United States alone.[5] The implications of this are clear — all managers, including CIOs, will be chasing a scarce resource. Because of the shortage, there will be a greater appetite for hiring and retaining older workers within the next few years. At the same time, having many generations coexisting in the same organization will present a human relations challenge.

Some of the challenges include the following:

■ Huge differences in upbringing. Later generations were raised (at least those from middle class and above families) with much more parental involvement. Some may be accustomed to considerably more praise than received by, for example, baby boomers in their childhood.

- Technology preferences. Telephone, instant messaging (IM), facebook, e-mail, text messaging — all different forms of communications with marked differences in popularity between groups.
- Resistance to perceived arbitrary rules. For example, the idea of staying late just to impress the boss is dying. Generation Y through the Millenials think it is a stupid idea and will resist blatant, nonwork-related "organization man" cultural norms.
- Motivational techniques vary between the generations. Some need praise; some need intense direction and management. Some want to be part of an organization that is green and socially responsible.

These differences are substantial and relevant. In general, the closer an employee is to the millennial age bracket, the more management effort and sensitivity to their perspective is required. It may be that social responsibility is the attribute that keeps a talented developer from jumping ship, rather than the salary. Mentoring will become an increasingly important part of your job — after all, you cannot move up the ladder yourself unless you have someone competent in line to take over.

What Affects Compensation?

Richard Florida's book, *Who's Your City?: How the Creative Economy Is Making Where to Live the Most Important Decision of Your Life*, discusses the importance of location to just about everything in life. Pundits predicted a few years back that global telecommunications would make where you live irrelevant. The reality is just the opposite. Certain deep sociological and economic processes are building up some areas of the world dramatically faster than others. Using a "light map" — a satellite reading of the light intensity of the world superimposed on a map — shows that certain megaregions are responsible for most of the economic growth of the world. When a region becomes known for something, say aerospace engineering, then it attracts talent from other locations. That talent generates wealth and attracts further talent. The city or region spirals upward and even high real estate prices will not dampen the growth. The creative class likes to be with the creative class. So what does this have to do with compensation? Several factors apply:

- You personally will earn more in a megaregion, such as Boston–New York– Washington or San Antonio–Austin–Dallas–Houston. Not only now but for the rest of your career. Money is not everything, but you should be conscious of what you are giving up if you choose to live in less-populated areas.
- On the flip side, you may not be able to offer recruits as much compensation if your organization is located in a medium- or small-sized town. Some ways to compensate include:

- Recruit from a local college.
- Stress that the new hire will have more variety of work than would be the case for a much larger organization.
- Ensure that your shop's technology is not too far behind — small town and old technology is a death knell for your recruiting efforts.
- Be more explicit in career path opportunities.
- Move staff around to give them a chance to learn new technologies.

■ Education matters. A November 2007 *Computerworld* analysis of a bachelor's degree versus a master's degree showed a substantial increase across a number of IT jobs for those with the advanced degree.[6] For example, a computer hardware engineer with 5 to 9 years experience earns $84,200 with a bachelor's degree and $95,300 with a master's degree (13% increase). A database administrator shows a 15% increase for a master's degree. Presumably such numbers apply to CIOs as well. In addition, an MBA demonstrates a commitment to business strategic knowledge which most certainly garners the approval of management.

■ Your business orientation will greatly influence your compensation. If you are perceived as a techie and not interested in the "mundane" problems of the organization, your compensation will be capped. It is good to show enthusiasm for technology but always sandwich that fervor in a bun of practical business value.

■ The profit margins of your firm will dictate the ability of your superior (CEO or perhaps the chief financial officer [CFO]) to adjust your bonus and salary. Some firms just do not have the margins to be generous. Investigate before signing on.

■ Your likeability affects your income. How good it would be if compensation were truly objective and based solely on organizational contribution. As one of Sir Thomas Moore's servants said in the movie *A Man for All Seasons*, "I wish rainwater was beer, but it ain't." It is really not as hard as one would think to increase likeability. Do you greet international business associates in their own language? Do you talk about family or tell yet another late night drinking story? Are you pleasant to subordinates, especially administrative assistants? *Side note:* It is the kiss of death to be harsh with them; they have a powerful network that eventually ties into the CEO. Of course, there are CIOs with high incomes who ignore these guidelines. They are exceptions. The great majority of businesspeople improve their careers and compensation by respectful and considerate behavior. In his popular *Harvard Business Review* article "Harnessing the Science of Persuasion," Robert B. Cialdini, Regents' Professor of Psychology at Arizona State University, notes the following[7]:

> Managers can use similarities to create bonds with a recent hire, the head of another department, or even a new boss. Informal conversations during the workday create an ideal opportunity to discover at least one

common area of enjoyment, be it a hobby, a college basketball team, or reruns of Seinfeld. The important thing is to establish the bond early because it creates a presumption of goodwill and trustworthiness in every subsequent encounter. It's much easier to build support for a new project when the people you're trying to persuade are already inclined in your favor.

■ Never forget Tom Sawyer. Tom was pretty good at generating enthusiasm for whitewashing fence boards. It is hard to duplicate his success, but your success will depend in part on maintaining a stable infrastructure and completing projects on time. Enthusiasm is infectious and ultimately affects compensation by improving your department's execution of the plan. Catch a junior developer doing something right; get one of your managers to find some code that he has documented well. Send the developer an e-mail — "Good documentation, Fred. Keep it up." You have just gotten 10% more work out of the guy for the next 6 months.

There are some indirect factors that affect compensation as well. Network strength is probably the most important and includes not only your direct associates but the associates of your associates. Oddly enough, the value of your network, in terms of obtaining promising career opportunities, depends more on second- and third-tier relationships than on primary relationships. These second- and third-tier segments of your personal network, called "weak ties" because they are friend-of-a-friend, provide a sufficiently different contact environment to provide real benefit. In contrast, your immediate friends probably run in the same circles, both physically and socially, as you. So you and they are aware of the same opportunities. Of course, from a mathematical perspective, secondary and tertiary contacts are proportional to your primary population, so it makes sense to keep up your network at all times. One of the most significant career errors CIOs can make is to drop contacts when the current job feels secure and then try to quickly ramp them up ("remember me") if it is time to move on. Networks can include former peers, subordinates, bosses, and association contacts.

CIO Viruses

There are all sorts of viruses. Some are mental constructs that damage the host's career. Three of the most insidious are the following:

■ Information cocooning. The CIO hides out in his or her office and communicates primarily electronically. He or she cuts him- or herself off from information other than what he or she wants to hear. He or she has noise cancellation headphones on when the honking bus is headed his or her way.

- Technology isolation. Building and maintaining systems that are proprietary and quirky, not able to be integrated into any new hardware or software. The implications are horrendous: staff has to be maintained who will work on technology that becomes increasingly irrelevant to the rest of the world. Business options are limited, change becomes difficult, and, of course, vendor support begins to slip.
- Zealotry temptations. Highly technical people, particularly those new to the workforce, tend to become enthused with a "religion" of technology. They may love Microsoft and distrust open source or vice versa. Maybe MySQL is perceived as the preferred tool over some other database. The CIO should steer clear of emotional approaches to technology. Decisions should be made based on standardized architecture, which itself changes based on business needs.

The Magic "AND"

What is so great about the "AND" word? It is your ticket to a more interesting and challenging job. If you can be CIO and "X," then your job just got expanded, possibly a lot. For example, David Finn at Texas Children's Hospital has the title "VP *and* CIO/Privacy and Information Security Officer." As we mentioned earlier, Michael Hites, CIO for New Mexico State University, is Vice President of Planning *and* Technology. Proactive CIOs can create many opportunities for themselves, far beyond the traditional IT management role. Examples of additional roles include VP or executive vice president (EVP) for the following:

- Business process
- Enterprise risk
- Business development (new product lines, acquisitions, etc.)
- Global outsourcing (not merely IT)
- Strategic planning
- Research
- Advanced projects
- Knowledge management

The point we are making is that if you view the IT organization as a pyramid with yourself at the top, it might appear there is nowhere else to go. The reality is that organizations can create titles and responsibilities that help them and you succeed. If you are a strong manager and go beyond the IT perimeter, you will find plenty of opportunities. After all, if lawyers (a specialty group) can become CEOs, why not CIOs?

References

1. Overby, Stephanie. Strategic Planning in the Real World. *CIO Magazine* (February 1, 2008): 32.
2. In the middle ages, some upper-class women took belladonna, which artificially enlarged the pupils. Larger pupils implied a stronger romantic interest in the person being courted. Unfortunately, it also led to vision damage and heart palpitations.
3. We both have great respect for English teachers, who with great effort push back the tides of ignorance and civilize our children!
4. Overby, Stephanie. Strategic Planning in the Real World. *CIO Magazine* (February 1, 2008): 25.
5. Canton, James. *The Extreme Future* (New York: Dutton, 2006), 95.
6. The Value of a Degree. *Computerworld* (November 12, 2007): 66.
7. Cialdini, Robert. Harnessing the Science of Persuasion. *Harvard Business Review* (October 1, 2001): 2.

Chapter 2

Information Technology Governance

Companies with effective IT governance have profits that are 20% higher than companies pursuing similar strategies.

Peter Weill, Jeanne Ross, *IT Governance*

CIO Success Pills — For Best Results, Take with Governance

You cannot be successful without governance. On second thought, perhaps that statement is too broad. If you are literally a one-person shop where development, priority setting, budgeting, operational controls, and strategy are all inside your own head, then formal governance is not required; for all others, implementing effective governance is the only option.

Information technology governance is for practical people. Once the structure is in place, the effort to maintain it pales in comparison to the rehabilitation effort, costs, and lack of performance caused by poor alignment with business objectives, inability to manage projects, and mishaps that could have been prevented by good controls.

If you put the term "IT governance" into Google, you will find a landscape of articles, tools, and somewhat abstract constructs, with an example here and there to make a point. In writing this book, we have assumed that real chief information officers are very busy people who do not have the time to wade through abstractions;

instead, they need answers or at least actionable ideas. With that philosophy in mind, the following sections describe some of the more common components of a strong governance system. The areas of emphasis will vary greatly between organizations, but the governance elements will apply to all.

By implementing strong governance, you will also join the ranks of highly successful executives in many U.S. and international firms. One McKinsey study found that investors pay large premiums for investments in firms with high governance standards. Premiums ranged from an average of 13% in North America and Western Europe to 20% to 25% in Asia and Latin America and even higher in Eastern Europe and Africa.[1]

Alignment — How to Avoid Growing Weeds

If you water and fertilize a plot of soil in your backyard, you will certainly get plant growth. If the plants are weeds rather than vegetables or flowers, you have spent time and effort with no benefit. That is a pretty close analogy to IT groups whose activities are not constantly tuned and monitored so that they support what is important to the business. A classic example (we cannot remember where we heard this) was the systems programmer in a large hospital who was told to improve response time for the back office accounting functions. He succeeded. Unfortunately, the solution was to reconfigure the customer information control system (CICS) so that priority was always given to accounting; meanwhile, patients were lined up and out the door trying to get admitted into the hospital. Alignment is the number one principle of governance. Figure 2.1 illustrates some actions and processes for improving alignment.

First Step — Make Sure a *Business* Strategy Exists

We could logically assume that IT needs to line up with a well-established, fully articulated business strategy. But what if the organization lacks a nuanced business strategy? What if the strategy is a one-liner — "Sell more stuff" or "buy raw materials cheap and maintain a big margin?" If so, the CIO must then coax his or her management peers to fill in the details. IT simply cannot provide optimum value if the goals are unclear — are we trying to reduce the speed of delivery, dramatically improve product design, ease the barriers to financial cross-selling, or provide a service that is not available today? To help the organization articulate business goals in a way that enables the CIO to create the right *actionable* strategy, tiers of responsibility should be created:

- Operational/day-to-day advisory groups
- Business unit steering committees
- Executive committees

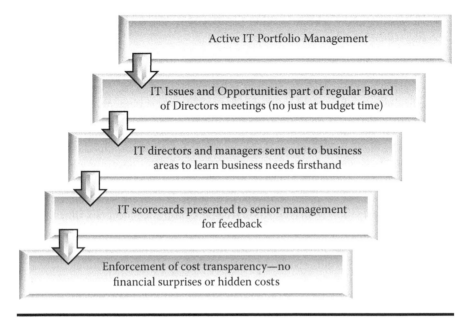

Figure 2.1 Example techniques to improve alignment.

All three tiers are necessary. The executive committees provide a forum for discussing the most global directives and serve to mitigate against suboptimization by competing business units. The business unit steering committees need to define and allocate resources based on immediate needs and an assessment of competitive strategies — how can IT improve our market penetration, reduce costs, identify opportunities, and perhaps create an entirely new market? In Chapter 14 we will discuss some of the demographic changes that will drive change in even the most staid industries. The early 21st century is not your father's world. Japanese teenagers may be driving technologies that will be adopted 3 to 5 years from now; if changes like these will eventually affect the business, the CIO needs to introduce the potential impact to appropriate levels of management. The third level, operations and small department groups, represents the ground-level stakeholders who shape the day-to-day activities of the IT function. If a clerk in payables notices that the percentage of invoices that do not match receiving documents is increasing, there needs to be a forum where such early warnings can be vetted. Some functions of an executive-level steering committee include:

- Budgeting and spending
- Approving projects, both business and infrastructure oriented
- Monitoring the progress of key projects and the overall IT strategic road map
- Communicating strategic goals to all parties so that IT activities can be properly aligned to those goals

- Reviewing and decision making for special issues, such as acquisition and divestment of IT-related resources
- Monitoring IT scorecard metrics; this includes a periodic report on IT operational issues
- Observing potential opportunities from emerging technologies (must be specifically related to the business, not broad-brush statements such as "total Internet content is growing exponentially")

Figure 2.2 shows a typical steering committee structure for a medium-to-large organization. In some cases, there are subcommittees by business unit which report up to the enterprise-wide committees.

Committees need to meet relatively frequently. For example, at CHRISTUS Health, the Information Management Oversight Committee meets six times a year.

IT projects, as one of the major indirect costs in most organizations, should be managed as a portfolio, much as a mutual fund manager matches his or her assets to the strategy of the fund. The basics of portfolio management include:

- Maintain a listing of current and previous investments (projects, infrastructure). Provide information at a relatively granular level — total cost, ongoing maintenance, business issues, and return on investment (ROI).
- Perform an annual or semiannual review of effectiveness. Did the investment provide the intended benefits?
- Target future projects or enhancements based on future state. Try to gracefully retire "the dogs."
- Balance the portfolio based on risk. Basic probability theory says that expected value from any activity equals the probability of success times its cost. "Squeaky wheel" business executives who push through high-risk projects without a corresponding high payoff are misusing or at least suboptimizing the organization's capital.

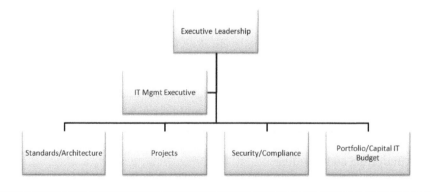

Figure 2.2   Example committee structure for a medium-to-large organization.

- Bring in traditional financial measures of capital investment. For example, ROI, payback period, and capital allocation policy can help make decisions more objective.
- Identify redundant and mutually exclusive projects.
- Provide an easy tool for discussion by business executives. With a reasonably objective portfolio ranking based on enterprise-wide return, the CIO has the support he or she needs. No need for the heroic but doomed role of "enterprise savior."

Figure 2.3 shows one example of how IT strategy is conceptually linked to the organization's mission. For-profit firms seek to maximize the wealth of the shareholder; nonprofits seek to provide services to their constituents in an efficient and cost-effective manner. Traversing down the pyramid from these ultimate goals, IT's role is defined in increasingly concrete objectives. This format reinforces the need for infrastructure expenditure, whose value may not always be clear to the business executive ultimately funding the IT group.

Constructing a pyramid or similar conceptual structure assumes that you understand your firm's economic drivers. In fact, knowing the drivers and related metrics used by the business units simplifies your strategic planning — the metrics of IT should mesh with those of its stakeholders. In *The New CIO Leader,* Marianne Broadbent uses the example of customer retention.[2] Assume a firm invests in new customers, expecting a loss in the first year but profits over the lifetime of the relationship. The lifetime value of the customer is essential to understand so that pricing, marketing, and other business initiatives can be appropriately targeted. IT's systems should be sufficiently robust to provide such information.

Prioritization

Prioritization of effort, not merely projects, is a component of alignment. The choice of projects is not a decision based on "useful" versus "useless"; it is making the distinction between multiple worthy efforts. Although egos and influence will always play a part, having a defined prioritization process will help IT focus on high ROI activities. Figure 2.4 illustrates the general methodology.

Alignment Tools

Alignment has its own set of psychological tools. Being a good sport and "hail-fellow-well-met" is not sufficient. The CIO needs to develop specific techniques for ensuring his or her model of business reality is congruent with his or her business peers and executive superiors.

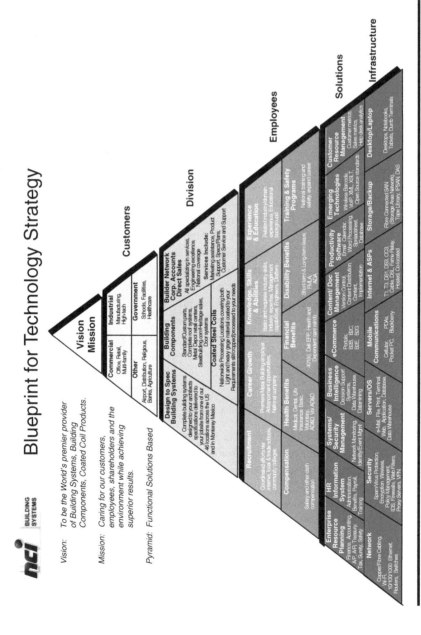

Figure 2.3   Blueprint linking information technology strategy to enterprise mission.

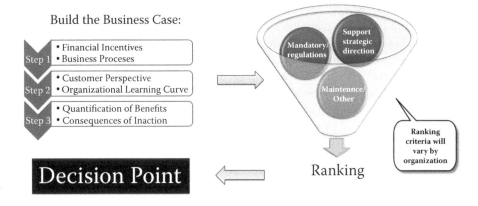

Figure 2.4 General methodology for prioritizing information technology projects and activities.

- Observe what they read, what conferences they attend, and what is communicated to the press and shareholders. For example, page 5 of NCI's 2006 annual report states the following:

  > We have accelerated our efforts to achieve another major synergy, which is the migration of RCC's automated engineering system to NCI's engineered building systems division. This advanced system should enable an unprecedented reduction in the cycle time of our engineering design, pricing and detailing functions, as automated tasks that previously took weeks are completed in minutes.

- Follow the dictates of "emotional intelligence." Get to know their interests, preferences, and needs. Find opportunities for social interaction.
- Make the rounds — communications requires both physical presence and delivering the message. The message needs to be clear — IT lives only by its success in serving the firm's business goals.
- Avoid emotion (except enthusiasm) in e-mails and formal communications. During the Civil War, the dashing Confederate cavalry general, J.E.B. Stuart, failed to keep Robert E. Lee informed of Union troop movements, partially contributing to Lee's defeat at Gettysburg. Afterward, Lee quietly reproached Stuart; no harshness was necessary — Stuart was thoroughly humbled. Any more emotion would have reduced the effectiveness of an otherwise capable general.
- Identify the metrics that drive their compensation. For example, one firm's tax department insisted that a much needed new version of their sales tax software be implemented at fiscal year-end. What was not completely clear during the planning phase was that implementing the new version at that time would delay last-minute sales order processing for the year, which meant that executive compensation would be adversely affected. Avoid tugging on Superman's cape.

■ Make sure their connectivity, laptops, handheld devices, and so forth are current and working properly. Busy executives, by the nature of their positions, will evaluate the CIO in a series of success and failure points. Because humans are not particularly good at assigning weights to events, there is a tendency to see a series of small successes (e.g., getting their iPhone to work properly) can outweigh a negative event that may have much higher actual impact, such as a missed deadline on a project. Nassim Nicholas Taleb presents an entertaining discussion of this flaw in his book *Fooled by Randomness.*[3]

Value Delivery

Are we doing things that make sense for the business and getting payback for the investment? The CIO needs tools and methods to identify the most productive investments and then to communicate the value to stakeholders at all levels of the organization. According to the IT Governance Institute,[4] there are four critical questions for value delivery:

■ Are we doing the right things?
■ Are we getting the benefits?
■ Are we getting them done well?
■ Are we doing them the right way?

Whenever practical people read such questions, the initial response is "isn't all this rather obvious?" Actually, it is, unless, of course, you have been so focused on delivery that you have not been able to gather perspective. As an aside, one of the quickest ways to evaluate an organization is to look for grease boards, small conference rooms, and sketch pads. If they are missing, the organization may not be one that supports thinking and strategy. Blank, dull walls are anathema to creativity. So the first step to value is to say what value is. And how is that done?

■ Understanding the business drivers
■ Understanding the industry
■ Learning to ignore the loud but unimportant voices
■ Maintaining the right balance between day-to-day operations and strategic functions

Value delivery meshes with strategic planning and the implementation of an enterprise architecture to support the business mission. An important part of value delivery is measurement. This includes traditional measures of project efficiency — was the system produced on time, within budget, and at an acceptable level of quality? These are easy questions to ask but harder to answer than is generally understood. For example, what does "on time" mean when systems specifications change excessively during construction? What does quality mean? Only 2% of code backed out? Happy users? An Oracle database system that avoids duplicating item numbers across various subsidiaries? A highly maintainable, reproducible, sharable, and efficient collection of processes and software which reduces long-term total cost of ownership?

In the world of politics, the pejorative term "demagoguery" implies an amoral pandering to the emotions of the crowd, knowing the end result may likely result in harm to the populace but provide power or position to the demagogue. The counterpart in IT is to provide users exactly what they ask for, regardless of long-term costs or disruption in strategic direction. How many CIOs have been bullied into maintaining antiquated platforms because "everyone is comfortable with the old system's screens," or been forced to postpone architectural consolidations that are clearly in the best economic interests of the enterprise?

At this point, we have aligned IT with the business and refined our understanding of value. Now we need to look at how we avoid getting struck by lightning as we walk away from the state lottery office with our $5 million check — in other words, how do we manage risk?

IT Risk Management

Many CIOs and even auditors have had the nagging feeling that the traditional IT risk analysis — if the truth be told — starts out with what the analyst thinks is the answer. Then the details, weightings, and issues are aligned to show the applications, infrastructure components, and projects that score the highest risk. Such thoughts may be laced with cynicism, but they reflect a central concern — how do I make an ostensibly objective analysis generate results that I know are reasonable, given the organization's technical, business, and regulatory environment?

Consider the following somewhat facetious example: An auditor or someone in the CIO's organization accepts the conventional wisdom that the number of transactions in an application is a factor affecting risk. Further assume that the organization sports a good sense of humor and tolerates a football pool on its intranet, where employees use play money to bet on their favorite teams. Given a large number of sports enthusiasts creating hundreds or thousands of transactions, is the football pool now a higher-risk application?

George Westerman and Richard Hunter, in their book *IT Risk, Turning Business Threats into Competitive Advantage,* argue that IT risk is not based on specific volumes of transactions, dollars, or events. Instead, IT risk is purely based on the *strategic* goals of the enterprise. They identify four key business requirements (the 4A framework[5]) that IT must deliver in order for the organization to succeed:

- ■ Availability. Systems must be up and running. Recovery from failure should be rapid, based on the firm's business requirements.
- ■ Access. Systems should be sufficiently secure to prevent loss and destruction of data but flexible enough to enable employees to do their job.

- Accuracy. Information must be timely, complete, and correct when presented to both internal and external users.
- Agility. Ability to change IT systems to meet new business requirements with requisite speed and reasonable cost.

The last item, agility, is often not included in risk assessments but can have a major impact on a firm's profitability and ability to make strategic changes. For example, suppose an unprofitable division needs to be divested but cannot (without great expense) because the IT systems are so intertwined with corporate functions? What if a major investment in a proprietary solution solves an immediate problem but makes it more difficult to create new products or customer offerings?

The philosophy of risk has often been based on the probability of some cataclysmic, point-in-time event. Those risks continue to exist, but the quiet risks — such as Enron's decision to siphon off unprofitable projects to "Raptor" and "Condor" special-purpose entities, backed up by Enron stock — may have an equal impact.

Another factor perpetrating the traditional quantitative approach to risk assessment is the "comfort of numbers syndrome." At the end of the 19th century, Lord Kelvin said "When you can measure what you are speaking about, and express it in numbers, you know something about it; but when you cannot measure it, when you cannot express it in numbers, your knowledge of it is of a meager and unsatisfactory kind; it may be the beginning of knowledge, but you have scarcely, in your thoughts, advanced it to the stage of science."[6] Roll forward to the 1970s when Harvard MBAs began using HP calculators with near missionary zeal — the conventional wisdom said numbers up, soft concepts down. Then the inevitable reaction began. John Cotter, in his book *The General Managers*, pointed out that most of the vital decisions in business are only partially supported by hard numbers. Business reality is simply too complex to be reduced to equations (although quantitative information is most helpful when available). Bottom line for the CIO: do not settle for counts, transactions, numbers, or the like; they may be useful, but they are not a substitute for strategic risk assessment.

Risk assessment should be a part of any significant IT development project. In Chapter 4, we provide specifics on some models and example calculations. A sample questionnaire for a preliminary risk assessment is shown in Appendix D.

Compliance

The 1997 movie *Titanic* resulted in such emotional outpouring from some viewers that cynics began wearing T-shirts saying "The boat sank, get over it." A comparable IT T-shirt might say "compliance is here to stay, get on with it." CIOs in banking, defense industries, and other highly regulated industries grew up with a compliance mind-set, but some firms, particularly those newly required to meet

Sarbanes-Oxley (SOX) regulations, struggle to adjust. Regulatory compliance is one of the core governance disciplines. Let us use SOX as an example.

Ten Steps to Sarbanes-Oxley Compliance

Anyone reading business magazines and newspapers comes away with the impression that Sarbanes-Oxley requirements are onerous. Section 404 requires both the chief executive officer (CEO) and the chief financial officer (CFO) vouch for the adequacy of internal controls. The external auditors must then independently review management's assertion of adequate internal controls. If there are "material weaknesses" or too many "significant deficiencies," they will not certify compliance (see below for a description of these levels of control weakness).

One problem with the implementation of SOX is that it tends to set a standard for compliance that may be inadequate. Meeting SOX standards (i.e., passing 404) does not imply that a firm or an IT department has the processes in place required to manage its business. Nor does it mean that an optimal level of control exists anymore than having a pulse signifies good health. SOX compliance is the minimum standard, not an optimum standard.

Regardless of your firm's current maturity level, you will need to demonstrate SOX compliance efficiently and honestly. Following are typical steps required to pass section 404:

1. Identify your framework. Most U.S. organizations use CobIT[7] (see www.isaca.org) as a starting point for objectives. The legislation does not specifically require CobIT, but it is accepted by all the major auditing firms.
2. Using CobIT as a reference point, develop a list of controls that are "key" to the successful operation of information technology. These key controls support, ultimately, accurate financial statements.
3. Split key controls into two categories: (a) general controls, which are pervasive across all or most platforms and applications, and (b) application controls. Appendices A and B list example general and application controls, respectively.
4. Review the list with your external auditor. In the first year of SOX compliance for accelerated filers,[8] many firms, fearing the unknown, defined far too many controls as key. As a result, the quantity of testing and consequent funds expended to support 404 compliance was excessive. If you define a control as key, it has to be tested, documented, and remediated if found ineffective and then tested again. At NCI, for example, we started with 165 general controls and as of this writing are down to 32.
5. The external auditors will also be interested in "environmental" practices and organizational structures that strengthen the overall control environment. Unlike the general and application controls discussed earlier, these entity-level controls are typically measured in degrees of compliance and often not

precisely measureable. For example, it is easier to form an opinion on the question "Does your accounts payable system have a built-in check for duplicate payments" than to state unequivocally that "the audit committee represents an informed, vigilant and effective overseer of the financial reporting process." Following is a partial list of representative entity-level questions:

- Are there appropriate policies for developing and modifying accounting systems and controls (including changes to and use of computer programs and data files)?
- Are there defined responsibilities for individuals responsible for implementing, documenting, testing, and approving changes to computer programs that are purchased or developed by information systems personnel or users?
- Are systems conversions well controlled (e.g., completed pursuant to written procedures or plans)?
- Are appropriate approvals from management required prior to allowing an individual access to specific applications and databases?
- Are IT personnel prohibited from having incompatible responsibilities or duties in user departments?
- Has management established procedures to prevent unauthorized access to, or destruction of, documents, records (including computer programs and data files), and assets?
- Is data processing access to nondata-processing assets restricted (e.g., blank checks)?
- Is physical security over IT assets (both IT department and users) reasonable given the nature of the company's business?
- Is there a dedicated security officer function that monitors IT processing activities and are there periodic reports to the board of directors and audit committee on the current state of IT security at the company?
- Are there systems to monitor and respond to potential business interruptions due to incidents stemming from malicious intrusions, and to update security protocols to prevent them? Are security violations and other incidents automatically logged and reviewed?
- Does the company conduct periodic reviews or audits of IT security? If yes, are the results of the review or audit reported to the board of directors or audit committee?

6. In order for the external auditors to acknowledge that your firm is in compliance with section 404 of Sarbanes-Oxley requirements, detailed testing of the controls is necessary. From their perspective, the value and reliability of IT controls testing falls into three tiers:
   - Lowest reliance: Self-testing done by the IT group. This does not imply lack of professionalism or expertise in the testing. Indeed, IT self-testing is likely to be the most effective, because the team members have a strong level of systems knowledge. But the external auditors consider it to be the

least independent, because IT is essentially auditing itself. An example of IT testing might be a review of change control compliance — out of ten programs with a compile date in the current year, how many have corresponding authorization and testing documented in the change management system?

■ Medium reliance: Internal Audit performs a set of well-defined tests to show the compliance of each key control, both general and application. Standard workpaper format and adherence to statistical guidelines for sampling are expected. As a practical matter, the performance of Internal Audit's SOX testers can affect the cost of the external audit. If the workpapers are highly organized, well annotated and easy to review, then E&Y, PwC, KPMG, or other outside firms develop confidence in the results and minimize their own independent testing. In a review of NCI's SOX workpapers a few years ago, one of our external auditors jokingly remarked "we were tempted to use some of your work for our own but you used some annotation software that would give it away." Clearly, the big auditing firms hire bright and energetic people. Nonetheless, those same people are typically young, overworked, and rushed to get results out. Anything that can be done to make it easy for them works in the CIO's and the organization's favor.

■ Highest reliance: The work performed by the external auditors is the most independent and therefore counts more than work performed by the client's management. For IT, focus areas are usually security, change management, and data integrity (including backup). If there is a significant variance between their testing and management's self-testing, two unpleasant consequences will occur: (1) the external auditors will significantly expand their testing — at their then current billing rates, and (2) the integrity of management will be brought into question.

7. Sometimes key controls fail. When they do, a remediation plan is created, put in place, and the control is retested. For example, a key control may state that "periodic, formal restore testing is performed to ensure that backups are effective." During examination of this control, the auditor may find no evidence of a *systematic* restore testing. Perhaps the individuals in IT operations responsible for restore testing thought that incidental restores that happen during the year, due to some random mishap, are sufficient. Unfortunately, such informal activities do not constitute formal restore testing, where systems and applications are methodically restored to ensure compliance across all critical applications. A simple remediation plan may state "Effective 6/30/08, a quarterly restore testing process will be initiated and documentation retained to demonstrate all critical applications can be restored on demand." After a "cure" period, the control is retested for effectiveness. Cure time is a duration required before the control can safely be considered effective. After the control has been in place for the specified number of days and the retest is

Cycle	Control No.	Control Description	Environment
07GL	KC2	Individuals who access and make changes to XYZ's general ledger are appropriately authorized. They have no more access than is required to perform their assigned duties. In addition, they do not have rights to the general ledger which conflict with other rights, based on requirements for proper segregation of duties. FR C 02 FR C 64	SAP

Exception: Excessive number of developers have full access to general ledger production files (read, write, update). From an IT perspective, only an administrator and a backup should have permanent access.

XYZ Corp Remediation:

Application developer's access has been removed. Only the administrator and a backup have access rights to administer security. Accounting user access conflicts have been removed per the segregation of duties project. Conclusion: The control is now in place and effective.

Figure 2.5   Example remediation work-paper entry.

successful, then it is has been remediated and will not result in a deficiency. Note that compliance to section 404 is at a "point in time." This means that if you get your IT control failures fixed early on, you can get a clean bill of health at the end of your fiscal year — at least from a SOX perspective.[9] Figure 2.5 shows an example remediation work-paper entry.

8. Combining the results of their own work, Internal Audit's testing, and IT self-testing, the external auditors will assess the strength of IT controls and whether they are adequate to support management's contention that the system of internal controls supports accurate and timely financial statements. IT controls mesh with traditional financial and operational controls to create the combined control environment. In some cases, a weak IT control can be compensated for by a strong compensating manual control. For example, in organizations where receipt of goods is a significant part of the business, auditors typically look for the well-known "three way match" — that the purchase order, physical receipt, and invoice from the vendor all match before the invoice is paid. If an application does not include this control, a manual three-way match can compensate for the lack of computer control. When controls fail, the results are ranked at one of three levels:

■ Deficiency. A control breakdown prevents management or employees from preventing or detecting financial misstatements within a reasonable time frame. This lowest level of failure will not preclude a successful 404 outcome. For example, a key control states that emergency program changes to applications are permitted if they are required to repair a "broken" production system (e.g., a critical batch process aborts at midnight); however, they must be approved by IT management in advance and by an appropriate user within 48 hours of the change. The requirement for user approval was not built into the change control system as an automated process. The auditor discovered emergency application changes approved by IT management but not by a user. The finding was noted as a deficiency and was remediated by automating the reminder for user approval — the e-mails continue and escalate until the user's electronic signature is obtained.

■ Significant deficiency. An important control is not working and the organization's ability to initiate, record, process, or report financial data to the public is compromised. In addition, a significant deficiency may prevent compliance with generally accepted accounting principles (GAAP). A significant deficiency must be reported to the audit committee of the board of directors. A single significant deficiency may not cause a "404 failure," but multiple, unresolved, significant deficiencies could convince the external auditors that the system of internal controls is not adequate to support the financial statements. For example, a firm's enterprise resource planning (ERP) security system was configured to permit sales personnel to alter standard shipping terms on contracts. An auditor found three instances where revenue had been recorded in advance of shipment, thus slightly distorting both revenue and inventory in the period reviewed. Because there was a manual review of variances after the period (compensating control) and the magnitude of the distortion was not "material" at the entity level, this control weakness was designated as a significant deficiency rather than a material weakness. The problem was remediated by restricting full contract modification capability to a limited number of individuals. A new transaction capability ("responsibility" in Oracle terms) was created to allow sales representatives to change some other terms, which are routinely modified as part of the sales cycle.

■ Material weakness. One or more control failures at this level will result in a 404 failure. A material weakness represents, according to the AICPA,[10] "more than a remote likelihood that a material misstatement of the financials will not be prevented or detected." The control failure must be reported to the audit committee of the board of directors as well as the investing public (via the 10K). Material weaknesses usually, but not always, arise from business practices rather than IT control failures. For example, auditors performed a test of change control authorization for one firm and found more than a dozen application program changes with no user approvals and testing documents. This same deficiency was noted in the previous year's review. The remediation plan that management had developed in the prior year had apparently not been implemented. Accordingly, the auditors concluded that the likelihood of financial misstatement was more than remote *and* management's inaction implied a lack of commitment to maintaining a strong system of internal controls.

9. Within a month or two of the close of the fiscal year, the external auditors will review their findings, discuss areas for control improvements (not necessarily

related to key controls), and examine management's retest results. Because SOX testing typically takes place throughout the year, a selected subset needs to be retested at the end of the year in order to demonstrate that the control environment has not deteriorated. The external auditors will also review the results of remediation efforts and related tests.

10. After the close of the fiscal year, the auditors will render an opinion. This will include an opinion on the accuracy of the financial statements and management's assertion that its system of internal controls that will properly identify and correct material financial inaccuracies. The following text is copied from NCI Building Systems' 2006 annual report:

> We have evaluated the effectiveness of our internal control over financial reporting as of October 29, 2006. This evaluation was performed using the internal control evaluation framework developed by the Committee of Sponsoring Organizations of the Treadway Commission. Based on such evaluation, management has concluded that, as of such date, our internal control over financial reporting was effective.

> Pursuant to Section 404 of the Sarbanes-Oxley Act of 2002, we included a report of management's assessment of the design and effectiveness of our internal controls as part of this Annual Report on Form 10-K for the fiscal year ended October 29, 2006. Ernst & Young, LLP, our independent registered public accounting firm, also attested to, and reported on, management's assessment of the effectiveness of internal control over financial reporting. Management's and Ernst & Young's reports are included in our 2006 Consolidated Financial Statements on pages 39 and 40 of our Form 10-K under the captions entitled "Management's Report on Internal Control Over Financial Reporting" and "Report of Independent Registered Public Accounting Firm on Internal Control Over Financial Reporting" and are incorporated herein by reference.

The corresponding text in the 10K is an example of the external auditor's opinion on both the system of internal controls and the financial statements:

> In our opinion, management's assessment that the Company maintained effective internal control over financial reporting as of October 29, 2006, is fairly stated, in all material respects, based on the COSO criteria. Also, in our opinion, the Company maintained, in all material respects, effective internal control over financial reporting as of October 29, 2006, based on the COSO criteria.

> We also have audited, in accordance with the standards of the Public Company Accounting Oversight Board (United States), the consolidated balance sheets of the Company as of October 29, 2006 and October 29, 2005, and the related consolidated statements of operations, stockholders' equity, cash flows and comprehensive income for each of the

three years in the period ended October 29, 2006 and our report dated January 8, 2007 expressed an unqualified opinion thereon.

The above text is the formal equivalent to "Hurray! We passed 404!" Of course, IT is only one component, albeit an important one, of the system of internal controls.

For new CIOs, SOX can be a tense process. The CEO and CFO have to *personally* sign a statement that, to the best of their knowledge, the system of internal controls is adequate. IT is expected to pass with few deficiencies, no significant deficiencies, and certainly no material weaknesses. It reminds one of us (Yarberry) of tenure as Enron Corp's Telecom Director — not once did anyone call to say "I just picked up the phone and it worked — gee thanks." SOX compliance is a baseline, expected part of your job. One bright spot is that it gets significantly easier over time. Key controls should not change much, except to get more streamlined. Testing becomes routine. So long as the data, screen shots, and so forth originate from the current fiscal year, testing processes can be the same from year to year.

Resource Management

Governance includes responsible management of the organization's resources. Following are some methods and tools that should be included in this governance domain:

- Strategic sourcing (see Chapter 8)
- Supply-chain management
- Appropriate use of suppliers (competitive bidding, carefully monitoring contract compliance, etc.)
- Training to ensure resources are used efficiently
- Services automation
- "Front door" control — demand management for services
- Replacement of obsolete systems
- Leverage via common standards (e.g., for data, voice, video, workflow)

Performance Management

We will discuss this subject matter in more depth in Chapter 13, but it squarely belongs as a domain within IT governance. To paraphrase Socrates, unexamined performance is likely to be poor performance. Numbers, frequently updated, are essential to optimal performance. Some of the factors driving performance management include:

- Key performance indicators (metrics)
- Management dashboard

- IT balanced scorecard (popularized by Kaplan and Norton)
- Tools for efficient decision making
- Tools to ensure repeatable, efficient execution

The Nut-and-Bolt Stuff — Managing Your Own Department with Governance

Governance in your own shop is a little easier than ramping up processes involving senior management. Following are some governance processes you should have in place, and they should be at the maturity level of "consistent, repeatable, accurate and testable by a third party." When governance permeates your department, you will have more moral authority to pitch the message to your executive peers. Here is the list.

- Change management. Program modifications, new systems, database changes, and any other function that directly affects how information is generated should be processed through a change management system. Key components include:
  - Request for projects or changes to existing systems come from preauthorized users, except for pure infrastructure changes (e.g., to repair a server). Infrastructure changes may be initiated by IT staff, but their implementation is normally approved in advance by IT operations management.
  - "Unit" testing and sometimes integration/regression testing must be performed by the development/infrastructure personnel. The results of the tests should be documented.
  - User acceptance testing (UAT) is performed by competent users outside IT. Results are also documented.
  - Approval of testing results by an approved user and a final review by IT management are required before the change can go into production.
  - A "mover," an individual separate from the developer, physically transfers code and other production elements into the production library for execution.
  - A mechanism exists to handle emergency changes. All emergency changes should be authorized, even if after the fact.
  - All steps are documented for later review. Typically a system such as Remedy is used to house the steps. Workflow provides a reliable way to keep all the authorizations and processing steps in sync.
- Security. Network, database, and application security systems are in place. As we discuss in Chapter 10, a layered approach to defense is the most effective approach, as no single defense is considered adequate.
- Data management. Standards, monitoring, and proactive analysis of databases is essential. Many firms, particularly those that have grown more via

acquisition than accretive growth, have redundant databases. Standards include do's and don'ts; for example, needless replication of ERP environments (instances) is a colossal waste of IT resources. There should be some mechanism to review database design, for both application effectiveness and overall efficiency. For example, if the same item is used in three divisions, there should be one item descriptor with flags indicating the applicable divisions; providing this functionality using three records is inefficient.

■ Incident management. Incidents are recorded, prioritized, and tracked to resolution. Also, the change management system includes links to incident management because production problems are the initial reason for many changes.

■ Systems development life cycle. A standard methodology with a defined process and artifacts helps improve the quality and integrity of the system (or change) to be implemented. See Chapter 4 for more details.

■ Vendor management and procurement standards. Contracts are reviewed by legal and maintained centrally. Purchasing for IT software, hardware, and services is centralized. Because purchasing is centralized for the enterprise, volume discounts can be obtained. For major vendors, service-level agreements are established and monitored for compliance. Finally, the organization is protected from loss of intellectual property by nondisclosure agreements and other caveats.

■ Policies and procedures. IT documents policies and procedures, including important controls. Staff and users are aware of the most critical policies.

■ Operational dashboards and performance management. IT provides line and executive management with easy-to-read dashboards that clearly show progress on goals (projects on target, uptime, etc.). See Dennis Klinger's use of metrics in Chapter 15.

■ Merger and acquisition methodology. IT has an established process for integrating the acquired firm's technology and business functions into the enterprise. Reasonable timelines to eliminate redundant systems are enforced.

■ Disaster recovery and business continuity (at least the IT part). Risk calculations are frequently performed showing the probability of some disaster and its impact. In reality, the organization either has computing services or it does not. The capacity to provide services after a damaging event — and it could be a nasty malware attack rather than a hurricane — is essential. Business continuity requires the participation of the entire enterprise, but IT is a critical part of the response.

■ Capacity management and planning. Resources are monitored and tracked over time to ensure that services continue to be available even when many new users, transactions, or storage elements are added to the data center's load. The Information Systems Audit and Control Association (ISACA) had a humorous video just before the year 2000. An old man, a former Cobol programmer, was pictured in a bare room lit by a naked light bulb. Two tough-looking guys were questioning him. One of them said "And Mr. Smith just *when* did you know that these year 2000 problems were going to show up." He gulped and said "OK, we knew it back in the sixties!" Running out of capacity is somewhat like year 2000 being a surprise.

■ User training/IT staff training. Application and technical training are provided as needed. Even though on-the-job training is important, users also need a safe test environment to become familiar with applications. Do you want a new user on day 1 to enter transactions on an unfamiliar system? The need for IT training is almost obvious, particularly if the organization is adopting new technologies or standards.

■ Network management. Tools and expertise are in place to ensure that network uptime meets business requirements and that assets are protected from outside attack. Network analytical packages permit rationalization of bandwidth, detection of unauthorized devices, and identification of throughput chokepoints.

■ Infrastructure for analytics. A data warehouse is available and organized appropriately for quantitative analysis required by the business units. Alternative methods for data access may be employed, but the end result is that high-quality data are available as needed for analytics.

We confess that governance is not as exciting as some of the customer-facing projects that are easily visible and understood by senior management. Nonetheless, governance is the rock upon which the house of IT rests.

Authors of writing books use an interesting technique to improve creativity: change the word-processing font color to white and type away. The theory is that if you cannot see what you are doing, you will not feel constrained, and writer's block will vanish. Of course, anyone who does this will note that upon changing the font back to black, many mistakes have been made in grammar and spelling. In essence, the novice writer has removed "governance" from his or her environment. An IT environment without governance policies in place has about the same result — possibly more activity, but the error rate is unacceptably high.

References

1. Weill, Peter and Jeanne W. Ross. *IT Governance. How Top Performers Manage IT Decision Rights for Superior Results* (Boston: Harvard Business School Press, 2004), 4.
2. Broadbent, Marianne and Ellen S. Kitzis. *The New CIO Leader* (Boston: Harvard Business School Press, 2004).
3. Taleb, Nassim Nicholas. *Fooled by Randomness: The Hidden Role of Change in Life and in the Markets* (New York: Texere, 2005), 82.
4. IT Governance Institute. 2006. Enterprise Value: Governance of IT Investments. http://www.isaca.org (accessed July 12, 2007).
5. Westerman, George and Richard Hunter. *IT Risk, Turning Business Threats into Competitive Advantage* (Boston: Harvard Business School Press, 2007), 23.
6. http://zapatopi.net/kelvin/quotes/ (accessed August 24, 2008).

7. Control objectives for information technology.

8. A U.S. company with market capitalization over $75 million.

9. It is a different matter for the traditional audit of the financial statements. To render an opinion on the overall balance sheet, income statement, and cash flows, the auditors need confidence that controls were in place during each quarter so that they can rely on the numbers. If the controls were not functioning in, for example, the first quarter, the external auditors will need to perform many more "substantive" or detailed tests on the data in order to feel comfortable expressing an opinion on the financial statements. This extra effort will undoubtedly increase audit fees.

10. AICPA (American Institute of Certified Professional Accountants). 2005. SOX Section 404: Responding to an Adverse Report-A Checklist for the Audit Committee. www.aicpa.org/audcommctr/spotlight/SOX_Section_404.htm (accessed April 22, 2007).

Chapter 3

Information Technology Finance

People who don't respect money don't have any.

J. Paul Getty

When a feller says "It ain't the money, but the principle of the thing" — it's the money.

Kin Hubbard

Money management must be one of your core skills. In some cases, financial acumen is the critical competence separating the chief technology officer (CTO) from the chief information officer (CIO). Even the most visionary leader must operate in an environment of funding limits. For example, at Amazon.com, "all the desks are still modeled after the one Bezos built for himself in the early days (and still uses): a cheap wooden door as the top, connected by metal brackets to sawed-off two-by-fours as the legs."[1] The chief executive officer (CEO) and your business unit customers expect you to use money wisely and effectively — and *show* that you do so. Image is often as important as reality. One of our clients was delivering an important presentation for some potential Indian partners. During an informal working session, the CIO's administrative assistant ordered too much pizza. Later the CEO noticed the investors glancing at the leftover food and then privately criticized the CIO — not because of the trivial cost but for leaving the impression that the firm was unconcerned with expenses. Dollars matter.

Budgeting

Budgeting is the first step and the primary tool for cost management. In economist-speak, it is a *macro* tool because problems show up in budget reports after they are significant enough to stand out. So it is essentially a front-and-back tool. Capital projects and expenses are set up at the beginning of the fiscal year and then historical results are compared to budget to identify variances. There are always variances unless someone is "smoothing" the numbers — it is not reasonable to expect the CIO to be a soothsayer. Variances do, however, provide a shorthand method for monitoring expense outliers. If you have only a limited time to review your department's financial progress, a review of the largest variances is the best use of your time. Either the initial estimate was bad or something unexpected happened.

Table 3.1, adapted from a $3 billion in sales services firm, shows typical rolled-up budget categories and expenditures for a cost-conscious information technology (IT) department.

Typically the accounting department provides a ready-made template, including some categories that may not apply (for example, utilities may be an unallocated overhead item). The financial reporting process may not be as smooth or efficient as you would expect. Some of the impediments to accurate tracking of expenses include:

- Other departments may inadvertently charge IT for unrelated expenses or they did not budget enough and now corporate IT picks up the tab.
- Vendor invoices may not come in on a regular schedule, resulting in unexpected monthly variances.
- Costs may not be recorded in the accounting system at sufficient granularity to understand the expenses without delving into the invoices.
- Subordinates may not be tracking expenses carefully, so that you are surprised at month- or quarter-end.
- The accounting department may inadvertently allocate expenses to the wrong general ledger code, as a result of a user input error or initial general ledger coding setup error.

Senior management and board members feel better about any IT budget if it falls within some reasonable industry standard. For example, Kevin Kearns, the former CIO at Health Choice Networks in Miami, Florida, satisfied his board members by showing his IT budget was approximately 2.5% of revenue, below the 3% to 4% industry average.[2] Rick Omartian, Information Technology Chief Financial Officer and Chief of Staff for Guardian Life Insurance Company, evaluates every project over $100,000 against a return on investment (ROI) hurdle and a payback criterion of less than 3 years. Projects above $1,000,000 require approval of the Corporate Finance Department.[3] The more financial metrics from your industry you have, the more successful your budget will be. Any numbers that exceed the

Table 3.1   Example Information Technology (IT) Annual Expense Budget

NCI Building Systems
Fallbrook, TX — Period 09
G&A Corporate   --------------- Current Month ----------------

Account	Actual	Budget	Variance	% Variance
Wages — Hourly	0	59,000-	59,000-	100.00
Wages — O.T.Premium	0	0	0	0.00
Wages — Salaries	393,241	424,123	30,882	7.28
Wages — Benefits Pay	36,986	0	36,586-	0.00
Payroll Taxes	30,689	27,968	2,721-	9.73-
Contract Labor	57,201	89,177	31,976	35.86
Outsource Services	41,070	85,722	44,652	52.09
Professional Services	5,000	65,100	60,100	92.32
Consulting Fees	0	0	0	0.00
Certification Fees	0	0	0	0.00
401k Administrative	0	0	0	0.00
Vehicles (Excludes Depr.)	0	0	0	0.00
Disaster Contingency	27,269	10,167	17,102-	168.21-
Professional Development	22,418	12,917	9,501-	73.56-
Business Meetings	0	0	0	0.00
Rentals & Leases	162,712	161,273	1,439-	0.89-
Supplies	34,078	18,300	15,778-	86.22-
Entertainment & Promotion	1,212	0	1,212-	0.00
Employee Benefits	0	0	0	0.00
Telephone	78,294	20,000	58,294-	291.47-
Depreciation	106,353	87,193	19,160-	21.97-
Travel	9,068	47,208	38,140	80.79
Employee Relocation	0	0	0	0.00
Repairs & Maintenance	19	3,600	3,581	99.47
Officers' Life Insurance	0	0	0	0.00
Workers' Compenation Insurance	0	0	0	0.00
Property & Casualty Insurance	0	0	0	0.00
Health & Life Insurance	0	0	0	0.00
Other Insurance	0	0	0	0.00
Health Insurance (as of 4/01)	0	0	0	0.00
Compensation Exp-Rabbi Tst	0	0	0	0.00
Employees' Benefit Expense	0	0	0	0.00
Taxes — General	0	0	0	0.00
Bonuses	0	0	0	0.00
Restricted Stock	0	0	0	0.00
401k Company Contributions	0	0	0	0.00
Stock Transfer Costs	0	0	0	0.00
Public Reporting Costs	0	0	0	0.00
Dues & Subscriptions	5,830	1,650	4,180-	253.33-
Donations	0	0	0	0.00

(continued on next page)

Table 3.1 (continued)   Example Information Technology (IT) Annual Expense Budget

Account	Actual	Budget	Variance	% Variance
Postage	0	0	0	0.00
Bank Service Charges	0	0	0	0.00
Janitorial Services	0	0	0	0.00
Utilities	0	0	0	0.00
Advertising	0	0	0	0.00
Literature	0	0	0	0.00
Overnight & Special Delivery	811	1,200	389	32.44
Research & Development	0	0	0	0.00
Covenant Not to Compete Amort.	0	0	0	0.00
Employee Education Asst.	0	0	0	0.00
NCHA Sponsorship	0	0	0	0.00
Green Initiative	0	0	0	0.00
End Marketing Expenses	0	0	0	0.00
Miscellaneous	3,787	0	3,787-	0.00
Environmental Expenses	0	0	0	0.00
Allocated — Corp Billing	0	0	0	0.00
Software	0	0	0	0.00
Lease Communication Lines	154,080	154,000	80-	0.05-
Rental & Leased Buildings — MIS	435	349	86-	24.60-
Hardware Maintenance	64,450	80,633	16,183	20.07
Software Maintenance	262,566	228,463	34,103-	14.93-
Implementation Costs	0	0	0	0.00
Programming Costs	0	0	0	0.00
Employee Educational Asst.	0	0	0	0.00
Grand Total:	**1,497,567**	**1,460,043**	**37,524-**	**2.57-**

(continued on next page)

industry should be explainable (one time infrastructure upgrade, consolidation of data centers, and so forth).

Directors or managers within IT usually work within a subbudget and compare monthly or quarterly expenses to line items under their control. For example, the operations director may have a budget specifically devoted to disaster recovery/business continuity, and the program management office (PMO) director typically tracks capital projects with a project budget.

Constructing the Budget

The budget shown in Table 3.1 is a cumulative, enterprise-wide spreadsheet and is a summation of various subbudgets. The totals roll up to equal the CIO's entire

Table 3.1 (continued) Example Information Technology (IT) Annual Expense Budget

Account	Actual	Budget	Variance	% Variance	Fiscal Yr Budget
	------------------- Year to Date -------------------------------------				
Wages — Hourly	25,272-	531,000-	505,728-	95.24	708,000-
Wages — O.T.Premium	0	0	0	0.00	0
Wages — Salaries	3,003,839	3,261,316	257,477	7.89	4,448,862
Wages — Benefits Pay	295,953	0	295,953-	0.00	0
Payroll Taxes	246,798	268,546	21,748	8.10	349,390
Contract Labor	544,819	802,593	257,774	32.12	1,070,124
Outsource Services	275,972	771,498	495,526	64.23	1,028,664
Professional Services	201,598	493,400	291,802	59.14	688,700
Consulting Fees	0	0	0	0.00	0
Certification Fees	0	0	0	0.00	0
401k Administrative	0	0	0	0.00	0
Vehicles (Excludes Depr.)	0	0	0	0.00	0
Disaster Contingency	187,747	91,503	96,244-	105.18-	122,004
Professional Development	82,129	121,653	39,524	32.49	150,904
Business Meetings	0	0	0	0.00	0
Rentals & Leases	1,416,919	1,526,634	109,715	7.19	2,010,453
Supplies	282,576	173,200	109,376-	63.15-	228,100
Entertainment & Promotion	11,065	0	11,065-	0.00	0
Employee Benefits	0	0	0	0.00	0
Telephone	243,018	180,000	63,018-	35.01-	240,000
Depreciation	869,394	803,347	66,047-	8.22-	1,058,427
Travel	121,010	345,072	224,062	64.93	458,796
Employee Relocation	0	0	0	0.00	0
Repairs & Maintenance	1,600	32,400	30,800	95.06	43,200
Officers' Life Insurance	0	0	0	0.00	0
Workers' Compenation Insurance	0	0	0	0.00	0
Property & Casualty Insurance	0	0	0	0.00	0
Health & Life Insurance	0	0	0	0.00	0
Other Insurance	0	0	0	0.00	0
Health Insurance (as of 4/01)	0	0	0	0.00	0
Compensation Exp-Rabbi Tst	0	0	0	0.00	0
Employees' Benefit Expense	4,778-	0	4,778	0.00	0
Taxes — General	0	0	0	0.00	0
Bonuses	0	0	0	0.00	0
Restricted Stock	0	0	0	0.00	0
401k Company Contributions	0	0	0	0.00	0
Stock Transfer Costs	0	0	0	0.00	0
Public Reporting Costs	0	0	0	0.00	0
Dues & Subscriptions	74,011	115,748	41,737	36.06	120,698
Donations	0	0	0	0.00	0

(continued on next page)

Table 3.1 (continued)   Example Information Technology (IT) Annual Expense Budget

Account	Actual	Budget	Variance	% Variance	Fiscal Yr Budget
Postage	0	0	0	0.00	0
Bank Service Charges	0	0	0	0.00	0
Janitorial Services	0	0	0	0.00	0
Utilities	0	0	0	0.00	0
Advertising	0	0	0	0.00	0
Literature	0	0	0	0.00	0
Overnight & Special Delivery	15,231	10,800	4,431-	41.02-	14,400
Research & Development	0	0	0	0.00	0
Covenant Not to Compete Amort.	0	0	0	0.00	0
Employee Education Asst.	0	0	0	0.00	0
NCHA Sponsorship	0	0	0	0.00	0
Green Initiative	0	0	0	0.00	0
End Marketing Expenses	0	0	0	0.00	0
Miscellaneous	119,898	0	119,898-	0.00	0
Environmential Expenses	0	0	0	0.00	0
Allocated — Corp Billing	0	0	0	0.00	0
Software	8,190	0	8,190-	0.00	0
Lease Communication Lines	1,194,671	1,386,000	191,329	13.80	1,848,000
Rental & Leased Buildings — MIS	3,914	3,141	773-	24.60-	4,188
Hardware Maintenance	560,649	725,067	164,418	22.68	963,466
Software Maintenance	2,016,957	2,191,626	174,669	7.97	2,884,713
Implementation Costs	0	0	0	0.00	0
Programming Costs	0	0	0	0.00	0
Employee Educational Asst.	510	0	510-	0.00	0
Grand Total:	**11,748,418**	**12,772,544**	**1,024,126**	**8.02**	**17,025,089**

budget for the year. Subbudgets, which the CIO asks subordinates to prepare (at least for the first pass), may reflect a variety of organizational perspectives:

- Geographical coverage — by office, plant, district, etc.
- Insourced versus outsourced functions
- Functional units such as accounting, human resources (HR), operating units
- Projects versus operations
- Contingency budget based on potential acquisitions

The budget is typically contingent on major business decisions, such as the trajectory of growth (both accretive and organic), any significantly greater service-level demands, new technology areas, increased security requirements, and other changes.

To the extent possible, budgets should be tied to deliverables. In some cases, the deliverables will be multiyear projects, so it makes sense to project costs across the life of the project. Capital budgets can be broken down into infrastructure investments, which allow IT to meet its service-level objectives and strategic investments, which provide new functionality for the business. Some typical infrastructure (maintenance) investments include:

- Network equipment replacement
- Security devices
- Disaster recovery equipment and services
- Routine backup capacity
- Redundancy in order to improve service levels

The line between operating expenses and capital expenses can sometimes blur. Keeping the lights on is an expense; a forklift replacement of underpowered routers would be a capital line item on the budget.

Budgets for hardware and software follow a different trajectory. The cost to maintain hardware will likely increase over time, but its capabilities — at least relative to a comparable device currently on the market — will decline. Software, on the other hand, does not wear out and theoretically provides the same level of service year over year. In practice, software maintenance costs (mostly employee resource costs) will be highest in the early years, decline in midlife, and eventually rise as technology, interfaces, and business requirements change. So you should always recognize and budget for not only the initial cost of software but also varying future maintenance costs. This may not prove true for some isolated systems, but it will certainly hold for major systems at the core of your business. Table 3.2 shows an example capital budget and includes some multiyear projects.

Rational Buying

The process of acquiring IT hardware, software, and services follows the same logic individuals should follow when spending their own money — without some rational philosophy of buying, the return on investment is often low. In his book *Boiling the IT Frog,* Harwell Thrasher recommends asking the following fundamental questions about major expenditures[4]:

- Is it clear what the product or service does and how it functions?
- Is the vendor financially strong? Can you count on future services and maintenance?
- Can you obtain the human skills to service the product (consultants, in-house, and so forth)?
- Is the product a good fit with your organization?

Table 3.2 Example Capital Budget

Description	Justification	Priority	Approval Amount	Q1	Q2	Q3	Q4	FY2008 Total	Carry Forward to 2009
Corporate Telecom (Avaya) system project: hardware and deployment costs	Other	High	4,549	797	797	61	61	1,717	2,832
Citrix Server Upgrade project: licenses and software to upgrade current Citrix environment to latest version	IT infrastructure	High	473	—	473	—	—	473	—
License upgrade for test system	Growth/capacity	High	51	51	—	—	—	51	—
License true-up for systems software	Growth/capacity	High	92	92	—	—	—	92	—
Sales Tax software: Enterprise DB License portion	Cost reduction	High	98	98	—	—	—	98	—

Engineering system	Cost reduction	High	1,000	333	333	334	—	1,000	—
Drafting system development	Cost reduction	Medium	3,300	500	500	500	500	2,000	1,300
Web system: Phase II	Growth/capacity	Medium	186	90	96	—	—	186	—
Major ERP upgrade	Essential maintenance	Medium	4,003	1,001	1,001	1,001	1,001	4,003	—
Common job number project	Growth/capacity	High	259	259	—	—	—	259	—
CER Tracking Project: implementation	IT internal	Low	165	83	83	—	—	165	—
Web system: Phase III for XYZ	Growth/capacity	High	135	68	68	—	—	135	—
End user engineering system, workstation based	Growth/capacity	High	445	111	111	111	111	444	—
		Total	14,755	14,755	14,755	14,755	14,755	14,755	14,755

- Will it integrate with existing systems (from both a technical and business process perspective)?
- How much effort will be required to transition from your current system or process to the new one?
- What is the total cost of ownership, including initial purchase, maintenance, and support?
- If the system is implemented, will it increase sales or at least prevent loss of sales? Will it affect any first-to-market strategies?

These sensible questions notwithstanding, we know that emotion and the influence of powerful executives can skew decisions. The trick is to set up a rational process, knowing that reality will be short of the ideal. With the proper tools and standard analytics in place, at least highly irrational projects or acquisitions will be highlighted.

The IT Governance Institute's flagship standard, CobIT 4.1, outlines in section AI5 a standard approach to IT investment and procurement[5]:

- Develop IT procurement policies and procedures
- Establish a list of preferred suppliers
- Evaluate suppliers via a request for proposal process
- Use contract terms that protect the organization's interests
- Buy in compliance with policy

Figure 3.1 and Figure 3.2 show examples of policies and procedures for IT procurement.

Managing the IT Investment

Every IT organization should have a standard set of templates for project evaluation. By using the same templates over time, your stakeholders become accustomed to the presentation and your message is clearer. Typically, financial analysis hinges on standard metrics such as ROI, payback, internal rate of return (IRR), and net present value (NPV). Current versions of Excel and other spreadsheets offer a wealth of financial functions. See Table 3.3.

Of course, project selection only starts with straightforward financials, such as labor hours saved, increase in high-value sales, number of customers served faster resulting in X% more sales, and so forth. Alignment with the enterprise business strategy is equally important. In fact, some organizations multiply by an "alignment parameter" when evaluating projects. For example, if calculated benefits are $1 million over 3 years and the system is a one-off project not well aligned with the corporate strategy, the benefits are knocked down to $0.5 million by multiplying by 0.5. On the other hand, if a project is clearly strategic and permits expansion into new profit-making opportunities, a "strong alignment" parameter of 2.0 may be used.

**HARDWARE & SOFTWARE
PURCHASE POLICY**

---

1   Hardware and Software Purchase Policy

1.1   Policy and Direction

a. All hardware and software purchases will be reviewed for compliance to XYZ CORP's technical architecture prior to purchase
b. Any deviations from the approved software and hardware list must be approved by the CIO or his designee.
c. XYZ CORP Maintains a Standard Hardware/Software List
d. No software will be acquired without the requisite license/proof of right to use.
e. No software or hardware is to be acquired outside the standard purchase process.
f. Hardware and software purchases will be centralized in order to provide greater standardization, lower maintenance costs and increased purchasing power.
g. Implementation of major hardware or software purchases will be planned and sufficient notice given to affected parties.
h. Records (licenses) will be maintained such that a review by an outside party, such as the Business Software Alliance, will demonstrate XYZ CORP's compliance with all applicable agreements and legal regulations.

Peripheral hardware, such as a PDA, is included in this policy if it attaches to the network. If purchased individually, it must nonetheless conform to XYZ CORP's technical architecture before linking to the network.

Capital expenditures will conform to XYZ CORP's capital appropriation policy.

Figure 3.1   Information technology procurement policies.

The title of R.B. Sheridan's 1777 play, *The School for Scandal*, seems appropriate for some of the tricks used by sponsors to put a positive spin on their favorite projects. It is understandable that people would do this in an environment where everyone else does it. Following are some of the intentional and often unintentional spins used to get projects to the starting line:

■ Using the "oops" factor — forgetting to mention that an interface needs to be developed or purchased.
■ Omitting underlying infrastructure costs.

1.2   Software

1.2.1   General

a. All software and hardware must be purchased via Corporate IT.
b. Users obtain supervisor approval to order software or hardware
c. An email or fax showing approval is sent to the software/hardware purchase coordinator
d. The hardware/software purchase coordinator compares the request to the current list of standard, approved software.
e. If the cost for an individual order exceeds $1,000 and the item(s) are not considered expense items, a capital expenditure form (CER) must be completed and signed by the requestor and immediate supervisor or department head. The request is sent to the IT purchase coordinator, who reviews and forwards to the CIO of Operations (alternatively the VP & CIO). The CIO signs if it meets standards for IT software and is otherwise appropriate. The form is then sent to accounting for a CER number, which serves to chargeback the business unit. After assignment of a CER number, the document is sent back to the IT hardware/software purchase coordinator for actual ordering (an email may be used to expedite ordering).
f. If the request matches the approved list and does not exceed $1,000, the purchase coordinator orders the software from the approved vendor(s) and sends an email to the original requestor.
g. Purchases for IT equipment, software and services up to $150,000 may be approved by the Director of Operations. Larger amounts must be approved by the CIO.
h. For "one off" items not on the approved software list, the purchase coordinator maintains an inventory to demonstrate compliance with license agreements and legal restrictions.
i. Annually, the purchase coordinator requests printouts or electronic records from vendors supplying software (e.g., CDW). Combined with the "one off" items mentioned above, these records constitute an informal software licensing database.
j. Time sensitive requests: On an exception basis, software can be ordered prior to receipt of a CER number for chargeback. Such exceptions must be approved by the CIO.
k. Overall corporate purchase policy. All capital purchases must conform to the enterprise-wide capital procurement policy.

Figure 3.2   Information technology procurement detailed procedures.

■ Setting unrealistic time commitments for key users or developers. Good people are already busy. If you take away their time, something that costs money will likely be needed to compensate.

■ Adopting a perspective of near certainty. The sponsor sees that everything is for the best and discounts potential failure points. Any project without at least 10% contingency is probably underfunded.

Table 3.3   Example Financial Metrics for Projects Using Microsoft Excel

Function/ Calculation	Inputs	Results	Comments
Net present value (NPV)	Rate: discount or hurdle rate. Often provided by your finance department Cash flows: dollars coming in or going out, by month or year	A single value representing the discounted sum of cash flows (either positive or negative) associated with the project. NPV answers the question "what will this project cost if I funded the entire project in one lump sum on the front end."	For highly profitable firms with a high discount rate, some projects may not make the cut even though they would save money in the long run. The firm simply has better uses for its capital. Net present value has the advantage of showing the scale of a project (volume of dollars), whereas internal rate of return (IRR) indicates only that any given dollar invested will be profitable or lose money.
Payback	Initial cost Savings per month	A multiple, such as 6.5, meaning that the initial expenditure will be recovered in 6.5 months.	This is the granddaddy of funding analytics. It has the advantage of "back of the envelope" simplicity but ignores the cost of capital.
Internal rate of return (IRR or XIRR* for irregular flows)	Cash flows: dollars coming in or going out, by month or year	Shows a rate of return arising from negative or positive cash flows	If IRR exceeds the firm's cost of capital, the project is acceptable from a financial perspective.

* Returns the internal rate of return for a schedule of cash flows that may not be periodic or equal. For example, cash may be expended for 60 months on a regular schedule but a balloon payment is to be made at the end of the 60th month.

To maintain a sense of fairness and adjudicate between powerful user executives, you should use and promote a standardized prioritization process. The process will be imperfect, but it serves as a focus for rational discussion. If time and the political environment permit, a routine post implementation review further promotes an atmosphere of IT as an investment vehicle in its own right. If the organization invested $3 million in a particular project, were the results promised in the original business requirements document actually realized?

SOP No. 98-1

Should you capitalize or expense new systems? The answer directly affects net profits for the current year and future years. SOP 98-1, a standard created by the American Institute of Certified Public Accountants (AICPA), governs the method of accounting for the costs of internal-use software. It comes into play when you develop or purchase new systems. Table 3.4 provides a thumbnail sketch of the rules.

This area of accounting pegs the "fuzzy meter." The AICPA has written a plethora of rules to help firms correctly capitalize or expense costs associated with an internal software project. If you are implementing a multimillion dollar project, it is worth your time to get into the minutia of the regulations — or at least ensure

Table 3.4   High-Level Summary of SOP 98-1

Stage of Project	Typical Activities	Capitalize or Expense
Preliminary	• Vendor presentations • Identifying potential technologies to meet requirements • Selecting a consultant(s) to perform the work • Strategic decisions to allocated resources between alternative projects • Preliminary steering committee meetings	Expense as occurs
Data preparation	• Purge or clean existing data • Create new data • Convert old data to the new format • Reconciliation and balancing old and new data	Expense as occurs
Obtain or develop software for internal use	• Payroll and related costs for individuals who are primarily responsible for project development • Direct cost of software and consulting services purchased from outside suppliers • Interest on funds used during development • Any direct cost of materials or services related to development	Capitalize
Operations (after implementation)	• Routine operations • User training • Maintenance and cleanup • Post implementation documentation	Expense as occurs

that you have someone in accounting well versed in its nuances. Following are some (by no means all) of the factors that should be considered:

■ Capitalized costs should be amortized on a straight-line basis
■ A major upgrade falls under the rules of SOP 98-1 so long as it enables the software to perform significant (nontrivial) tasks previously outside its capabilities
■ Hardware costs, even if the new application has its own server, are not part of the SOP 98-1 treatment. But as a side note, you can capitalize hardware costs related to rollouts if you purchase (not lease) the equipment. This includes development, testing, production servers, PCs, laptops, and printers. Also, software costs related to the project can be capitalized — just not maintenance fees associated with the project.
■ Maintenance is always an expense.
■ Amortization of each module of the system starts when the module is ready to go into production, even if it is to be placed into service later in the period. But it must be ready and not dependent on other modules that have not yet been completed. Yes, it gets a little unclear at the detail level.
■ Software can be impaired. If there are programming or technical difficulties that essentially shelve the system, the rules change. If this happens, Financial Accounting Standards Board (FASB) Statement number 121, which accounts for assets abandoned, takes over. Because it is not likely to have value, you are probably stuck with a write-off. However, we are deep into accounting here, so please find an expert before you adjust the books.

Clare Cooper, a Houston, Texas-based project management consultant and owner of Aircoop Technologies, suggests the following for IT projects using the SOP 98 guidelines:

■ Be careful with rewrites and refactoring[6] — their treatment can be ambiguous. If processes are only slightly modified or rationalized, you cannot capitalize the software costs. The changes must add additional functionality, not merely improve the efficiency of an existing capability.
■ Capitalize IT elements such as high-level and detailed requirements, design, development, testing, training materials (computer-based training, manuals, etc.), training class creation, and production support enhancements.
■ Do *not* capitalize IT elements such as initial discovery, training, rollout, and production support (bug fixes).
■ Keep good records for capital projects. Time sheets, detailed work plans, and receipts should be retained in an easily accessible format. Work plans should be sufficiently detailed so that each task can be categorized as a capital or expense item. Early on, the project managers and team members should meet with the accountants (and perhaps auditors) to define the information that should be kept and the appropriate level of detail.

- Establish checkpoints throughout the project where accountants and auditors can review the record keeping and make timely adjustments as needed.
- Ensure that all appropriate documents are centrally stored and protected. Project documentation tends to follow the law of entropy and become scattered. If the accounting treatment of a large project is challenged by auditors (Internal Revenue Service [IRS], external, etc.), the documentation should be easy to find. Otherwise, an unpleasant scramble for documents across the organization may ensue. Although documentation will rarely be deleted outright, its location may become obscure. Sometimes vital information is stored on local drives rather than the network.

Cooper makes a final plea, based on her years in the project management trenches: avoid the typical lopsided focus on capital dollars. Be sure to include enough expense allocation to properly maintain hardware and software. Otherwise, costs will rise over time, as emergency fixes and potential business disruptions result from inadequately maintained systems.

Cost Management

Making good use of a budget is a necessary but not sufficient condition for success. Variances against budget provide financial eyesight and general awareness of expenses gone south. A budget does not, however, help you reduce costs over the long term. For example, many organizations pay too much for telecom services because no one looks critically at the services offered or the competitive offerings. If the bills are roughly the same as last period and no budget variances are noticed, the invoices get paid month after month without question. Frank Marino, a Houston, Texas-based telecommunications consultant, states that he is routinely able to reduce his clients' expenses by 25% to 30% without a reduction in services and in many cases *without even changing providers*. One major carrier, for example, still maintains accounts charging 60 cents per minute for domestic calls. Other carriers have miscellaneous services with similar wildly priced services. The point is that every cost element in the CIO's portfolio of expenses must be examined critically — "same as last time" is the way of bloated costs. Figure 3.3 illustrates a telecom bill that will continue into perpetuity unless specifically canceled by the customer.

Cost reduction is implemented primarily in two areas:

- IT operations. Hardware, network operations, telecommunications, help desk, e-mail, and desktop and laptop provisioning are all subject to decreased

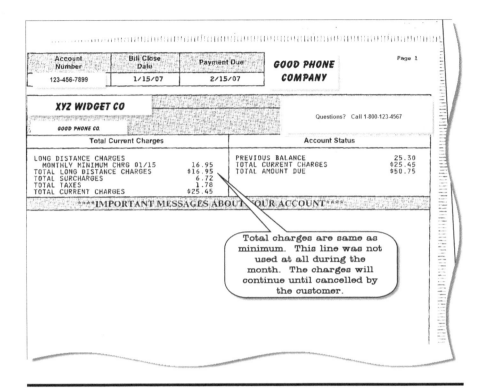

Figure 3.3   Example of a telecom bill with recurring but unnecessary charges.

unit costs as the IT organization matures and stabilizes its architecture. There is simply no cheaper way to provide IT services than to impose standards, which in turn integrate into an enterprise architecture.

■ User applications maintenance and upgrades. Business and engineering software must be maintained, even if the business requirements do not change — the technical environment relentlessly evolves. Without these regular upgrades, costs will "lurch" upward when an application, several releases out of date, must be updated quickly. Some business or regulatory requirement may present itself or perhaps the application may have to be modified just to continue functioning. Doing things in IT with extreme speed is almost always costly. Marathoners could run another mile at the end; sprinters, having run a far shorter distance, have to stop.

Another management tool to drive down costs is the consistent and relentless use of metrics to keep score. Dennis Klinger, Vice President of Information Management Services at Florida Power & Light (FPL), maintains a database of failure rates, mean time to repair, number of changes that failed, frequency of outages, and many other performance elements. This enables him to make informed purchase and vendor contract decisions. To ensure all his managers take the metrics seriously, he ties compensation, in part, to the infrastructure/operations performance measures.

In addition to the reasons listed above, there are plenty of common-sense reasons for runaway IT expenses:

- Too many pet projects, without a clear business justification
- Poor project governance practices
- Excessive zeal for "cool" technologies, regardless of financial value
- Inability to accurately estimate the total cost of ownership for projects
- Political inability to kill projects that will not deliver promised results or will experience cost overruns that exceed their benefits

One survey revealed that 84% of companies do not have business cases for their IT projects or perform them only for a few projects.[7] In short, just by doing the basics, you will be ahead of many other organizations.

Gray Areas and the Tilt

Of necessity, accountants approximate. Although debits equal credits, to the penny, even for the largest corporations, many of the underlying accounts and activities are estimates. There is no choice. Accounting, like any other mental model, must start with a numbingly complex array of real events and condense them into rules simple enough to run a business every day. As a result, there will be areas of ambiguity. Consider, for example, Enron's large IT outsourcing agreement with EDS in the early 1990s. In addition to seeking the quality, technology, and other benefits of the billion dollar outsourcing agreement, Enron needed a financial boost. Classifying various computer services — mainframe central processing unit (CPU) time, disk space, and time-sharing operation (TSO) time as CRUs (computer resource units), a plot of any one of these CRUs over the life of the contract shows the following change in unit price over the (initial) 10-year duration of the contract.

Pricing arrangements, so long as they are arrived at by arms-length negotiations with no kickbacks, are perfectly legal. However, if the initial cost of services is well below market pricing and the final year's pricing is above market, the net effect is to provide an off balance sheet loan, improving the profitability and cash flow of the purchaser — in the early years. Enron, formed in the late 1980s as a merger between Houston Natural Gas and Northern Natural Gas Company, struggled to earn a profit in its first few years (and of course in its last, disastrous year). The "tilt" (see Figure 3.4) helped its financial image. In today's regulatory environment, such arrangements (if material) would need to be shown in the financial notes of the annual report. Such was not the case in the early 1990s.

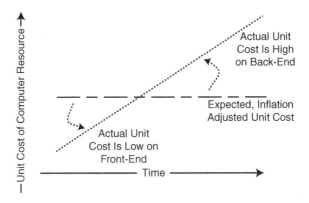

Figure 3.4 The "tilt" enables lower costs on the front-end of a contract but results in high costs in later years.

The point of this story is not to pound the carcass of a once successful company but to show that even the CIO can become enmeshed in gray decision areas. Any major agreements that could materially affect the financial statements should be reviewed by legal, accounting, and — if any questions arise — by your external auditors.

And yet, there are routine situations where treatment of assets and depreciation is not clear. For example:

- Capitalization of expenses. Small expenditures on meals, travel, and miscellaneous employee expenses are typically expensed. However, beyond a limit (usually set by the Accounting department), all those items can be lumped together and capitalized. The limit varies by organization ($1,000, $5,000, or higher). In the past, more industries were regulated and there was an incentive to capitalize more expenses. Regulated gas pipelines were at one time jokingly accused of capitalizing wastebaskets because the costs could be passed on to the consumer.

- Lease versus purchase. Firms often lease assets in order to stay technically up-to-date and to meet capacity requirements that may change sharply over time. Leases are shown on the books somewhat like debt obligation — you must show both the total lease obligation and the periodic payments. Otherwise, a firm could simply lease everything and show a fabulous (but inaccurate) picture of financial strength to the investing public. Purchase of IT assets may also be appropriate. To calculate which alternative is best for the organization, it is probably best to leave it to people who do it all the time. Unless you are comfortable with terms like MACRS (Modified Accelerated Cost Recovery System) and CCA (Clinger-Cohen Act), leave it to the accountants. The Internet has a plethora of sites devoted to this topic. For example, www.lease-vs-buy.com/ provides a handy calculator if you are looking for a quick answer.

■ Operating versus capital lease. There are two methods of lease accounting. The operating lease permits the lessee (your firm) to *use* the asset but provides no ownership of any kind. At the end of the operating lease, the property goes back to the owner (lessor). The operating lease never affects the balance sheet and is considered an operating expense during the lease period. In contrast, the capital lease permits the lessee to enjoy some of the benefits of ownership (along with the risks). The lease is recognized as both an asset and a liability for the lease payments. Depreciation as well as the interest expense component of the lease payments can be claimed each year. Most firms prefer to keep leases off the books and so there is a tendency to attempt to treat most leases as operating leases. Accounting and tax advice is beyond the scope of this book, but as a rule of thumb, keep the following guidelines in mind. The lease should be considered as a capital lease if:

  – Lease life is greater than 75% of the life of the asset.
  – There is a transfer of ownership to the lessee at the end of the contracted lease period.
  – The asset can be purchased by the lessee at a very low price at the end of the lease period.
  – The sum of the lease payments (discounted appropriately) is greater than 90% of the fair market value of the asset.

Chargeback

Chargeback has a logical allure — it seems to make sense to charge user departments for the systems and operations that support their operations. If, for example, the trading group is the rainmaker this year, they should be able to get the most powerful servers, brand new trading turrets with automatic ring downs, and a robotic cappuccino maker to boot — so long as they pay for it. On the flip side, chargeback discourages departments from irresponsibly asking for services that are not cost effective. It might be cheaper to do some things with temporary manual help.

Chargeback is certainly not universally deployed. It is more common in larger organizations but is frequently limited to specific, large-dollar projects rather than ongoing operations. Generally, the results of chargeback are mixed. Following are some of the disadvantages found in chargeback systems:

■ It costs money to implement. The more refined the chargeback system, the more effort to identify, measure, and bill direct and indirect costs.
■ It can lead to shadow IT departments if user management believes charges are excessive. To use an extreme example, a business department head may think routers and other bargain-priced equipment purchased on eBay are satisfactory. When he then computes all his apparent costs, he erroneously concludes that the central IT group is overcharging. His next step is to set up

a shadow IT department and drop out of the primary IT structure. It is only when this approach fails that the true cost of computing becomes visible. A classic example is the failure of out-of-date or insufficient memory routers in high-transaction-volume environments.

■ Architectural standards can be bypassed and the entity-wide effectiveness of IT compromised as a result of "cowboy" activities outside the structure of professional IT management.

■ IT spending can go up, yet remain hidden, due to "off balance sheet" hiring of IT specialists.

■ Chargeback may promote an adversarial culture and interfere with IT/business strategic alignment.

If you are going to work nights and weekends, spend your time developing strategies to help the business achieve its core objectives. Unlike the Nike commercial, our advice regarding chargeback, based on experience, would be "just don't do it."

Looking Financially Smart

A few years back, *Saturday Night Live* featured a comedian whose repetitive line was "you have to *look* good." The joke was that he did not actually know anything — it was enough simply to sport a cool look. CIOs, of course, need to know a lot about many different areas of business, but looking financially smart gives you the edge. Knowing a few financial ratios, especially their trend over the last few years, suggests to senior management that you are financially savvy and aware of the firm's monetary status. The French term *au courant* ("being in the know") describes the CIO who knows the numbers. Table 3.5 lists some common ratios you can easily calculate from your annual or quarterly financials.

The following 2006 (annual) ratios for NCI Building Systems were obtained from the Google Finance Web site[8]:

Net Profit Margin	4.70%
Return on Average Assets	6.43%
Return on Average Equity	15.66%

It also helps to keep key figures in your head. For example, in the metal building industry, handy facts include:

■ Market cap
■ Revenues

Table 3.5   Basic Financial Ratios

Category	Ratio Name	Formula
Liquidity	Current ratio	Current assets/current liabilities
	Quick (or acid) ratio	(Cash + net receivables)/current liabilities
	Inventory turnover ratio	Cost of sales/average inventory
	Average collection period	(Net receivables/annual sales) × 365
Solvency	Debt-to-equity ratio	Long-term debt/(long-term debt + shareholder's equity)
	Times-interest-earned (indicates whether the firm can meet debt payments)	Operating income/annual interest expense associated with long-term debt
Profitability	Net profit margin	Net income/annual net sales
	Gross margin	Gross profit/annual net sales
	Return on average equity	Net income/shareholder's average equity throughout the year
	Return on total investment	(Net income + interest expense after tax)/total capital
	Return on average assets	Adjusted net income/total average assets

- Price of a ton of steel
- Number of metal buildings sold
- Tons of steel sold
- Plant capacity in tons
- Cost of goods sold as a percentage of steel costs

Analysts provide a wealth of financial detail. UBS, Bank of America, Edgar, and similar sources provide perspective. Industry-specific information, such as the Dodge report, allows for comparison to your firm's peers. If your budget is cut due to a downturn, you can at least say "well, sales of the industry are down 13% this year, so I'll do my part to get us past this." When the grim budget reaper comes, you will likely not escape, so you might as well acquiesce with panache.

Because SG&A (selling, general, and administrative) expense includes the IT budget, you should understand how your department's expenses affect the earnings per share (EPS). On the revenue side, knowing how top-line growth (revenue) affects EPS may help put your projects in a positive light — "if we implement this online portal, we estimate our sales to increase by 3%, which will equal a .02 increase in EPS."

Think in terms of the financial elevator pitch. After listening or reviewing your firm's quarterly report, you will be able to chat about progress — how many tons of product have been sold, how does this compare to the competition, what segments of the business are doing well or declining? If you combine this with core knowledge of the annual income statement, balance sheet, and cash flow statement, you will see the big picture and share the "secret handshake" of those who hold the financial cards of the firm.

Managing Contracts

As CIO you are certainly awash in contracts of all types, sizes, and terms. By mastering a few basics, you can save thousands to hundreds of thousands of dollars each year. The following suggestions are provided by Alison Meyer Vann, a Houston, Texas-based attorney specializing in IT contracts and negotiations:

- Avoid the trap of thinking contracts from large vendors are fixed in stone. They follow the laws of buyer and seller and are almost always negotiable.
- Review software contracts, even small ones. They are much easier to modify on the front end, because typically subsequent purchases are merely addendums to an original master agreement.
- Vendors often provide contracts in unalterable form, such as PDF. Do not let this contrivance deter you from making important changes. (*Author's note:* Consider investing in a desktop utility, such as the professional version of Able2Extract, to convert the PDF to Word, then modify and print back to a PDF.)
- Set up a contract repository system. Time and again I have seen buyers stymied because they have lost the original contract and do not know specific terms or their rights. You should keep a PDF of the contract with original signatures (the executed contract) as well as a paper copy. Some organizations use a content management system such as Microsoft Share Point to maintain contracts.
- Try to centralize software/hardware purchases as much as possible. Although the central purchasing group may have experience in IT contract negotiations, individual business units tend to pay the price asked by the vendor — for both the product and related maintenance.
- Consider carefully the entity name(s) to be used for the purchase, as well as "affiliate language" (e.g., XYZ Corp and its affiliates). Software vendors are not typically lax with regard to terms. If you do not use the right name (e.g., XYZ Group versus XYZ Inc.), you could owe the vendor more money if the software is used in more locations/business units than anticipated. For

example, you may buy each copy of ABC software for $50 a seat for XYZ Group but the same software will cost $75 a seat for XYZ Inc.

■ Insert language related to U.S. versus worldwide usage if applicable. Some contracts will say "Usage in United States only" and may charge additional fees or prohibit use outside the United States.

■ To the extent that you can look into the future (18 to 24 months), consider possible rollout scenarios. Who will be using the software? What about new acquisitions?

■ Create a price list and insert price holds (called "rate stability" in telecom contracts) for a reasonable period, such as 1 year or more. This will allow you to purchase software or hardware at a discount for a period of time in the future, when you may have a better sense of the quantity of product required.

■ Carefully manage maintenance charges and ask for caps on increases.

■ Beware of autorenewals. Telecom contracts, for example, will transition from a negotiated, reasonable rate to an expensive month-to-month rate unless you take decisive action.

■ Remain skeptical about "quarter-end deals." Sometimes there is no deal — the salesperson simply wants to make his or her target and is betting that you will assume you are getting a better deal close to a period end.

■ Push out maintenance so that it is billed upon deployment. So if you start out with 1,000 devices and then deploy 1,000 more 6 months later, you want to pay only for maintenance on the first 1,000 for 6 months, not maintenance on 2,000 devices for 6 months.

■ Pay attention to vendor audit clauses. Of course, the vendor has the right to ensure that you are paying for all the licenses used, but the terms should not be draconian. You should ask for an advance notice of the audit; 30 days is reasonable. Do not allow a "due immediately" term in the contract. If you are found in violation, you should have a reasonable amount of time to get payment to the vendor.

■ Stridently resist extreme audit measures. One software vendor pressured a customer to install software that opened up a communication link to the vendor's "mother ship" in order to monitor compliance. This is an extreme and unnecessary security risk. Manual audits are perfectly acceptable and less of a fraud exposure.

■ Do your own self-audit so that there are no surprises if the vendor performs its own audit. It can be damaging to your career if a large discrepancy is found, resulting in an out-of-budget outlay of cash as well as institutional embarrassment. Count IDs and clean up those associated with departed employees and contractors — no need to pay for someone not using the system.

■ Focus on data quality that affects the bill from the vendor. For example, you might have Jane Smith and Jane Doe, the same person but on the system twice as a result of a name change. Run scripts to keep the data as good as possible. You really do not want to depend on the vendor's auditors to sanitize your user lists.

- Do not depend on specific individuals, with no backup, to maintain contracts. When they leave the firm, contracts get lost. One firm I know got into trouble at a customs checkpoint because they could not show that their software contract permitted them to use the software outside the United States. Had they used a contracts library/repository, the contract could have been readily located.
- Periodically review contracts to ensure that you are taking full advantage of terms and that you are in compliance with the number of licenses specified. Some vendors are amenable to a routine "true up" on licenses, but others may require you to pay top dollar for unanticipated (not previously negotiated) growth. A built-in price hold is a good defense against excessive costs from unanticipated growth.

We also discussed with Meyer Vann some recommended good practices to ensure the organization's assets are fully protected. She suggested the following:

- Make sure consultants and contractors sign nondisclosure agreements (NDAs). For larger consulting firms, just an agreement with the firm may be required rather than an NDA for each consultant doing the work.
- Use common sense regarding who owns the code. Assume, for example, a contractor develops a tool that connects two of your ERPs together. If this tool is not strategic for your firm, there is probably no reason for you to own that code. Of course, you need the rights to use it perpetually for your own use. However, if the code is important to your business (i.e., intellectual property) and helps you maintain a competitive edge, you should specifically address ownership in any agreement. It is no secret that some consulting firms have developed important business software for one client and then modified it slightly for another client. That may or may not be acceptable, but the economic impact needs to be considered in your contract negotiations. Sometimes cross-licenses can be useful for Internet protocol (IP) sharing.
- Trademark and copyright registrations are not that difficult to obtain; use them when needed.
- Go with a mid-to-upper tier, known vendor if you are concerned about performance. Reputable vendors do not want negative talk on the street.
- If you are concerned about a small vendor's viability, look for errors and omissions and other business insurance.
- Finally, as an umbrella piece of advice — always ASK for what you want.

Summary

To be an effective CIO, you must achieve certain core financial goals and competencies. These include improving IT cost efficiency, making budgeting and maintenance costs transparent, showing the business payback on the IT investment, defining a prioritization process for competing investments, and tracking deviations from expectations. A large part of managing the IT function is simply buying things — consulting services, hardware, software, training — the list goes on and on. Having a good grasp of accounting and financial fundamentals will distinguish you from your technology peers who lack financial acumen. Get a practical book, such as Robert Rachlin's and Allen Sweeny's *Accounting and Financial Fundamentals for Nonfinancial Executives*[9] and keep it next to your desk. If you are a good steward of your firm's money and buy the right things, you will be well rewarded. Compensation follows success.

References

1. Alan Deutschman. Inside the Mind of Jeff Bezos, *Fast Company*. www.fastcompany.com/magazine/85/bezos_2.html (accessed August 5, 2007).
2. Fitzgerald, Michael. The Fabric of the Company. *CIO Magazine*. www.cio.com/article/104609 (accessed September 2, 2007).
3. Bock, Geoffrey E. 2003. The Guardian Life Insurance Company of America — Improving Business Responsiveness with an Extensive Enterprise Infrastructure. ftp://ftp.software.ibm.com/software/solutions/pdfs/IBM_Guardian_casestudy12-17-03.pdf (accessed August 26, 2007).
4. Thrasher, Harwell. *Boiling the IT Frog: How to Make Your Business Information Technology Wildly Successful without Having to Learn Anything Technical* (Deluth: MakingITClear, 2007), 48.
5. CobiT 4.1, Framework, Control Objectives, Management Guidelines and Maturity Models. 2007. IT Governance Institute. www.isaca.org (accessed August 19, 2007).
6. According to Wikipedia (www.wikipedia.org [accessed October 7, 2007]), "A code refactoring is any change to a computer program's code which improves its readability or simplifies its structure without changing its results."
7. Maizlish, Bryan and Robert Handler. *IT Portfolio Management Step-by-Step* (Hoboken, NJ: John Wiley & Sons, 2005), 10.
8. http://finance.google.com/finance?client=ob&q=NCS (accessed October 29, 2007).
9. Rachlin, Robert and Allen Sweeny. *Accounting and Financial Fundamentals for Non-Financial Executives* (New York: Amacom, 1996).

Chapter 4

Project Management

Adding manpower to a late software project makes it later.

Fred Brooks, *The Mythical Man-Month*

Involve people in meaningful projects.

Stephen Covey, *Thirty Methods of Influence*

Books on self-promotion and success nearly always mention the "elevator speech." This is the 30 seconds of attention span you are given by someone forcibly confined and willing to listen to your accomplishments. For the chief information officer, nothing is more memorable than the completion of some major, universally acknowledged and appreciated project, on time, within budget, and functioning as intended. Unfortunately, this happens only 16.2% of the time, according to the 1994 Standish Group CHAOS report.[1] Fifty-two percent of projects are actually completed but are either late, over budget, or have a reduced feature set. An amazing 31.1% are never completed. Although these statistics are dated, there is no evidence that project delivery has improved.

Although these dismal statistics are a serious black eye for the IT profession, they suggest an opportunity for you — just do a little better and your management reputation will grow accordingly. In some organizations, the PMO (program management office) does not report to the CIO. Where it reports is not that critical. Either you are responsible for the PMO or you are its most vital, internal customer. Knowing and implementing effective project management methods is a core part of your personal management portfolio.

Figure 4.1   The Program Management Office value proposition.

Figure 4.1, adapted from a presentation by Chris Chambliss, Vice President of the Program Management Office for NCI Building Systems, Inc., shows the PMO value proposition discussed in this chapter. Done well, good project management delivers a plethora of benefits. But it will not occur spontaneously — you will need to continually promote the structured approach adopted by your organization.

Project Organization

Figure 4.2 shows a typical organizational chart for a specific project. The steering committee sits at the top, providing direction and feedback to the team doing the work. Although names have been changed (except for Brown and Chambliss), the example was selected from an eCommerce application development project at NCI Building Systems.

The first step to success is assembling the right team with the right expectations. As we will see later in the chapter, human factors play as important a role in project success as anywhere in information technology.

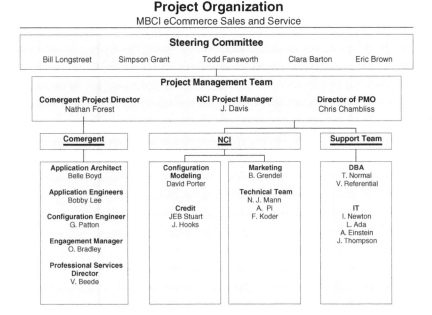

Figure 4.2   Example of an organizational structure for an individual project.

Systems Development Methodologies

Even the smallest IT organization needs to select a standard methodology for development. There may be variations based on size and other factors, but a published and communicated standard provides the shared vision necessary to create useful and timely systems. Figure 4.3 illustrates the methodology the authors use at NCI, which includes feedback, iteration, and sign-off at many points in the cycle. In later sections we will show examples of models used in the industry.

Model #1: Informal Approach — Code First, Fix Later

This approach is the equivalent of no methodology. For some small projects with very low risk to the organization, this may indeed be the best approach. Because of the small upfront investment, the work can usually be discarded if not useful or repaired quickly. However, this approach is obviously not recommended for most projects. If the system gets larger than its intended "micro" size, inadvertent errors (due to lack of design, "quick and dirty" methods) may significantly increase maintenance costs.

Developers and IT personnel with little professional experience, perhaps just out of school, may need to be coached out of the informal mind-set. In programming classes, every program is *private* in the sense that only the author has written

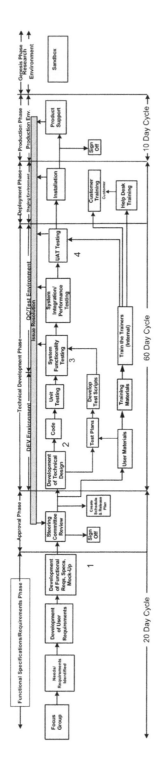

Special review points:

1. SOX and SOD (segregation of duties) compliance – design level only. High level internal control review. Reviewers: Security & Internal Audit

2. Technical architecture compliance review. Reviewers: IT Infrastructure Group

3. Internal control, SOX and SOD compliance. Reviewers: Internal Audit, Security

4. Final artifact review. Reviewers: Internal Audit, Security

Figure 4.3   Example of a systems development methodology.

any of the code, it does not need to be passed onto anyone else, and documentation is seen as an unnecessary add-on. The student owns the program. In contrast, in commercial environments, the organization owns the code, it must be maintained by multiple developers, and its function must be documented to ensure it will integrate into larger systems. The requirements for these *public* programs are far more stringent, as they are an asset and a working component of the organization's business systems.

Model #2: Traditional Approach — Waterfall

As the granddaddy of project development methods, the waterfall approach has proven successful for large development since the 1970s. The name derives from the flow of activity from one phase to another, much the way water flows over one ledge after another, down to the river below. Figure 4.4 shows the basic waterfall flow.

The waterfall method appears to work best in a slower-moving environment where requirements do not change quickly (e.g., from market-driven functionality changes). Testing and quality assurance occur at the end of each phase. It depends heavily on written specifications and is expensive to revise if design modifications are needed. Since the 1990s, this methodology has been declining in popularity due to its need for complete finalization at each stage and cost to revise specifications should new business requirements or technological changes occur. This methodology also runs into the limits of documentation. Pictures, words, and diagrams are

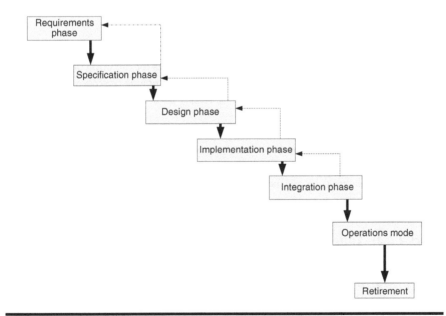

Figure 4.4 Waterfall development model.

valuable, but the dynamics of business sometimes require a more vivid projection of functionality. At some level it becomes difficult for the user to articulate exactly what he or she needs. IT documentation can be abstract, so the "oops" moment, indicating that the project has gone awry, may not occur at the intended early stages. Prototypes and models help visualize the anticipated outcome. Waterfall methodology also suffers from inflexibility because of the sharp separation of the project into strict phases. Late changes become expensive.

If you are building the pyramids, the waterfall model is the way to go. But if the goal is to develop a Web-based retail system to respond to the volatile tastes of Japanese teenagers, who frequent Harajuku station on a Sunday, other methodologies are a better fit.

Model #3: Rapid Prototyping/Rapid Application Development (RAD)

Building a product model in a few months helps users and management comprehend the deliverables as a unified product. The interaction improves specifications and elicits further dialogue and requirements from the end users. If the original concept becomes completely unworkable, the model can be discarded and a new one created. Or the model can be refined until it becomes the final product. James Martin championed this method during the 1980s.

Figure 4.5 shows a high-level perspective of the RAD process. Some of the characteristics of RAD include:

- Relies on small, well-trained teams
- Uses evolutionary prototypes
- Sets strict limits on development completion times for each function or module
- Uses tools for prototyping. These tools typically include the following features:
  - Application simulation (mock screens, with tools to create text boxes, tabs, calendars, sliders, etc.)
  - Prototype execution, showing flow of the program(s)
  - Connection of prototype screens to show a complete A-to-Z application, as a first cut of the final application
  - Templates/styles so that even the prototype has a consistent look and feel for reports, screens, etc.

Model #4: Agile Methodologies

Agile is a development framework that emphasizes quick development of software in iterative steps (see Figure 4.6). It stresses personal communications, with developers, users, and testers in the same or nearby rooms.

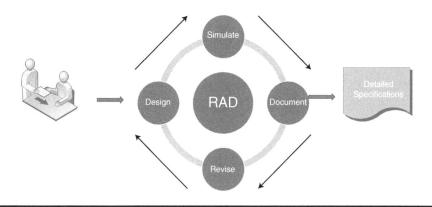

Figure 4.5   Core process for the Rapid Application Development approach.

Agile development depends far less on written documents than traditional development methods and is focused on quick adaptation to business changes. The difference from previous rapid development models is in the speed of each iteration — measured in weeks rather than months. Working software is considered the measure of progress and even late changes in specifications are included in the working code. Agile methods work best in "emergent" requirement environments where business conditions include ambiguity. These methods are less effective in systems where safety, extreme accuracy, or critical security features must be present. For example, NASA and the nuclear energy industry tend to use older systems for certain functions because the extreme attention to detail at every step of development and testing makes quick replacement of systems difficult. Scale also affects suitability — when the number of project participants exceeds about fifty, the close interpersonal communications required for Agile development to work begin to break down. Finally, this approach may not be as effective with a distributed insource/outsource workforce, because much of its power stems from direct contact of all participants.

Agile methods seem to have momentum, even though their penetration into major U.S. firms is still limited. *CIO Magazine* reports that 81% of firms using Agile methods found their projects to be "somewhat successful" or "very successful."[2]

For those firms adopting Agile as a philosophy/culture, its implementation is carried out by specific submethods, such as Scrum, which provides project management. The term "Scrum," short for scrimmage, comes from the sports of Rugby Union and Rugby League and is a way of restarting the game by using a scrum formation. Figure 4.7 illustrates this methodology's core cycle. Its components include:

- A backlog of work to be accomplished, in priority sequence
- Completion of a certain number of these tasks in short *sprints*

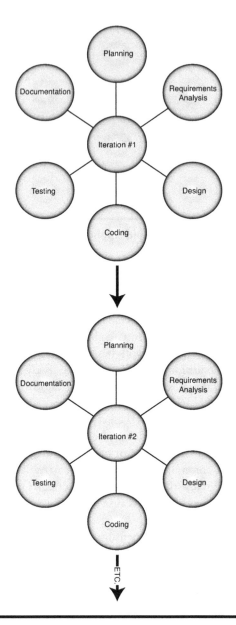

Figure 4.6   Agile methodology.

■ Daily meetings to communicate progress and identify roadblocks
■ A *sprint* planning session to define a new set of backlog tasks
■ A *sprint retrospective* that represents a postmortem for the past sprint

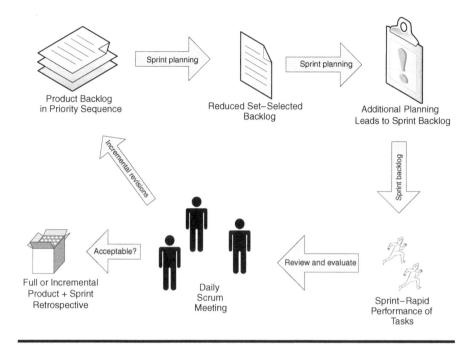

Figure 4.7   Scrum project flow.

Model #5: Rational Unified Process (RUP)

RUP is another iterative software development process, created by Rational Software Corporation, a division of IBM. It is both a process and a commercial package (framework), with extensive sample artifacts for various activities. The use of modeling (via Unified Modeling Language [UML]) provides a rich source of requirements, architecture, and designs to each member of the development team. According to IBM,[3] RUP uses six key principles to develop systems:

1. Adapt the process
2. Balance competing stakeholder priorities
3. Collaborate across teams
4. Demonstrate value iteratively
5. Elevate the level of abstraction
6. Focus continuously on quality

These principles are straightforward: Tailor the process to your organization's size and needs; get the competing parties to agree on what is important; share knowledge between teams; show results in increments; keep the design at a reasonably high level of abstraction in order to encourage reusable modules rather than

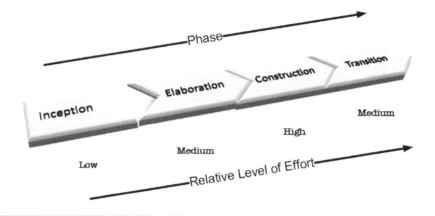

Figure 4.8 RUP project phases.

create custom code for similar functions; and finally evaluate quality throughout the project.

These principles are expressed in a four-phase model, as shown in Figure 4.8. The phases include the following core elements:

■ *Inception*: Obtain buy in from all parties — especially the end users; ensure requirements are clear; review any prototypes to further solidify consensus on the final product; make sure that the mechanism to track variances between budgeted and actual expenditures is in place; develop an initial risk analysis.

■ *Elaboration*: Develop detailed use-case models; develop and describe the software architecture; finalize the business case; identify project risks and eliminate the highest ones found; create a detailed project plan with dates, responsible parties, and man-hours required per step.

■ *Construction*: Perform the majority of coding/development; prepare for the first release of software to be tested by end users. This represents the bulk of the work and may require several iterations for complex systems.

■ *Transition*: Move the system into beta release for final testing by users; complete training and quality review; after approvals, move system into production status via standard change management procedures.

Each phase can have one or more iterations, somewhat analogous to the Agile approach. The iterations are subdivided into nine core process workflows, as follows:

■ Engineering Workflows:
  – Business modeling
  – Requirements
  – Analysis

- – Implementation
- – Testing
- – Deployment
■ Supporting Workflows:
    - – Change management
    - – Environment (tools, kits for the developers)
    - – Project management

IBM's Rational Unified Process package includes templates, guidelines, tools, and visual models for developers. By the time this book goes to print, there will likely be a new development methodology, supported by one or more major vendors. As CIO, you will need to select the package that fits your environment, based on total cost of ownership, speed, quality, staff size, and organizational temperament.

Model #6: Out of Scope/Embedded Project

Like any good mathematician, we must have a "null" value to complete our analysis — the absence of a development methodology. A reasonably large percentage of any IT group's work will fit into this category. Routine upgrades, simple maintenance efforts, or other extremely routine tasks may be considered "embedded" in existing infrastructures. Superimposing a full life cycle on top of these activities does not make economic or practical sense. This is not to say those changes should be exempted from standard change control procedures. Good IT governance requires all production changes to be approved and documented. But they do not require, for example, a financial analysis on the front end of the task. When your server crashes, you simply fix it or buy a new one.

Project Dynamics

Why Do Projects Fail?

In the Russian classic *Anna Karenina*, Leo Tolstoy remarks "Happy families are all alike; every unhappy family is unhappy in its own way." The same concept can be applied to projects. Successful projects have certain core features in common, whereas failed projects can fail for any number of reasons. Some reasons for project failure include:

■ Missing requirements
■ Ignorance of business or technical risks
■ Rigid, inflexible architecture
■ Insufficient manpower or expertise

- Poor governance practices (e.g., bad change management)
- Lack of rigorous scheduling and hours tracking
- Lack of tools — either technical software/hardware or business modeling tools
- Estimating honesty on the part of the project manager may be punished by upfront disqualification of the project
- Management fatigue — a realistic plan includes unknowns that have to be explained in too much detail for the management time available. As a result, the project manager is pressured to present a "Pollyanna" scenario
- Supplier breakdowns, including late deliveries, poor quality, or personnel changes
- General dependencies (on some action within or outside of the organization)
- Failure to consider downstream effects of the project
- Missing or inconsistent executive buy-in and oversight
- Political infighting
- Personality differences within the team
- Lack of outsource coordination and oversight

Few would argue with Fred Brook's classic statement that manpower added to a late project makes it later. Each new person added, regardless of expertise, must be briefed on the specifics of the projects and will temporarily consume more resources than he or she contributes. And project administration increases with each resource added. Another perspective on this problem comes from the mathematics of social networking. Assuming that some interaction time is spent between each participant, the number of interpersonal communication channels increases almost with the square of the number of participants — a rapid rise in administrative effort (see Figure 4.9).

In a 2003 presentation at MIT,[4] James Lyneis noted some of the problems that create "vicious circles" in a late project:

- Schedule acceleration causes out-of-sequence work, work-site congestion, coordination, and decline in morale
- Overtime causes fatigue and burnout
- Quality and productivity decline
- Undiscovered rework appears
- Scope changes affect the project in ways that cannot be immediately understood
- Twenty-four months are required to gain full experience for complex systems new to the team member
- Inexperienced staff work at 50% of the productivity and quality of experienced staff

Given all these depressing failure points and reasons why they happen, we quickly turn to the basics of project management and some suggested good practices.

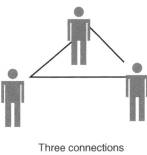

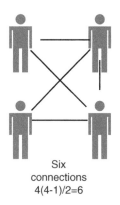

Three connections
N(N-1)/2=
3(3-1)/2=3

Six
connections
4(4-1)/2=6

N = Number of
individuals assigned to a
project

Number of
communication channels
= N(N-1)/2

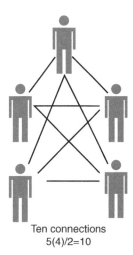

Ten connections
5(4)/2=10

**Figure 4.9   The number of connections (interpersonal communication channels)
grows geometrically with the number of project participants.**

Planning the Work

Planning succeeds. To get started you do three things:

1. Describe what is to be done.
2. Develop a schedule for the work, including dates, people, hours, and contingencies.
3. Create a budget by phases or other milestones.

Large organizations and large projects use specialized project management software. For many, however, a desktop package such as MS Project is more than

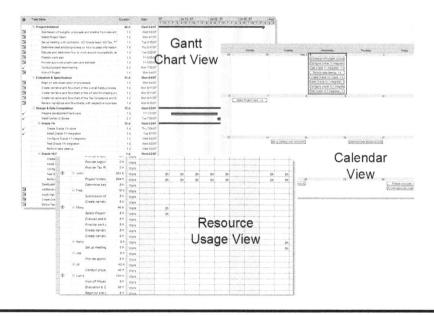

Figure 4.10 Three MS project views of a software implementation project.

adequate. It includes multiple views (Gantt, PERT, and so forth), scheduling, manpower planning, and many options for tracking progress and exceptions. A handy secondary package is the latest release of Visio, which provides attractive timeline shapes for executive presentations. Figure 4.10 shows three partial views of a Gantt chart for a tax software implementation.

Earlier in this chapter we discussed some of the varied development methodologies used. In practice, there are some life-cycle steps that should be followed as part of the administration and effective operation under any methodology. Figure 4.11 shows some of these base tasks using a simplified timeline.

Project Risk Assessment

Every project carries a hidden question: How much effort is required and appropriate to do the job properly? Does a "project" to create three new views of budget data need a requirements document? Does it need a unit, integration, regression, and user acceptance test? At the other end of the spectrum, how much testing and documentation is needed for our integrated, customer-request-to-factory-delivery system? There are no absolute lines of demarcation, but it is clear that high-risk projects require far more total effort than do low-risk ones.

On June 28, 1911, a very unlucky dog was hit and killed by a meteorite in Nakhla, Egypt. The point is, no matter how good your risk model, it will not identify "out of the blue" incidents like this one. However, most *known* risks can be identified in broad outlines. By developing a risk assessment model based on business

The Project Life Cycle

1 Concept	2 Planning	3 Design and Development	4 Implementation	5 Closeout

■ Gather data
■ Identify need
■ Establish –
  ▪ Goals, objectives
  ▪ Basic economics, feasibility
  ▪ Stakeholders
  ▪ Risk level
  ▪ Strategy
  ▪ Potential team
■ Guesstimate resources
■ Identify alternatives
■ Present proposal
■ Obtain approval for next phase
	■ Appoint key team members
	■ Conduct studies
	■ Develop scope baseline –
	  ▪ End product(s)
	  ▪ Quality standards
	  ▪ Resources
	  ▪ Activities
	■ Establish –
	  ▪ Master Plan
	  ▪ Budget, cash flow
	  ▪ WBS
	  ▪ Policies and procedures
	■ Assess risks
	■ Confirm justification
	■ Present project brief
	■ Obtain approval to proceed
		■ Set up –
		  ▪ Organization
		  ▪ Communications
		■ Motivate team
		■ Detail technical requirements
		■ Establish –
		  ▪ Work packages
		  ▪ Information control systems
		■ Procure goods and services
		■ Execute work packages
			■ Direct/monitor/forecast/control –
			  ▪ Scope
			  ▪ Quality
			  ▪ Time
			  ▪ Cost
			■ Resolve problems
				■ Finalize product(s)
				■ Review and accept
				■ Settle final a/c's
				■ Transfer product responsibilities
				■ Evaluate project
				■ Document results
				■ Release/redirect resources
				■ Reassign project team

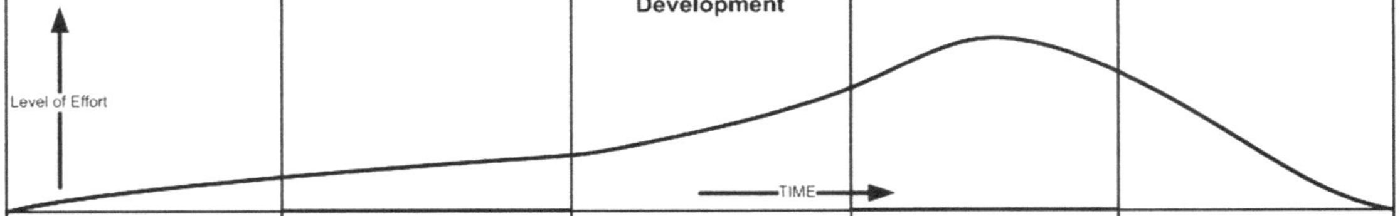

Level of Effort — TIME

Figure 4.11   Life-cycle steps and PMO operational tasks common to most development methodologies.

and technical factors, you can assess project risk and take measures to improve its chances for success. The risk model should provide at least the following:

- A consistent methodology to estimate risk.
- A set of guidelines that describe the additional resource/artifact/testing resources required as risk moves from low to medium to high.
- A periodic reevaluation of the model's weighting of factors and general effectiveness.

Although there are professional-strength risk assessment packages from firms such as Chordiant and Palisade, as well as government conceptual models, many IT organizations develop simple spreadsheet tools. One useful model, developed by George Westerman and Richard Huntsman,[5] condenses risk factors into four categories: availability, access, accuracy, and agility. In this "4A" model, *availability* includes disaster recovery, backup, online response time — are systems available to users when they need them? *Access* includes security and segregation of duties. *Accuracy* asks whether the outputs are correct, including financial statements, engineering calculations, and database inquiries. Finally, *agility* measures how flexible systems are — can they be integrated, duplicated in other business units, and modified easily for new uses?

To develop a working risk assessment process, you will need to identify factors in your organization which directly influence the 4As. Table 4.1 lists examples but should not be considered comprehensive.

A volume/impact category was added to the 4A categories in order to size the risk — the business unit affected may be too small to present a significant risk. Of course, judgments about size should be used with caution. For example, Nick Leeson, a 28-year-old employee in charge of the small Barrings Bank trading desk in Singapore, ran up such large losses that the entire bank folded.[6]

Each of these factors should be weighted based on importance to your organization. After weighting and assigning a risk rank (for example, H for high, M for medium, L for low), systems can be compared from a risk perspective. Figure 4.12 shows an example risk matrix after the rollup from individual risk factors. Typically, a spreadsheet with a tab for each risk category is used to generate the summary risk ranking. In Figure 4.12, ERP #1 is significantly more risky than another system, and therefore any projects associated with it should be more thoroughly tested, have more user involvement, and be managed more closely than usual.

There are many approaches to risk analysis and some are far more comprehensive than the methods discussed here. For example, Figure 4.13 shows the output of the PMO risk assessment used at NCI Building Systems. Regardless of sophistication, some assessment of risk is essential for both project management and IT governance. A risk assessment also provides you with a tool to slow user management who may want a project implemented before a reasonable level of

Table 4.1 Example Risk Factors Using the "4A" Method

Risk Category	Representative Factors
Availability	Included in DR[a]/offsite system or alternative offsite system?
	Excessive time to restore?
	Requires special equipment or unique environment?
	Supporting WAN telecom links are vital to system operations?
	Resources for essential/emergency maintenance are available?
Access	What is the financial impact of unauthorized modification of data?
	What is the impact of unauthorized disclosure of information?
	Are duties segregated so that a single individual cannot complete an important transaction from start to finish?
	Are job roles defined so that the access rights for any job can be easily replicated and controlled (e.g., security profile for an accountant, inventory manager, etc.)?
	Are most sensitive transactions restricted via programmatic controls?
	Is new technology in place for which adequate controls have not been developed (e.g., Web services)?
	Are audit trails and exception reporting fully developed for key applications?
	Is security-related information current? For example, do terminated employees or no longer active contractors remain as active IDs in Active Directory?
Accuracy	What is the financial impact of inaccurate calculations (General Ledger)?
	What is the effect of inaccuracy on customer-facing activities or organization's reputation?
	What regulatory and governmental compliance is required (e.g., taxes, reporting)?

(continued on next page)

Table 4.1 (continued)   Example Risk Factors Using the "4A" Method

Risk Category	Representative Factors
	What is the organizational maturity for business process (new to users?)
	Is data conversion a risk for the new system?
	Is there a high level of customization (modifications to vendor delivered code)?
	Are calculations performed by a third-party, offsite vendor (web services, etc.)?
Agility	Is the system hard coded with custom features difficult to replicate?
	Is the system/release supported by the vendor?
	Does system require hard to obtain resources (technical knowledge)?
	Can the system be scaled, both in terms of volume and number of business units using it?
	Is documentation adequate?
	Does the system require a specific/out-of-date operating system and hence cannot be easily upgraded?
	Is the system configurable (i.e., easily modified by user-controlled parameters)?
Volume/impact	What is the annual volume of the most important transactions?
	What is the largest dollar value of any account affected by the system (e.g., inventory)?

ª DR: disaster recovery.

testing and training has been completed. "Damn the torpedoes, full speed ahead" makes a great sound bite but in practice results mostly in sunk projects.

For IT projects, as is painfully clear, there are many pressures that conspire to delay or increase the cost:

- Programmatic risk
- Technical problems
- Schedule compression
- Fund limitations

Applications	Availability	Access	Accuracy	Agility	Vol/Final Impact	Composite Risk Ranking
ERP #1	2	2.25	3	3.35	5	15.6
ERP #2	1.5	2.25	2.25	1.6	3	10.6
ERP #3	2.6	2.25	2.35	1.55	2	10.75
Order Entry	2.4	1.8	1.85	1.7	2	9.75
CAMS-manufacturing	1.6	2.25	1.4	1.35	2	8.6
Job Tracking	1.5	1.6	1.85	1.9	3	9.85
Legacy financial system	1.5	2.25	2	1.9	3	10.65
Standalone financial system at subsidiary B	1.25	2.4	1.85	2.55	2	10.05
Payroll	1.5	2.25	1.85	1.15	2.5	9.25
Engineering system	1.4	1.1	1.25	1.55	2	7.3
Drafting system	1.4	2.25	1.25	1.35	2	8.25
Imaging	1.45	1.2	1.15	1.15	2.5	7.45
Drawing, engineering system #2	1.25	2.25	1	1.5	2	8

(— 4A Framework —)

Figure 4.12 Example of a Summary Risk Matrix showing high risk applications, requiring more testing, planning, user involvement, etc.

- Market changes
- Governmental regulation changes

Before a model is developed, some preliminary spade work will help organize the effort. Brainstorming will identify both business and technical risks. If all parties are included in the brainstorming effort, the results will be much better than an IT-only session. Consolidating the identified risks into a reasonable number of categories will facilitate model development. Then you can quantify them and insert into a model, such as the one recommended by Westerman.

Standard cost accounting techniques also help abate risk. Table 4.2 shows work/financial metrics that help monitor overall progress.

Scope of the Job — The Program Management Office's (PMO) Dilemma

In most complex systems implementations, users as well as IT have tasks essential to project completion. For example, a system conversion may require user effort to cleanse critical data, obtain regulatory permissions, or complete a marketing campaign or other jobs that IT cannot complete alone. So the question arises — does the project manager track only IT activities (assuming he or she reports to the CIO) or are all relevant activities managed, including required business steps?

This scope question can become a sensitive issue. If, for example, the tax department is late having sales tax certificates of exemptions scrubbed and loaded onto a database, is the project manager supposed to track the delay? Is it reasonable to expect project managers to escalate to management any delay caused by groups or

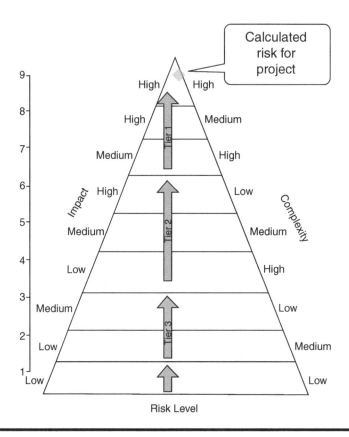

Figure 4.13 **Example of a risk analysis output showing the risk level for an application in development.**

Table 4.2 **Project Management Metrics**

Metric	Calculation Method
Cost variance	Budgeted cost — actual cost (for the work performed so far)
Plan schedule variance	Work performed — work scheduled (using budgeted dollars)
End-of-project variance	Total actual/expected cost — budgeted cost

departments threatening the go-live date? The answer will depend on the culture of the organization, but the scope of the job should be considered early on. The PMO charter is a good place to build the foundation and manage expectations.

To put this question in the most stark terms — if the project manager reports to the vice president of a particular business unit and that business unit, with the VP's knowledge, is holding up the project — where is the escalation point? There is no easy answer except that good project managers invariably bring effective human relations skills to the job at hand.

A Practitioner's Perspective

As the late historian Stephen Ambrose pointed out in his book *Citizen Soldier*, things look a lot different from the perspective of the soldier in the foxhole than what the general sees on the strategy board at headquarters. It is the same with project management — purists may not survive, and the successful project manager must almost always improvise. The following Q&A session with Chambliss, Vice President, Program Management Office, NCI Building Systems, Inc., provides some examples of how theory and practice merge into successful project management.

Q: Many studies have shown a large percentage of failed projects. What do you think are the primary causes for these failures, and how does the PMO improve the odds?

A: Oh, the dreaded statistics. 60%+ of projects fail due to everything from scope creep, lack of qualified resources, space aliens, and more. This is the core question every PMO leader has to face and formulate a strategy to address.

There are lists of reasons why projects can fail and they assign blame to various parts of the organization, but as the ultimate professional I will take responsibility for the high failure rate of projects. We, Project Management professionals, are one of the primary causes of project failure. Unqualified, undertrained Project Managers who lack the boldness, creativity, and vision to lead, direct, and steer a project through are the real culprits. This is the primary cause of project failure. Don't blame the business users, the stakeholders, scope creep, the guy who quit last week, or anything else. We, as certified PMP, PgMP, MBA professionals, are responsible for managing all aspects of a project from top to bottom and escalating anything that needs the attention of Executive Management.

In order to improve the odds of success, it starts with the PMO leader:

■ Know your company culture
■ Understand the business and the business unit personnel you're expected to work with
■ Hire the right people for the PMO team, be picky
■ Listen to what's working and adjust what's not working
■ Most importantly, communicate to the PMO team and the business team that the Project Managers are in charge of the project and take ultimate responsibility for the success of the project team

Q: The PMO function is often under the CIO but there is no inherent reason why project management needs to be strictly associated with IT. Do you see the scope of the PMO's responsibilities growing over time?

A: A PMO quite often is chartered by the CIO and funded by the IT organization in response to the wide array of projects that flow through IT. Naturally a PMO is expected to lead and succeed on IT projects in order to establish itself and build a reputation; however, many of these projects have a business unit element driving them to some extent. The result is a natural shift of an internally focused IT PMO to a broader-based PMO that gets involved in business unit project initiatives. A strong and successful PMO encourages the increased scope of responsibilities and makes the shift easily by hiring the right blend of Project Managers and Analysts with backgrounds that can cover the wide array of business initiatives.

Q: For small- to medium-sized firms that have not yet established a PMO, the introduction of strict project management methodologies would seem to be a wrenching cultural change. Do you have any recommendations to ease the pain as these firms move from informal methods to the use of detailed project plans, front-end design, checkpoints, user reviews, regression testing, and so forth?

A: Three major recommendations:

1. Never underestimate the concept of culture change regardless of organization size
2. Listen, listen, and listen again to your business community
3. Be flexible

Project Managers are taught and trained to leverage the PMBOK (Project Management Body of Knowledge) both for Project Management Professional (PMP) certification purposes and daily work execution, but the most valuable Project Managers are those that can balance the book knowledge with the vision and foresight to anticipate the impact of introducing methodology and processes into the organization.

I tend to focus my method of introducing project management structure, principles, and processes on a simple foundation, "Try something. If it doesn't stick, listen to the feedback, tailor it and try it again." Easy enough, right? It's been unbelievably successful for years and has moved our once fledgling $3 million PMO to an ever-growing $13 million PMO in the matter of 3 short years.

Q: There has been much written about various development methodologies, such as Agile, Waterfall, RAD, and RUP. Do you believe that the choice of a specific methodology is critical, or does the organization just need to pick one and enforce it?

A: Again, flexibility is the key message. Each organization and PMO is different. Our particular PMO crosses different software development boundaries that adhere to multiple development methodologies so we have to adapt our project management processes to work in sync with an Agile, Waterfall, or RUP development process.

For example, within our organization, Oracle Applications development tends more toward a Waterfall development approach based on the mechanics of implementing the Oracle ERP system; however, custom Engineering development lends itself to a highly repetitive development cycle with short release cycle times. The PMO tried to use standard requirements documents to encapsulate both processes and satisfy both development communities, but the feedback was negative from the Engineering development staff. They needed something that allowed for shorter requirement/development cycles, so as a PMO team, we tailored the requirements gathering documentation process to fit. Is it perfect? We're trying something. If it doesn't stick, we'll incorporate the feedback and build a better model.

Q: Our final question. When you are interviewing an individual for a project manager position, what traits and background do you look for?

A: There's a common saying around our IT organization, "Hire for attitude, train for skills." I can look for PMP certification, years of experience, project successes, communication skills, etc. All of these are obvious factors to consider when interviewing for a dynamic Project Manager. At the end of the day when I'm staring at two resumes of candidates I just interviewed who are on equal footing, it comes down to the candidate who has the better attitude and the willingness to stretch his or her skills and learn.

The Future of Project Management

Although projects have been part of human life since the beginning of recorded history, only in the last 40 years has this effort become a distinct professional function within both IT and business/government groups. As IT has become more pervasive in the life of the organization, the number of projects has risen and the demand for the PMO function has increased. In addition, the constant rationalization of manpower within most organizations means there are fewer spare "brain cycles" available to manage projects on a part-time basis.

The net result of these trends is to increase the need for project management skills and a more thorough penetration of the life-cycle philosophy into the fabric of the company. The science of project management is advancing, with more emphasis on resource leveling; an increasing recognition that projects are not inherently stable but subject to a plethora of internal and external changes; and more interest in portfolio management to ensure that resources are moved to the highest payoff areas at the right time. And do not forget those energetic academics, consultants, and mathematicians who are perennially throwing out new theories — some of them will develop tomorrow's tools of choice.

The effective CIO will use formal project management techniques as an essential tool for getting things done. No mechanic wants to be described as tinkerer, and no CIO wants to be accused of running projects by gut-feel emotions. PMO is the way to go.

References

1. Standish Group. 1994. The Chaos Report. www.standishgroup.com/sample_research/chaos_1994_1.php (accessed November 25, 2007).
2. Wailbru, Thomas. From Here to Agility. *CIO Magazine* (June 1, 2007).
3. Kroll, Per. *Key Principles for Business Driven Development*. www-128.ibm.com/developerworks/rational/library/oct05/kroll (accessed December 2, 2007).

4. Westerman, George and Richard Hunter. *IT Risk* (Boston: Harvard Business School Press, 2007).
5. Lyneis, James M. *Dynamics of Project Performance*. Power Point from a lecture at MIT on 10/2/2003 (ESD.36JSPM).
6. Nick Leeson. *Rogue Trader: How I Brought Down Barings Bank and Shook the Financial World* (Boston: Little Brown and Company, 1996).

Chapter 5

Creating Good Enough Code

Why did we not call this chapter "The Best Code on the Planet" or "The Top Ten List for Outstanding Code Development?" Well, those titles do not reflect reality. Certainly, the space shuttle needs outstanding code; medical equipment microcode needs to be as error free as humans can make it. But aside from those examples, most code needs to be at a merely appropriate level of quality. If you are 6 months late deploying a system your bank needs to be competitive, the chief executive officer (CEO) will not praise your project management skills, development effort, or quality control. On the flip side, your shop cannot produce unreliable junk; it has to work well enough to meet business needs. So our challenge is to find the middle ground — *good enough code* — and create working systems that serve the business, at a reasonable cost and within the correct time frame.

In Chapter 4, we discussed systems development from a high-level, project management perspective. And often strong project management will make or break the final product. But eventually the "thing" that actually does the work includes computer code, objects, parameters, and other elements of a computer-based system. We cannot ignore the nuts and bolts if we want to achieve success. The following sections outline techniques and factors that influence the essential plumbing of information technology systems.

How Do You Do Good Code?

Thick books describe some of the rather abstract and mathematical approaches to code development. Computer science has been a discipline since the Alan Turing and John von Neumann days; a vast literature has developed around the problems of creating quality, maintainable programs. We will leave those academic discussions to the specialists (see some of the books mentioned in the suggested reading). From a management perspective, following are some of the factors that will influence your developer's productivity:

- *Good architecture.* Code written in an environment of standards, up-to-date technology, uniform systems, and adequate documentation is likely to be less complex and more stable than otherwise.
- *Managers with the right background.* For some jobs, nontechnical functional managers are fine, even desirable. Developers on the other hand, generally fare better when their direct supervisor has a strong technical background.
- *Readability and documentation mandate.* Good code is readable by other developers, is documented, and is transferable. If the code is needlessly obscure and undocumented, logical errors are the likely result.
- *Mentoring and code reviews.* A system of mentoring and code reviews, even if informal, needs to be in place so that knowledge flows smoothly from senior to junior developers.
- *Tolerance of prima donnas.* Some of your best coders may not have a nuanced sensitivity to the social needs of others. If you can tolerate their personality "baggage," you may benefit from their outsized technical contribution. Nonetheless, if any developer's personality is so acerbic that it causes undue friction in the group, you may have to transfer or remove him or her.

How Important Are Coding Standards?

Certainly, compliance with standards will improve your code. The key is to avoid wholesale adoption of standards that come from some unknown party or third-party research bulletin. *For standards to be effective, you can start with a base but you need to tweak it in-house.* By taking the time to think and document standards, the entire development group has some buy in; they will not create impractical standards or ones that are not applicable in their own environment.

External standards may be excellent from a conceptual perspective. Each organization is different, however, so tailoring of a base set of standards is always necessary. Architecture standards in particular need to be customized by not only developers but also database administrators (DBAs), architects, and infrastructure staff. Use caution when adopting standards pushed by product vendors — some of these "standards" may be more for marketing than for real development. For example, some application vendors suggest that developers put all their logic into the application rather than the database. Presumably, this is so that you have complete flexibility to change out the database technology sometime in the future. How many times since the big bang has that happened?

Toolboxes Are Useful

Most development today is done in formal development environments. Examples include CA Plex, Ebase Platform, IBM Rational Business Developer Extension, LANSA RDML language, NetBeans, OpenROAD, and Microsoft Visual Studio. Even with these core tools, developers need peripheral utilities to help them through the day. Maybe they need something like PVCS to house all versions of source code so that they can see specific lines of code variations between any two versions of a module. Use of testing utilities, documentation software, multiple workstations, subscriptions to expert help Web sites, and other tools can speed development considerably.

Studies have shown that a good developer is two or three times more effective than an average developer, and an outstanding developer may be ten times more productive than a good developer. With that in mind, your top performer should certainly have the requisite tools.

Some Example Guidelines

As chief information officer, you will probably not be responsible for developing guidelines but may need a few examples to keep under your hat to ensure that the basics are being addressed. There are probably hundreds of recommendations in the literature, but here is a pupu platter (short sampler), based on a book by Ken Pugh[1]:

- Employ use cases to effectively capture user requirements.
- Define the "ilities" — reliability, testability, deployability, and performance.
- Do not reinvent the wheel — look for existing solutions.
- Use clearly defined names for each concept in the system.
- Do not "clump" too much functionality in a single place.
- Do clump related data.
- Avoid modeling with "primitive data types." For example, do not worry about specifications like INT or DOUBLE on the front end. Stay abstract until you are doing the actual coding.
- Do not hard code. Always use a symbolic name for a value.
- Use prototypes, including pictures and screen shots, to fully define what the system is supposed to do.

Release Philosophy

You should develop a release strategy appropriate to your business environment. Uncertainty as to which version is the "official" code base and confusion about what is or is not to be included in the release can disrupt the business. One useful change management approach is to extend the concept of "release" to collections of small changes, even if they are in multiple systems. By bunching all changes together, a comprehensive regression test can cover all changes at the same time. This provides the benefit of formal testing to low-risk changes which would not otherwise justify extensive tests.

Releases are usually classified as follows:

- Major
  - Functionality changes
  - Interface changes
  - Platform changes (e.g., rewrite or port to a different hardware/software base)
- Minor
  - Fixes to bugs that are irritants but do not significantly affect the validity of the output
  - Performance enhancements
  - Interface changes
- Emergency
  - Fix critical bugs that affect normal operation and uptime

Porting

We discussed project management and systems development life cycle in Chapter 4. Porting an existing system to another platform is a specialized activity, with a higher than average risk profile. By "another platform" we do not mean moving from one hardware server to another, but a wholesale change in operating system or database. Examples include a move from Unix to Linux or from Sybase to Oracle. Following are some general recommendations:

- Avoid it if possible. The outcome may be ugly and many hidden bugs are likely.
- Migrate in chunks, to the extent it is practical.
  - User interface
  - Data storage (generally to a database)
  - Core logic
- Ensure that your technical architects are deeply involved.
- Configure the modules within the ported system to be as "loosely coupled" as possible. This means that they are not linked in too many places. A car is a good analogy. The tires are loosely coupled to the car because there is only one place where they attach; the engine, in contrast, attaches in many ways physically and across many engineering systems and is therefore *not* loosely coupled to the car. Following is a rather technical list of practices that promote loose coupling.[2]
  - Vendor and platform independent messages
  - Coarse-grained, self-describing, and self-contained messages

- Well-defined interfaces
- Extensible versionable interfaces
- Constrained interfaces
- Human readable strings (URIs) for service and instance addresses
- Stateless messaging where possible and appropriate
- Humans controlling clients, called late-bound in this article, where possible and appropriate
- Asynchronous exchange patterns where possible and appropriate

The Ultimate Answer — Hire Good Developers and Keep Them Happy

At the end of the day, nothing works like good developers coding well-defined projects. Robert Sandifer, retired Vice President of MIS at Malone & Hyde in Memphis, Tennessee, once asked Yarberry, "What does it mean when a good programmer is quiet and not doing much?" Answer: "It means he's sick." The point was that good developers are *active* people, who enjoy creating efficient and easy-to-use systems. They will tolerate governance requirements because they know it improves quality and throughput in the long run. What they will not tolerate is lack of support, confused direction, and inadequate tools to do their job. If you can supply these tools and hire the right people (see Dennis Klinger's comments in Chapter 15), your code will be "good enough" to run the business and advance your career.

References

1. Pugh, Ken. *Prefactoring* (New York: O'Reilly Media, Inc., 2005), 7–22.
2. Orchard, David. *Achieving Loose Coupling.* http://dev2dev.bea.com/pub/a/2004/02/orchard.html (accessed May 11, 2008).

Chapter 6

Enterprise Architecture

> The role of enterprise architecture is changing. When it started off it was simply an IT-centric function, whereas today it aims to align IT with business.

Sohel Aziz, AVP and Head — Strategic Technology & Architecture Consulting, EMEA at Infosys

Enterprise architecture (EA) is viewed by some as abstract and "board room entertainment," not relevant to the day-to-day functioning of the information technology group. And certainly if it were not so important, we could pay some consulting firm to write a few thousand clever sounding words and then put it on the shelf. Reality says that it is vital to your success as a chief information officer, and you need to be intimately involved in its development. Let us begin our discussion with some down-to-earth questions:

- Can management view data from an enterprise perspective? For example, is the entire relationship for a single customer visible across multiple business units? How much does ABC Corporation really owe us?
- Are your computing infrastructure costs high because of needless multiplication of hardware and software vendors?
- Do users routinely "cut and paste" in order to transfer data between applications which should be electronically and seamlessly communicating?
- Can users rotate between business units without significant retraining on software?
- Can your computer systems tell you when they have run out of processing power or disk space before they reach that point?

- Can your computer systems scale if transactions or database records must increase dramatically due to the addition of more subsidiaries to the existing application base?
- Are your in-house systems or custom modifications to off-the-shelf software so "quirky" that they cannot be quickly modified to meet changes in the marketplace?
- Is IT the bottleneck for new business initiatives? Is your lead time excessive for new projects?
- Is inventory, sales, and other information available on a timely basis to business units? Do they have enough information to make key decisions?
- Does senior management spend an inordinate amount of time worrying about IT issues?
- If your company decides to divest an unprofitable or nonstrategic subsidiary, are application dependencies to corporate services so deeply embedded that it would interfere with (delay) the divestiture?
- Are acquisitions needlessly difficult because your applications are hard to scale or modify to fit a new business?
- Do you have a strong foundation for execution?
- Are you able to spend time accomplishing business goals using your *existing* set of IT assets rather than having to develop new ones for business initiatives?

Consider, as an example, telecom billing. It is a wonderfully instructive example of what happens over time if no plan or architecture exists. In the beginning, before AT&T was broken up in the early 1980s, there were a reasonably small number of services offered, and these were billed by running batch Cobol mainframe programs. After the breakup and especially after the Telecommunications Act of 1996, the number of players and products offered in the marketplace exploded. The billing systems groaned under the weight of change, resulting in incorrect or sometimes inexplicable billing algorithms. These systems became increasingly complex and failed to serve the telcos, who needed to rapidly create new products as technology and regulations changed. In the parlance of old-line programmers, the billing systems were inflexible landmines of nested "IF" statements and haphazard design.

We can learn some basic lessons from the telco billing debacle:

- Complexity does not add value.
- Operations and services can be hobbled by missing, nonstandard, or ineffective architecture.
- Fundamental change in IT environments without a clear road map happens in painful lurches and is often accompanied by a forklift approach/level of effort.

Without a platform for execution, many issues, such as those suggested above, will not be resolved. Investment decisions, standards, timing of projects, and alignment with the business all depend on a clear IT architecture. One recent study of 103 U.S. and European firms found that a strong architecture combined with digitization of core processes resulted in a 25% reduction of IT costs relative to those with less robust configurations. Those same successful firms had higher profitability, faster times to market, and higher values from their IT projects.[1]

Pursued vigorously, enterprise architecture can provide dramatic results. Following are example benefits that have accrued to organizations in various industries:

- Reduced number of application servers.
- Information warehouse consolidation.
- Consolidation of data centers.
- Reduction in software inventory — fewer applications to maintain.
- Reduction in development technologies, with fewer platforms to maintain and reduced need to maintain a skill base for obsolete technologies.
- Faster response time for new development.
- Improved ability to show IT compliance with Sarbanes-Oxley (SOX), Health Insurance Portability and Accountability Act (HIPAA), Graham Leachy, and other regulations.
- Proactive system and application alerts, resulting in reduction of costly downtime.
- Consolidation of portals, reducing maintenance effort.
- Improvement in risk management: business exposure to downtime, ability to respond to disaster, and defense against security breaches are all strengthened by a robust architecture.

Mergers and acquisitions do not always work as intended. Sometimes the two firms may actually do worse as a unit than as separate entities. The poor results may be due, in part, to an inadequate or contradictory technical foundation. Without a base of systems and databases that can be expanded and adapted (agility) easily, the two organizations must dance like two porcupines, careful to avoid the sharp needles of ad hoc applications and rigid infrastructure. One red flag is a history of few new IT/business products prior to the merger. If a company is mired in the muck of applications and infrastructure built without consistent standards and an enterprise view, it is much more difficult to merge or acquire.

In the sections below, we show how you can build and tailor the IT architecture to meet the demands of your firm's business operations.

Start with an umbrella structure for enterprise architecture. Gartner identifies three starting points for developing an EA[2]:

1. Business architecture viewpoint
2. Information architecture viewpoint
3. Technology architecture viewpoint

Keeping these perspectives separate simplifies the development of the architecture and ensures that each component will be given appropriate attention. We will start with the business perspective.

Develop the Business Model

The first step in developing an IT architecture is to understand your firm's business model. Following are some characteristics that typically drive the organization's core processes and services:

- What do business units have in common — customers, suppliers, regulatory environment?
- Are customers serviced across the enterprise? For example, can receivables from XYZ Corporation be consolidated across business units? Do we know how much they owe us in total?
- Are strategic business needs defined in detail? For example, Harrah's must have detailed, real-time information on gambling customers who may be "discouraged" due to a consistent string of losses. With this information, special measures, such as providing premium meal vouchers, can be taken to keep the customer in the casino.
- Are data typically shared across the enterprise? Are there common data standards? For example, assume a manufacturing company is composed of three different business units, all of which were previously independent firms (prior to a merger). When they order a widget from a supplier, do they all use the same item number, job number, or general ledger codes? Can the enterprise track and aggregate purchases to reduce costs?
- Are acquisitions customized in terms of accounting, finance, and IT, or is the model to cookie cutter each acquisition, even to the point of yanking out working infrastructure to install common platforms?
- Are business processes, such as payables, inventory accounting, and sales techniques, uniform?
- Are engineering manufacturing processes the same?
- What are the "hot buttons" of the business — instant response to the customer, providing maximum information of orders in process, superlative artistic or engineering design, or most reliable raw materials sourcing?

The single word that describes the effective match between IT and business processes is *alignment*. As the CIO you cannot effectively align the two without considerable help from the business executives. To move forward you will need to employ standard but effective management skills:

- *Show thought leadership.* Businesspeople are smart, but they do not live in your world of IT abstraction. You must lead and explain the concepts, over and over again.
- *Demand, as politely as you can, participation in key architectural decisions.* If your business really demands a strong customer relationship management (CRM) system, let your customers drive the requirements and the capabilities. CRM can range from a few copies of ACT! on sales desktops to an enterprise-wide Siebel solution. Sometimes the Band-Aid solution works, but if they choose it, explain the consequences.
- *Understand business processes.* The term "MBWA" still applies — *management by walking around* helps you to understand the core business. Visit your firm's plants, offices, and sales outlets. It will help your alignment efforts and increase your popularity to boot.

Before IT and business can be aligned, the basic architecture type(s) of the organization need to be established. Following are potential variations; real organizations will likely have bits and pieces of each one, but there should be a predominate model:

- *Distributed and diverse.* Sites have different infrastructures and little sharing of customers or suppliers. It has the advantage, at least from the business unit's perspective, of complete local control for each site. This is the least strategic and usually the most expensive architectural option.
- *Distributed but similar.* There are multiple sites, largely independent but using standard infrastructure and applications. Works best when customers are not shared and only limited data aggregation is required. Provides for reduced infrastructure cost and faster implementation for newly acquired business units (cookie cutter approach).
- *Coordinated with consensus building.* Customers and vendors are common to many business units. Local control over design and process retained but considerable sharing/impact on other business units. Strong effort to share data across all business units. Infrastructure decisions still made at the local level.
- *Top-down integration.* Customers and suppliers may be shared and geographically distributed. Centralized IT management accompanied by integrated business strategy and processes. Databases are centrally managed. Information easily available from an enterprise perspective. Needless duplication of IT and business services largely eliminated. IT training is standardized as is IT knowledge (hardware, software, general technologies).

The temptation in developing an architecture is to start with the technical components first. These are the least abstract and the easiest to put on paper. And in fact an effective design must have the nuts and bolts at its base — WAN configuration, computing platforms, software development methodologies, database design, and so on. However, the best way to get there is to thoroughly understand the business' economic drivers. An article written by the Patrician Seybold Group describes some of the challenges facing The Guardian Life Insurance Company of America in the 2001–2002 economic downturn[3]:

■ Independent agents had no consistent view of their clients and the products those clients were purchasing. They had to look through multiple databases in different systems before they could decide what products to offer their customers.
■ Guardian's business units failed to share sales information. So, for example, the life insurance groups could not see the equity investment group's data, and vice versa.

Clearly the sales channel was not where it needed to be. The firm created, as part of its architecture, an integrated enterprise information infrastructure. The components included a common platform running on a company-wide intranet and a single suite of software resources. The eventual success of the architectural overhaul was based on direct, immediate business need (that is, keeping the firm alive) and not on a techie-driven vision of a new rack of blades, a virtual tape library, and the latest enterprise management tools with call-home capabilities.

Business Drivers and Selling the Enterprise Architecture (EA)

CIOs, like any other executive, must spend time selling. Capital dollars are always less than capital needs, and an EA project must stand in line at the trough like any other. So you must show the value to your peer executives and in some cases your boss. (If it is an IT-only architecture, its value will be a harder sell.)

Start with the basics. A good EA results in alignment to business strategy, ability to respond to the market with new products (opening up new sales channels), capacity to rapidly expand existing services, easier consolidation of data, creation of enterprise rather than silo views of customers, improved security, and reduced time to market. Offsetting these benefits, according to the naysayers, are bureaucracy, rigid procedures, additional costs, and the dangers of stifling innovation. Lack of vision from key decision makers may be a perennial challenge in some organizations.

To sell EA, you will need to provide business examples and repeated explanations of the negative consequences of having no road map. Some selling points include:

■ *An EA provides a rough filter to eliminate projects that are likely to fail.* Perhaps a technology cannot scale, has security flaws, is a one-off custom design, or will require new, ongoing staffing, dramatically increasing the total cost of ownership.

■ *IT costs may decrease in the long run.* However, it is difficult to objectively prove that an EA directly reduces costs. An EA simply has too many moving parts to calculate its exact contribution. To use an analogy, many studies have shown a significant financial benefit of a college education. But we have no way to prove that any specific college course, semester, or teacher contributed X% to the lifetime earnings increase from a college education. Education is holistic and so is EA.

■ *Business performance will be improved.* Well-architected systems run faster and with fewer disruptions. They come with built-in tools so that they can be better monitored and managed. In addition, they have longer mean time between failures, shorter duration, preventive maintenance windows, and therefore a higher percentage of uptime.

■ *The net result of a strong business/information/IT architecture is better decision making, supporting both top-line and bottom-line revenue growth and business unit cost reduction.*

To address the concerns of your business peers, you can set up a postimplementation review for projects. In this review (and it can be very short and informal), determine the effect of compliance or noncompliance with the EA on the project. What are the lessons learned? Did noncompliance delay the project, increase its costs, or make integration into the rest of the user environment more difficult? Facts, like a spam musubi after a day of surfing in Hawaii, sell well.

Each constituent with a stake in the effectiveness of IT and hence the architecture has a core concern. The chief executive officer (CEO) and board of directors are worried about long-term stock price and the wealth of the shareholders; the chief financial officer (CFO) and senior business unit executives are concerned about profitability and market share attrition; IT fears that its systems are not flexible enough to keep up with changes in the market. One way to ensure these concerns are addressed is to maintain a practical set of metrics. Table 6.1 is a list of example benefits and potential metrics used to validate the effectiveness of the EA (not all inclusive).

Although Table 6.1 uses some IT measures, it is more oriented toward business executives than IT peers. Table 6.2, showing more specific IT metrics for the EA, is more granular and provides a better picture of progress.

Information Architecture and Process Modeling Perspective

After the business drivers are identified and documented, the design of your data environment should be reviewed. Even with a solid understanding of business

Table 6.1 Business Benefits and Enterprise Architecture Metrics

Expected Enterprise Architecture Benefit	Potential Metric to Evaluate Effectiveness
Faster delivery of new business projects, arising from use of common software elements	Number of times modules, designs, or even whole systems can be reused for new projects. Focus is on reuse. This is also a core element of SOA (service-oriented architecture).
Reduction in man-hours and hence cost to implement a new system or feature	Estimate man-hours required with and without compliance to the enterprise architecture (EA). This may be an imprecise calculation, but it will show roughly the impact of duplicate systems, extra interfaces, oddball one-off technologies, etc.
Improved ability to share information across the enterprise	Show number of interfaces/modules needed to consolidate information.
Increased ability to share a common infrastructure, reducing costs and simplifying maintenance	Show quantity of applications using common infrastructure versus the number of additional platforms that would be required in a silo environment.

strategy and a robust technical infrastructure, a poor information design will hamper IT's delivery of value.

Information and user access design should be an upfront function of all medium to large development projects. Your information architect needs to build information structures that are straightforward to use, technically feasible, and aligned with business requirements. Examples of information architecture concerns and deliverables include:

- *Database design.* Selected information used for inquiry only may be housed in a separate warehouse from core-transaction-based production databases. This simplifies user access and reduces the processing bottleneck caused by transaction and BI (business intelligence) users attempting to simultaneously access the same database tables. In some organizations, the data warehouses are located at their offsite disaster recovery facility, thus making use of the offsite facilities for daily work rather than only during a disaster or recovery event.
- *Inquiry flexibility.* Users and especially customers may ask for information in many ways. In addition, there may be errors in spelling or categorization that should be filtered and resolved in order to provide the information needed. Thomas Myer, an independent information design consultant, provides the following example (referring to a Web site for snow equipment): "snowboards and snow skis would be categories of products and content. And skiing might

Table 6.2   Enterprise Architecture Benefits from an IT Perspective

Expected Enterprise Architecture (EA) Benefits from an Information Technology (IT) Perspective	Potential Metric to Evaluate Effectiveness
IT maintenance cost reduced	Cost of products (software, hardware, services) decreased as needless duplication eliminated.
Emergency or last-minute infrastructure projects reduced, which in turn reduces operations disruption	Number of emergency projects to shore up failing or inadequate infrastructure.
Effort to install new releases reduced due to simpler architecture	Duration or man-hours to complete routine upgrades decreased (both for applications and infrastructure).
Interfaces from disparate but similar functioning applications reduced (e.g., duplicate payroll systems)	Man-hours to maintain interfaces and/or software purchases for interface maintenance decreased.
Proactive system and applications management now possible	System downtime reduced, problems and issues fixed prior to user awareness of the problem.
Fewer errors in applications and infrastructure because of simpler and more robust architecture	Number of errors reported via the problem/issue management system.

contain several subcategories, such as cross-country skiing and downhill skiing. The way that the site is structured from the top down can help make the content more navigable."[4]

■ *Content portals.* If customers need only a few lines of information at one time, the presentation will differ from environments where in-depth, lengthy text may be required. Web format and navigation are about as close to art as IT ever gets — with the exception of good programming.

■ *Input methods.* Scanning, bar-code readers, electronic sensing devices, and cash register transmissions are just a few examples of original inputs. How these systems of data, voice, and video content are entered and controlled is an important part of the architecture.

■ *Content management.* As the organization grows larger, content management needs to be formally addressed. How will shared knowledge be stored, indexed, and retrieved? Any system selected needs to import documents and multimedia material; assign roles to key users; track and manage multiple versions; support workflow associated with event messaging so that content managers know when changes have been introduced; and provide an effective search mechanism. Example content management packages include Stellent, Morello, SharePoint, Jadu, Infopark CMS Fiona, Documentum, and CoreMedia CMS.

■ *Use of the right tools.* The burden of categorization, storage, and versioning should not be placed too heavily with the user. Core library services such as check in and check out need to be included in your basic services. In addition, the content management architecture will be more effective if it integrates e-mail, Web sites, wikis, blogs, desktop documents, scanned documents, voicemails, selected data from enterprise resource planning (ERP) databases, and even video.

■ *Productive policies.* When data structures are revised, they should not simply meet parochial needs but should be designed for future use by the entire enterprise. So, for example, the changes to these structures should go through the change management system and be vetted/approved by relevant business units.

There are any number of information analysis and design tools that help manage the complexity of large, integrated environments. According to Gartner, market leaders include IDS Scheer, Proforma, Mega, iGrafx, Telelogic, IBM, and Microsoft.[5] These modeling tools help visualize the flow of information throughout the enterprise and bring into sharp relief the "as is" versus future state information architecture. Another benefit is the relatively speedy translation of processes into business and technical requirements for development, testing, training, and move into production.

The design tools vary in scope from simple documentation repositories to statistical business process simulators. The old saying "if the shoe fits, wear it" applies here — select the appropriate level of complexity. Some organizations really care whether a tool supports the DoDAF or Zachman model; others just want the basics. Example features for these tools include the following:

■ Visual, graphical, and relational model views providing change impact across organizational functions
■ Framework for data view
■ Documentation of business processes, organizational structure
■ Overview plans
■ End-to-end modeling from strategic process requirements to implementation
■ Ability to analyze the impact of failure for any specific IT element
■ Ability to link with other operational systems through standard interface languages such as XML and BPML (business process markup language)
■ General analysis and what-if capability
■ Storage of office documents and multimedia content
■ Support for process improvement initiatives such as Six Sigma and ISO certification

- Templates to kick start the process
- Ability to segregate users of the tool with access rights — viewers, chief architect, specific business unit owners, etc.

Information architecture is a tough job. It affects users where they live and requires changes in work habits. (We all love our spreadsheets and use them even when they are not the best tool.) Your best role is sponsor, communicator educator, supporter, and tool provider — all with the recognition that improving the design and effectiveness of information use within an organization is a long-term effort but one with measurable enterprise-wide benefits. A strong return-on-investment (ROI) is always a strong selling point. For example, Gartner reports in a 2006 presentation the following benefits[6]:

- $3.8 to $7.8 million in annual cost reduction for a university
- 25% to 30% reduction in infrastructure costs and 50% reduction in field service calls for a professional services firm
- $3 million in cost reduction for a charity

Technology Architecture Perspective

The third perspective, technology, is the traditional "technical architecture" found in most organizations.

Figure 6.1 shows sample sections from a typical IT architecture. It is difficult to present a generic technology architecture because of the wide variance in implementations throughout the United States and the rest of the world. Nonetheless, we can make some general observations:

- It should make technical direction perfectly clear and should include hardware, software, telecommunications, development platforms, testing tools, and so on.
- The technical architecture should create a road map that can be presented in two versions — one that is understandable by the CEO and board of directors and another intended for implementation by your department heads. We cannot stress enough the importance of gaining buy-in ahead of time by creating an "English" version of your architecture, with diagrams and a presentation that outlines as-is, to-be, ROI, and so forth. All executives and the board will appreciate the effort and gain a better understanding of your strategy and how it will benefit the company, employees, and shareholders.
- Frameworks and direction, such as service-oriented architecture (SOA), should be articulated.
- Developers need to work in an environment that is ambiguity-free from a technical perspective; at least that is the goal.

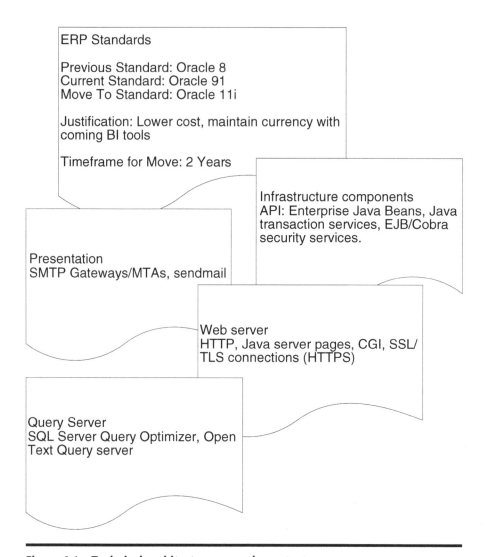

Figure 6.1 Technical architecture example contents.

You may want to arrange your IT/technical architecture by groupings related to technology or business function, such as:

- Common information and database structures
- Development tools (for ERP, Web, custom applications, distributed, etc.)
- Reusability, agility issues (SOA, documentation, avoidance of spurious uniqueness)
- Security/audit/control (e.g., encryption, payment card industry (PCI) standard, repudiation requirements)

- Business intelligence and analytics
- Telecommunications
- Hardware/infrastructure standards

Road Map to an Effective Architecture

Business Architecture

The first step is to create a business architecture team. This group is one level above the IT architecture team and provides the strategic knowledge to structure the plan. One has to know a great deal about the business to do this work — individuals recently entered into the business need not apply. So you need to convince your executive peers to contribute seasoned business people — analysts, senior managers, key users, and perhaps selected senior PMO staff.

To kickoff the process, start with some level set training for the team. Topics such as business processes, key business drivers, and application functions should be covered to ensure that all the members understand what exists from an enterprise perspective. If your firm does not have a culture of interaction between business units, this educational process is particularly important. You may even consider using resources from Internal Audit. If audits are performed by business cycle (revenue, treasury, conversion, purchase-to-pay, and so forth), extensive process flowcharts may be available. These can be a starting point for understanding the interaction between various business functions. If tools are to be used, training should be conducted at this point.

Next decide how various stakeholders and interested parties should work with the business architecture team. Define how much input, detailed work, and direction are provided by the CIO, IT Strategy Board, IT steering committees, PMO, and IT architecture team. This could be a simple "who does what" and a schedule of review points. Avoid silos in architecture work as you would anywhere else.

The general objectives of the business architecture team include the following:

- Understand business processes across the business units.
- Identify common points of processing/information flow — where do redundancies, synergies, and desired capabilities exist in the organization? Where do common patterns of activity show themselves across the organization?
- Consider potential business cases for strategic initiatives, integration, changes to functional design, and new requirements. These can then be communicated to the IT Steering committees for possible action.
- Ensure that all parties acknowledge the value and cost of the solutions presented. For example, assume a new, enterprise-wide sales tax system will significantly reduce potential state fines originating from tax calculation errors (wrong tax treatments for changes in online sales). Clearly this is a benefit to all

business units, but if the new system requires work flow changes, the stakeholders need to fully understand the impact. An architecture promulgated without feedback lasts as long as a bowl of Portuguese bean soup at a University of Hawaii tailgate party.

■ Document, organize, and communicate the results of the team's work to the IT architecture group. They can then develop the technical details enabling the business objectives. Of course, budgeting for the initiatives, creating an ROI, and informing key stakeholders are parallel and separate activities.

At the end of this process, there should be a business road map providing benefits such as integration of data across businesses, customer visibility across the organization, improved accounting/reporting, flexibility in acquiring/divesting subsidiaries, higher employee productivity, better sales channels and tools (e.g., a unified CRM system or an enterprise e-commerce system), elimination of redundant processes/consolidation, and reduced resource consumption (more efficient transportation network, product consolidation, SKU elimination, etc.). Everyone can understand these goals and they are specific enough to be actionable by the IT architecture team.

IT Architecture

Next, establish the IT architecture team. As with business architecture, experience and in-depth knowledge are essential. In some ways, the IT architecture is even more intellectually demanding than its business counterpart. The lead architect needs to be sufficiently business savvy to fully grasp the implications of the business requirements while understanding the breadth, width, and scope the latest technology has to offer. In addition to identifying the lead architect, you will need to accomplish the following:

■ Select the rest of the team, based on technical and business skill sets. If you are considering completely new initiatives, such as a major SOA implementation, you might consider bringing in outside help on the front end.
■ Create a structure that includes standards, policies, and procedures and guidelines for lease, acquisition, implementation, and enhancement of technology.
■ Develop detailed reference materials that shape the end result of IT projects for infrastructure (including intermediate architectures such as middleware), databases, unstructured information, and most importantly, applications.
■ Document interfaces and upstream/downstream data requirements.
■ Identify the core application functionality required to support business functions.
■ Develop a framework of alternative solutions and architectures. For example, some firms use SaaS (software as a service) to address a critical application

need. Products such as Oracle's On-Demand ERP software and Workday's HR software are examples of "ready to move in" solutions from outside providers.

■ Develop a map of where the organization needs to be from a technical perspective, based on the business architecture driving the IT architecture. That map includes direction at the very highest level, such as "we will provide retail management to include point of sale monitoring, inventory management, warehouse and distribution center reporting and data mining, using Celerant software" down to hard-core techie specifics, such as "we will use Microsoft COM+ runtime services for APIs."

The end results from the IT architecture should provide the business architecture team with a realistic perspective on the costs and effort required to implement business projects and strategies. Frameworks and guidelines will be available to development staff so they can proceed without having to consider fundamental technical decisions and have assurance that systems under development will mesh with one another as well as with business direction. In theory at least, the organization should receive the benefits of lower costs, higher interoperability, and greater agility. In practice, those things are hard to isolate and prove. However, as any executive knows, business life is about probabilities, not absolute proof. When senior management sees initiatives implemented quickly and new capabilities developed without excessive rework, that sends a strong signal that the architecture is working. It also demonstrates that the IT department knows what it is doing with the company's money.

Pushing Out the EA — Communicating with Management and Employees

Many organizations prefer to develop the enterprise architecture quietly, letting it seep through the ranks like the gentle Koolau mountain mist. Unfortunately, this approach rarely works. The CIO needs to get the mission and objectives in front of stakeholders frequently and with a consistent message. You should use some old fashioned marketing push techniques to kick-start the EA project and speed adoption:

■ Publish a description and expected benefits.
■ Give it a name — something *non*-IT like "12 speed, art deco, or Bahamas."
■ Devote a section of your intranet for benefits, schedules, plans, and detailed specifications.
■ Provide an online forum for discussions.
■ Hold meetings to educate stakeholders and generate enthusiasm.
■ Create a newsletter with stories. Love of stories is built into our genes as humans; a tale of success is more likely to be read than a set of bulletized admonitions..

■ T-shirts and gadgets with the EA logo create a sense of playfulness associated with the project. Pictures of Google's work areas, for example, show a nearly endless procession of gadgets, toys, and diversions. The Generation X-ers, Millennials, and younger workers, raised in the milieu of video games, respond more positively to colorful images than to standard business speak. Silly to some, but it works.

The Outsourcing Alternative

Opinion on outsourcing has changed over time. Once heralded as a way to deliver results by cutting through politics and stagnation, the trend has peaked, at least in its current forms. Firms found that sometimes the provider did not always have the customer's *long-term* benefit as part of its relationship management practices. Unsurprisingly, providers often attempted to focus on services for the client such that the *provider's* profits were maximized. On the flip side, some firms find outsourcing successfully fulfils basic needs such as:

■ Supplying variable capacity
■ Lowering costs
■ Reducing risk in specialized environments/applications
■ Improving processes in niche areas of business or technology
■ Freeing up staff to work on higher-value projects
■ Supplying expertise outside the core competency of the organization, eliminating the need for dedicated resources

Outsourcing arrangements vary from simply processing transactions (e.g., credit card processing) to a strategic partnership where the outsource firm provides key customer services. What should remain constant, however, is your firm's retention of the enterprise architecture (assuming, of course, that your firm has already developed one). The experiences of Enron and EDS in the early 1990s illustrate how control of the architecture can heavily influence end results.

In the late 1980s, Ken Lay and Rich Kinder negotiated a 10-year arrangement with EDS. Seven hundred Enron IT personnel either became EDS employees (the majority) or sought employment elsewhere. EDS at the time was the master of heavy, mainframe processing and was the logical choice, given Enron's many mainframe systems. Unfortunately, as Enron began moving into new business areas, including trading, EDS initially resisted the related move to client-server and object-oriented technologies. Such resistance was to be expected — their profit model was based on mainframe central processing unit (CPU) minutes, time-sharing operation (TSO) time, and other easily measurable computer resource units (CRUs). Of course, computer resources were not the only billable services. Developer and project management hours were a source of revenue but could not fill the gap from declining mainframe CRUs. This transition away from mainframe technology was not unique to these two firms — the late 1980s was a time of wrenching IT change for firms worldwide.

These trends set up years of arm wrestling between Enron and EDS. The original negotiations did not contemplate an explicit statement of who controls the architecture. Enron wanted to move quickly to new, more agile technologies. EDS was willing to change but often asked Enron to pay for extensive EDS staff training in order to develop new applications in Powerbuilder and other (at the time) new technologies. The EDS argument was "You brought us in to be the expert and to provide a service; now you are dictating how we do our business." Enron responded that EDS was too set in a mainframe mentality and could not provide the flexibility to meet rapidly changing business conditions. What was not clear — and should have been made very clear — was that the client, Enron, was the *owner* of the EA. Even if a firm has a staff of only three people to manage an outsource group of several hundred, the blueprint for IT direction must remain with the business, not the outsource firm. This does not denigrate outsource providers; many become strategic partners and provide outstanding advice on direction and alternatives. But in the long run, outsourcing is like the relationship you have with your doctor; though he or she may have vastly more medical knowledge than you, the ultimate control over the direction of treatment is yours alone.

Tools

As one would expect, a plethora of vendors have developed EA packages. Typically, these tools either focus on narrow segments of EA or provide a holistic view, accommodating models of business strategies, economic models, tasks, information flows, and technology infrastructure. Table 6.3 lists some example features found in many of these tools/environments.

Most packages use one or more frameworks, such as Zachman[7] and FEAF (Federal Enterprise Architecture Framework). Examples of EA tools include Corporate Modeler by Casewise, Aris Process Platform by IDS Scheer, and Avolution by Abacus.

Enforcement and Governance of the EA

"Enforcement" sounds harsh, but the "encouragement" approach is sometimes ineffective. To counteract the many forces that will weaken the implementation of the enterprise architecture, you can use a variety of carrot/stick approaches:

- Start with guidance. Power Points and grand words are fine, but at the grassroots level, technical and business direction need to be as concrete as possible. Sometimes direct, in-your-face guidelines are required — "high bandwidth, inefficient protocols will not be permitted on the network, as one of our business objectives is to provide the customer with quick response time."

Table 6.3　Common Features of Enterprise Architecture Toolkits

General Function/Scope	Example Capabilities
Software development	Visual modeling, including that of complex infrastructures
	Simulation based on assumptions
	Version control
	IDE (integrated development environment)
Knowledge management/repository	Search and archive
	Document management
	Maintain various objects and related documentation
Security and permissions	Technical options
	Role-based security standards
General analysis	Visually capture end-to-end business processes
	Document as-is and to-be architecture
	Creation and modification of diagrams. Use predefined modeling objects, including processes, business units, locations, applications, specific technologies, and information/data
	Create "what if" scenarios to show impact of decisions on the organization
Alignment/matrix analysis	Link people, processes, and IT (technology) in an understandable format
Discovery	Technical capability to obtain knowledge of the IT environment and map out enterprise applications in an easy to understand graphical format.
Best practices and design patterns	Templates showing example architectures
	Map the data, applications, and IT hardware used in process steps
	Suggestions for effective EA design
Return on investment/economic impact	Test the financial impact of alternative process redesigns

Table 6.3 (continued)   Common Features of Enterprise Architecture Toolkits

General Function/Scope	Example Capabilities
Data design	Model data reuse (eliminate redundancy)
	Show hierarchical data flow diagrams in order to shows data relationships and movement across the organization

- Tell would-be "cowboys" that systems developed or purchased outside the scope of the architecture will receive no support or bailout if they fail. It may be politically difficult to keep your resolve, but at least make that your going-in position.
- Eliminate funding for projects that are clearly outside the architecture. This is more difficult in a chargeback environment (another reason to think carefully about implementing a large-scale chargeback system).
- Provide technical support and encouragement for business segments transitioning to a standards-based architecture.
- Mandate that all technology providers must be approved by IT or the Accounting department will reject the provider's purchase orders.

Enforcement of the architecture is sometimes not straightforward with package providers. Consider whether your core infrastructure and applications are adversely affected by a third-party technology or business approach. If you can consider the service or application as a black box and if it is maintained by the provider, the risk of nonconformance may be less (e.g., Siebel CRM OnDemand).

A governance strategy is required for an effective EA. An executive steering committee sits at the top, providing guidance to subcommittees. Committee duties include setting direction, approving allocation of resources for EA initiatives, resolving any exceptions to the EA standards, and setting up the architecture core team as well as any subcommittees.

A working group/review committee, just below the executive steering committee, includes the organization's architect and representatives of IT management and business units. Typical duties include:

- Periodically, realign the EA with any new business requirements.
- Evaluate new technologies. Contrary to what some believe, the EA is not a brake on innovation. Instead, it channels innovation toward business goals.
- Review any recommended updates to the EA.
- Approve projects that incorporate new features or technologies supported by the architecture standards.
- Request feedback from stakeholders to ensure continuous improvement.

■ Develop or oversee the technical and business architecture supporting the overall EA.

■ Recruit IT and business subject matter experts to flesh out the details of the EA (it should not be so high level that lower-level personnel cannot make day-to-day decisions on technology, direction, etc.).

More than any other, the PMO needs to support, encourage, and enforce the EA initiative. A repository (such as Microsoft's Share Point) provides a central repository for documentation, templates, problem resolution, and training materials. Like security and internal audit, architecture should have its own review points within the systems development life cycle (SDLC). This provides a natural structure for comparison of the project's direction with the enterprise standard. Any significant deviations can then be resolved or forwarded to the EA review committee for disposition. Figure 6.2 illustrates one possible approach for the review and signoff. The SDLC is handy for controlling spurious changes in direction; your methodology requires you to bring up the issue. Finally, there is the sports/teamwork approach – "Bob, if you don't support the architecture, you don't support the company."

Architectural Maturity

A few years ago the U.S. Department of Commerce (DoC) developed a reference model for architectural maturity.[8] Certainly others exist, but this model is convenient and freely available. The DoC model rates maturity based on the following six levels and nine IT architecture characteristics:

■ Levels
  – None
  – Initial
  – Under development
  – Define
  – Managed
  – Measured
■ Characteristics
  – IT architecture process
  – IT architecture development
  – Business linkage
  – Senior management involvement
  – Operating unit participation
  – Architecture communication
  – IT security
  – Architecture governance
  – IT investment and acquisition strategy

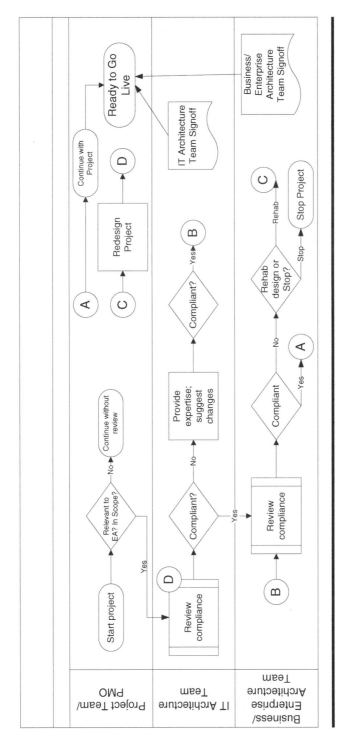

Figure 6.2 Enterprise architecture compliance. Software development review points by the information technology and business architecture teams.

Larger organizations may formalize their assessment of architectural maturity in the same way that the DoC requires federal agencies to rate themselves as part of their IT investment management and audit requirements. However, you may wish to simply use the concepts and target areas for an informal assessment. By assigning a numerical score to each characteristic based on the levels of maturity observed, a numeric ranking can be used to calculate progress year by year.

For another benchmark, you can use the IT Governance Institute's free IT governance standard, Control Objectives for IT (CobiT). This excellent document (available at www.itgi.org/) includes benchmarks and checklists to help you evaluate your success in any of the 34 areas deemed relevant to governance. For architecture/strategy specifically, it asks:

- Are databases designed for parochial needs only or are enterprise needs considered as well?
- How many redundant/duplicate data elements are found across the enterprise?
- Can applications be seamlessly integrated into business processes or is extensive modification required to fit software into a new business unit?
- Do standards exist for critical data (e.g., enterprise-wide item numbers) and are they enforced?

Putting It All Together

In this chapter, we discussed logical steps for developing a business-based enterprise architecture. The benefits range from agility, cost savings, alignment with business initiatives, to day-to-day efficiencies in project delivery. To get there, we need to develop an understanding of the organization's business model/objectives, link that to information needs, and then create a supporting IT architecture. The architectural diagram from NCI Building Systems, shown in Figure 6.3, provides an example of the structure and scope of an enterprise architecture/strategy:

Starting with a strong foundation, each layer supports the one above it to achieve the strategic vision of the company. There are many variations of the pyramid structure. Larger organizations may have more layers and complexity, but the theme is the same: everything the CIO does must be seen in the larger context of the organizational mission. Activities that do not contribute should be eliminated.

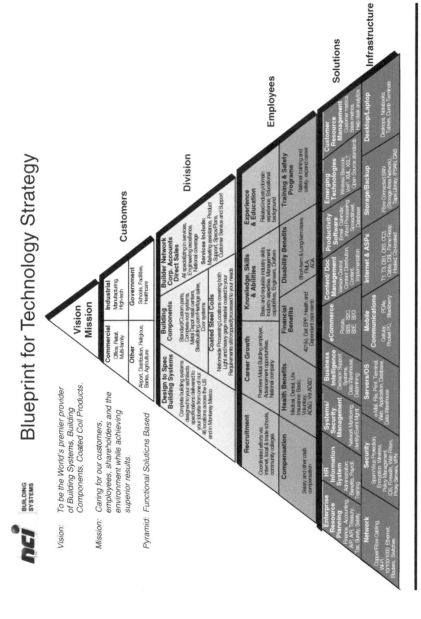

Figure 6.3   Example of an enterprise architecture concept. (Copyright © 2004, Eric J. Brown.)

References

1. Ross, Jeanne W., Peter Weill, and David C. Robertson. *Enterprise Architecture as Strategy*. (Boston: Harvard Business School Press, 2006), 9.
2. Gartner Leader's Toolkit: Bank XYZ Enterprise Architecture Framework. 2007. www.gartner.com (accessed October 17, 2007).
3. Bock, Geoffrey E. 2003. The Guardian Life Insurance Company of America. ftp://ftp.software.ibm.com/software/solutions/pdfs/IBM_Guardian_casestudy12-17-03.pdf (accessed September 2, 2007).
4. Myer, Thomas. 2002. Information Architecture Concepts. www.ibm.com/developer-works/library/us-inarch.html?dwzone=usability (accessed November 4, 2007).
5. Magic Quadrant for Business Process Analysis Tools. 2006. www.gartner.com (accessed November 4, 2007).
6. Selling Enterprise Architecture's Value to the Business. www.gartner.com (accessed October 20, 2007).
7. "The Zachman Institute for Framework Advancement (ZIFA) is a network of information professionals who understand the critical role of Enterprise Architecture in the ability of the enterprise to successfully participate in the global economy of the 21st century." www.zifa.com (accessed November 10, 2007).
8. www.opengroup.org/architecture/togaf8-doc/arch/chap27.html (accessed November 20, 2007).

Chapter 7

Mergers and Acquisitions

In the business world, the rearview mirror is always clearer than the windshield.

Warren Buffet

Haste in every business brings failures.

Herodotus, *The Histories of Herodotus*

In 1917 a gigantic new business was formed, "Russia, Inc." No one called it that but in effect the entire USSR became a single firm. There were no mergers or acquisitions; aside from the occasional direct state intervention, business managers felt no pressure to improve efficiency, develop new products, or become economically viable. The West, in contrast, developed the twin hammers of capitalism — bankruptcy to eliminate the really inefficient firms and merger/acquisitions to strengthen the weak ones or make the strong ones even stronger.

This history is relevant to the chief information officer because it reaffirms what we already know: mergers and acquisitions are part of the deep genetic structure of capitalism. You will never get away from them, even in government, as the post 9/11 creation of Homeland Security attests. In this chapter we discuss the process from both perspectives, acquiring and acquired firms, and how the alert CIO can negotiate the transition. And if your firm is acquiring or acquired *because* of specific information technology (IT) assets or expertise, then you have even more reason to understand the pros and cons of the process.

The CIO's Golden Opportunity

Individuals do not become CIOs because they want to be the "alpha ape" of technical prowess, nor do they wish to impress their friends with arcane IT expertise. Instead, most seek to play on a wider stage, directly affecting the success of the enterprise by enabling efficient execution of business strategies. Mergers and acquisitions (M&A) provide the CIO with an opportunity to create value by swift integration of environments, strong project management, effective human resource planning, and a good measure of cheerleading. Some organizations may not have the deep project management skills needed for complex business integration. So they either turn to you or go outside for the expertise.

M&As, as they happen, are virtually always periods of high stress for all concerned. First, there are the expected human issues. If you are the acquiring CIO, you must ensure that key IT personnel in the acquired firm are retained. If the economy is good and the physical location of the IT staff is a hot market, early departures can become a torrent of skill loss. Furthermore, you can stress your own staff by essentially making them work two jobs — their own plus extra tasks associated with the acquisition. Naturally, everyone involved worries about how it affects them personally, from compensation to reporting structure to medical benefits. These challenges give you the chance to demonstrate facility with communications and general human relations. M&A is a golden opportunity not so much for what you do but simply because you are on stage — the chief executive officer (CEO), chief financial officer (CFO), and vice presidents (VPs) of the business units — all are vitally interested in the outcome of the integration and are keenly observing your performance.

The CIO's Two Responsibilities

Typically, the CIO participates, to some extent, in the due diligence process and then as a major player in the integration if the M&A is successful (approved). The extent to which the CIO participates on the front end is a function of the relationship with the CEO and the senior management team. If the relationship is strong, you will be included in early activities such as visits to offices and plants, highly confidential meetings with key executives, strategic analysis of markets and customers, and other sensitive activities. Early participation is a significant advantage because it allows vital information to be gathered before the M&A trigger is pulled. For example, you need to know who are the key IT staff, based on either general IT competence, application knowledge, or both.

Responsibility #1: Due Diligence

Due diligence requires the teams (legal, IT, manufacturing, sales, and so forth) to learn quickly under a major constraint — the deal may fall through and the firm being acquired or merged wants to return to business as usual without providing trade secrets, strategic initiatives, or vital intellectual property (IP) to the acquiring firm (often a competitor). But just as you cannot assume that a small holiday gift package contains a diamond ring, the outward appearance of the products and services may hide the reality of the acquired firm's assets. For example, Gartner reports that one company significantly overpaid to acquire a firm with reportedly 9 million unique customer records. Independent review of customer records showed that indeed there were 9 million unique records there. Unfortunately, later analysis disclosed that only 250,000 of those customers were unique to the combined entity — the acquiring firm already had the rest as customers.[1]

We will discuss the M&A implementation plan in a later section, but to fulfill your due diligence responsibilities, you will need to understand in advance the IT approach if the acquisition goes through. Will the acquired firm's IT capability:

■ Remain as a standalone function, communicating with the rest of the enterprise through interfaces?
■ Be incorporated into the fabric of the existing enterprise IT function (assimilated into the Borg, for Star Trek fans)?
■ Be segregated into "keepers" — best of breed systems — and other applications to be replaced when it makes financial sense?

According to Jeanne Ross, Peter Weill, and David Robertson, in their book *Enterprise Architecture as Strategy*, the $7 billion Mexican cement manufacturer CEMEX is a good example of the second approach. When this firm acquires a new business, it implements a "rip and replace" strategy. Even if the acquired firm has a better widget than CEMEX, the corporate standard is used; it is the "CEMEX Way." This ensures that as CEMEX grows, its systems are standard and the synergies of size can be obtained on a world-wide scale.

UPS, on the other hand, adopts the first approach for many of its acquired firms. Although there is a standard core around the package network, many of the newly acquired or internally created businesses would not greatly benefit from adoption of the core network. For example, UPS Consulting and UPS Store/Mail Boxes do not depend on the corporate foundation to be successful.[2]

NCI Building Systems follows the last bullet — selecting best-of-breed systems as appropriate. The 2006 acquisition of Robertson Ceco Corporation provided NCI with engineering systems that, as stated on page 5 of NCI's 2006 annual report:

[S]hould enable an unprecedented reduction in the cycle time of our engineering design, pricing and detailing functions, as automated tasks that previously took weeks are completed in minutes. With two dedicated teams working to implement the components of the system, we now plan to complete the migration in early fiscal 2008, instead of by the end of fiscal 2008 as originally anticipated. We expect this system to greatly diminish the primary bottleneck in NCI's engineered building systems division and, thereby, to improve the efficiencies up to 300 basis points.

NCI already had an engineering design package; this one was selected as best-of-breed and is replacing the old one.

A due diligence checklist is an appropriate starting point. There are so many facts, figures, and issues to be resolved that a structured approach is essential. Your checklist should include at least the following:

- *Staffing.* What are the skills, tenure, education, and broad experience levels of the IT staff? How much overlap is there with the existing knowledge base? Is there a "bench" for critical systems or is all knowledge concentrated in one person/one application?
- *Architecture.* What does the technical infrastructure look like, including hardware, networks, software, databases, standards, and outside services (salesforce.com, payroll processing, etc.)? Are protocols, standards images, and so forth specified so that maintenance costs for the overall computing environment are reasonable? Is a data warehouse maintained?
- *Applications.* What custom and off-the-shelf applications are used? Are they documented and up to date? How much effort will be required to port them to your existing data center, if that is your strategy? Is the code structured and easily maintainable, or are programs written in a mish-mash of languages with little integration? Are a plethora of "one off" programs, such as old MS Access 98 systems, used in production?
- *Projects.* Identify both active and backlogged projects.
- *Governance.* Are standard practices, such as change control and security administration, separate from application development, user testing, and systems development life cycle, in place? Is all the code secure and accessible?
- *Contracts and obligations.* Is there a listing of all contracts and obligations, including maintenance costs? Does the organization to be acquired maintain good records and perform self-audits on licenses? If not, you may experience a nasty surprise when it comes time to true up the count. Long-term telecom contracts typically have minimum required usage clauses; this may abrogate some of the anticipated savings if you are unable to take advantage of your existing high-volume–low-unit-cost enterprise contracts for the acquired company.
- *Quality and value of data.* The ability to integrate the acquired firm's information into the enterprise has far-reaching strategic and financial ramifications. If data cannot be converted with a high degree of accuracy, there may be significant fallout, such as customer defection due to poor service, cost overruns as additional scrubbing is required, and overextension of credit because the same customer on both sets of books is not resolved into one. According

to a white paper from Innovative Systems, 80% of customer data integration projects fail.[3]

■ *Infrastructure.* What is the state of the hardware and software infrastructure? Have switches been purchased from a bargain retail outlet and hence do not include management features? Are servers loaded with a standard build or do they tend to be configured uniquely for every environment? Are standards for hardware/software maintained?

■ *Asset inventory.* A complete asset inventory should be obtained, with original cost and accumulated depreciation, if available.

■ *Financial information.* Are budgets accurate and tracked against actual expenditures? Is chargeback used and if so, for what? Some organizations chargeback for all services; others may only include major projects specifically requested by the business unit. If IT is highly decentralized, it may be difficult to determine which costs can be eliminated by an efficient, enterprise IT group and which will remain after the merger or acquisition.

■ *Key performance indicators (KPIs).* If available, obtain KPIs for operational activities. Examples include help desk statistics (average time to respond, number of abandoned calls, etc.), staffing levels, turnover, customer call center statistics, percentage of changes during the month that had to be backed out, and hardware/software outages. These KPIs will help benchmark performance after the acquisition.

At the end of this analysis, you need to ask yourself, "Do I have the information necessary to help my firm price the acquisition correctly?" The business executives leading the entire M&A project may be making some assumptions, such as reduction in combined back office costs. With the right information, you can support or challenge this assumption, helping to ensure an excessive price is not paid for the acquisition.

Staff Due Diligence

Who survives? You will have to answer that question, and, as they say in the old swashbuckler movies, "you'd best be quick about it, capt'n." Those with obvious talent are easy to spot, but there are other criteria that should be considered. If a core team needs to be held together, perhaps because vital product knowledge resides in their heads, team dynamics needs to be considered. Perhaps the leader should be retained and supported simply to ensure that the team does not become discouraged. On the other hand, from the perspective of the acquired CIO or VP of IT, an acquisition provides an opportunity to eliminate nonproductive staff without appearing overly harsh. Not every firm operates in the "big city." In smaller communities, where IT jobs are relatively scarce, firing nonperformers may not be as socially acceptable as in larger urban settings (where it is easier to find a new position and new recruits).

As IT groups are integrated, cultural and background differences are brought into focus. If the acquired IT group has been isolated by geography or opportunity, the effect is the same as a house with no mirrors. The inhabitants have no idea what they look like. So their idea of what a database administrator does may include simple configuration changes, and a more advanced IT group looks for best practices, domain/key normal form and row-level security. Again, you have to make a swift, conscious decision — who is to be retained? And those who are retained should be shown respect and a path for professional growth. Good people can be improved with education and opportunity.

As part of due diligence, existing deficiencies should be noted with an analysis of remediation requirements. For example, developers may have adequate technical skills but lack standard project management expertise. To the extent the acquired group needs to be fully integrated into existing practices, more investment will be needed for retained employees.

Cutting too deeply into IT staff who need to maintain acquired systems can backfire. Taking the "Chainsaw Al"[4] approach can disrupt IT so much that it harms the business, and then the CIO becomes the target of management ire. Sometimes an outside consultant can objectively identify the people and processes working effectively in the existing organization, so that staff reductions are at least somewhat based on objective facts rather than emotion or arbitrary preference.

Responsibility #2: IT Integration

After due diligence, management's final decision to proceed, regulatory OK, and any other hurdles have been overcome, you get the green light. The speculation and excitement are over, and the hard work of integration begins.

The integration plan should include at least the following elements:

- Decide on your strategic method and communicate to all relevant parties — will you "rip and replace," choose best of breed, or assimilate into the enterprise? Or choose some other strategic direction?
- Identify your integration team, including key IT, and business personnel from the acquired entity. The IT transition project manager should be full-time or near full-time.
- Develop an explicit plan of implementation — data center moves, network transition, firewall/security configurations, application transitions, etc.
- Be sure to integrate with other function groups such as HR, finance, accounting, property management, and security.
- Develop an organization chart for the combined entities. If the placement of specific individuals has not been decided, you can at least show organizational structure.

- Create an inventory of IT assets, including licenses, software, hardware, databases, and WAN links.
- Identify any clear duplication of duties. If it makes business sense, attempt to redeploy redundant staff.
- Scope out essential data integration projects. As mentioned earlier, quality problems with customer data can destroy some of the value of the acquisition.
- Communicate timing as much as possible. If you can say, for example, that the new IT organization and related responsibilities will be finalized by May 15, staff will have a sense of direction, and the exodus of skills may be reduced. In general, people hate uncertainty. That is why most people are employees rather than freelancers — they do not like to think of their compensation in terms of probabilities rather than a defined schedule.
- Face compensation issues head on. Whatever you decide, communicate it quickly and move on.
- Put on your cheerleader hat. This is the time to promote the company, discuss new learning opportunities, personal growth, and exciting future projects. The ancient Persians understood this very well. After they conquered a country, the king would typically appoint a member of the former ruling family to govern the new province. He stressed the benefits of being part of a larger, more sophisticated empire. Every attempt was made to reduce hostility and promote common interests. Resentment weakens both empires and businesses.

Culture change is probably the greatest challenge the CIO faces. One firm may have a culture of intense work effort with generally high compensation; the merger partner may be more laid back, unaccustomed to longer hours and close management scrutiny of projects. Governance maturity varies considerably, particularly between larger and smaller organizations. How do you fix the culture? There are no easy answers but here are some suggestions:

- *Explain the new culture repeatedly.* Overcommunicate if you have to. It is hard to win a game if you do not know whether mahjong or chess is being played.
- *Educate staff.* If coding is informal, systems are designed without long-term maintenance in mind — for example, bring in trainers, online education, books, whatever it takes to help them see the big picture.
- *Provide project management expertise.* A good PMO can provide the A-to-Z guidance needed to reshape thinking. Perhaps the acquired developers have never worked with business requirements, formal technical specifications, regression testing, and code reviews. Just bringing key artifacts to the table will go a long way toward maturing a less-experienced group.
- *Comingle the two groups to the extent possible.* Imagine a developer who has not worked in an environment with a strong change control system. His initial

feeling when forced to comply with standard practices is negative — how can I get my work done if I have to comply with this bureaucracy? Then he works alongside a developer who uses the change control system every day and seems to get work out on time without a problem. He sees that success is possible. Imitation is built into our genes; the effective CIO takes advantage of it.

One Approach to Integration

Figure 7.1 shows NCI Building System's approach to IT integration. The "SC³" methodology is based on the following:

- *Centralized infrastructure and development.* Centralized infrastructure and databases provide a clear economy of scale and enable decreasing unit costs as volume of transactions increases.
- *Standardized computing.* Hardware, software, and applications are standardized as soon as the business and economics permit. Second-tier, "one off," systems are the most difficult to standardize. Historical systems, for example those written in an old version of MS Access, may perform a minor but useful function supporting end users. These oddball systems challenge the standardization process and irritate technical architects.
- *Consolidation of systems and features.* NCI selects best-of-breed systems from the firms acquired and implements them across the enterprise. Realists will note that this is easier to say than to do. As one project manager said, in a casual conversation, "Fred" (not his real name) will simply not learn the new engineering system; he will have to retire or find something else to do.
- *Collaboration.* NCI ensures that all parties share information and participate in problem solving.

As Figure 7.1 shows, the consolidation process requires a comparison of the "as is" functionality of the acquiring firm with the "to be" desirable features from the acquired company. We discussed "CIO ego" in Chapter 1, but clearly there is little room for false pride under the best-of-breed scenario. If you are the big kahuna acquiring the little fish — and the little fish has a better widget — use it!

NCI uses a pyramid graphic to show how each layer of technology supports a layer above it, with the functions becoming increasingly more business/strategically oriented as you move up to the apex. This serves as a handy model during an acquisition. If IT systems, assets, and applications do not support the business at one or more levels in the pyramid, then they probably need to be converted or phased out. A manager at First Tennessee Bank, whose name we have forgotten, had a standard question when confronted with any IT activity — "are we growing weeds here?" In other words, do our actions support the business objectives in some way?

Appendices E and F list business and IT checklists for the due diligence process.

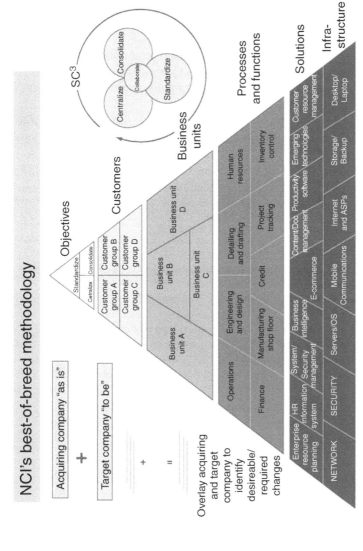

Figure 7.1 NCI Building Systems SC³ best-of-breed methodology. (Copyright © 2004, Eric J. Brown.)

Success Factors

In some organizations, growth by acquisition is a way of life. As CIO, you can easily be on either end of the table, acquiring or acquired. Success and advancement are possible under both scenarios. In general you need to:

- *Act quickly.* This is a time of high anxiety and risk. Employees on both sides of the fence need to know what to expect, especially in personal matters such as compensation. Do not delay critical decisions.
- *Go way beyond IT.* Although IT is your major responsibility, you need to have your global/strategic hat on at all times. How can you help retain customers, ensure that operations continue without a glitch, and obtain maximum value from the merger/acquisition?
- *Lead.* If there is one lesson we have learned from primate studies, it is that humans share many emotional characteristics with other social animals. When a predator threatens the pack, all look to the "alpha male" for direction and protection. This is an opportunity to manage the process and stem the loss of key IT staff by communication, support, and decisive action.

References

1. Timing is Everything in Mergers, Acquisitions and Divestments. Gartner EXP CIO Signature, August 2006. www.gartner.com (accessed February 23, 2008).
2. Ross, Jeanne W., Peter Weill, and David C. Robertson. *Enterprise Architecture as Strategy* (Boston: Harvard Business School Press, 2006).
3. Planning for Successful M&A — The Critical Role of Customer Data Quality. 2007. www.innovativesystems.com/docs/white_papers.php (accessed February 24, 2008).
4. The former Sunbeam Chairman and CEO Albert J. Dunlap had a reputation for ruthlessly and harmfully firing key employees. When Sunbeam's Board of Directors terminated his contract, employees, shareholders, and even his own family cheered, according to a July 1998 article in *Business Week*.

Chapter 8

Sourcing

IT people see most of the fun jobs going overseas, and many of the jobs left behind are just administrative roles for people who need to coordinate the offshore work.... Enrollment in IT degrees is in sharp decline [in the United States].

Harwell Thrasher, *Boiling the IT Frog*

The cost structure of the work being done offshore will continue to go down in the near future ... suppliers [are] getting more sophisticated about "lifting and shifting" work; they're also getting productivity costs out.

Joe Fernandes, *Sourcing Magazine*

The Pendulum of Opinion

The adoption of outsourcing seems to go in and out of favor, as one firm achieves success and another scrambles to take back the work in-house. Since information technology outsourcing first reached the market in the 1960s, the options have expanded into off-shoring, near-shoring; undoubtedly, when people one day live on Mars, off-planet-shoring may become popular. When opinion shifts back and forth on nearly any financial/operational topic, the reason often has to do with the complexity of causes "under the hood." Was a tightly defined IT service moved to Monterrey, Mexico, with outstanding results? Was a loose set of guidelines and a high-level specification "thrown over the fence" to developers in Hyderabad with poor results? Both involve outsourcing but have completely different outcomes. As

129

we will see throughout this chapter, generalization about sourcing is not particularly useful. To quote from one of the TV diet ads, "individual results may vary."

The Traditional Pros and Cons

To start our discussion, let us review the historical arguments for and against outsourcing IT.

Pro — From the Provider's Perspective (As Might Be Presented by a Provider to a Prospective Client Who Manufactures Surfboards)

- We are the experts in IT. You, on the other hand, are the expert in the manufacturing and marketing of the most advanced surfboards on the planet. Why do you not spend your time with what you do best and leave IT to us?
- We can do the job as well as you, but we are simply less expensive.
- There are jobs, such as network reconfiguration, that you do only occasionally. It is easier and less expensive to have us do "one off"-type work like this.
- Your developers, database administrators, and infrastructure staff have a limited career path inside your surfboard company. All those positions within our company, on the other hand, can lead straight to senior positions if the individual has the talent. We could even discuss bringing your existing staff on as employees, so no one gets laid off as part of the deal.
- Our size enables us to bring considerable expertise to the table. We have staff skilled in many different technologies and can afford to become experts across the board. Your IT staff has limited capabilities simply because there are not enough people in a typical in-house shop to cover all the technologies.
- We can do your IT processing work cheaper than you can do it yourself. With our cumulative volumes of transactions and large infrastructure, we gain economies of scale. As a result, we can offer a lower per transaction cost than you can achieve yourself.
- Using our infrastructure, you pay only for what capacity you use. If you divest part of the business and your volume goes down, so does your cost. You do not have a fixed investment in infrastructure which must be allocated over all your business units. If your business increases we are there with you to seamlessly increase IT capabilities and capacities as well.
- We offer a standard, highly controlled computing environment. This means that IT disaster recovery, infrastructure breakdowns, unexpected loss of technical personnel, and other IT concerns no longer demand senior management attention. Steering committees can now focus much more on business requirements; decisions such as whether it makes sense to build out a second data center are no longer relevant.

Con — From the Customer's Perspective *(As Might Be Shown on a Powerpoint Presentation at a Conference on Outsourcing)*

■ We can see where the outsource firm provides standard, well-defined transactions at a low cost. However, we are not a high-volume transaction business. Our mix of required IT services changes rapidly, so we must continually renegotiate the contract to address changing requirements.

■ We are concerned that the outsourcing "culture" is overly conservative in terms of bringing very new technologies to the table. Where are the real breakthrough ideas? If the outsource firm's revenue model is based on certain technologies and services, a change to a new IT environment (e.g., SOA) means extensive and additional training for their staff and perhaps even new hardware/software to support the applications. In all fairness, the provider could lose money if they do not negotiate properly; conversely, we could lose money by paying an unreasonably high-risk premium for leading-edge systems.

■ We are concerned that the provider's processes could become rigid and slow to change in response to marketplace demands. The provider may have a large amount of time and money invested in a specific approach to customer service, processing schedules, and so forth. It may be difficult to modify this process if we need to respond to external demands.

■ We worry about our risk. Putting all our systems in the hands of the provider creates a single point of failure. This is particularly true if the provider handles the primary interface with our customers.

■ We need to have regularly scheduled reviews of the work and the costs. If technology dramatically drops the cost of some service, we do not want to get locked into a noncompetitive rate.

■ In some cases, providers may want to insert a management layer between us as consumers and their IT staff doing the work. This could potentially slow work and reduce the clarity of business requirements. If our person "A" must go through the outsourcer's management person "B" in order to communicate requirements to the developer "C," then the opportunity for quality degradation increases significantly. "A" needs to be able to talk to and work with "C" *directly*, if required.

■ We have been told that the cost for a given project or specified piece of work will be based on the outsourcer's manpower estimates. If it takes 5 or 50 people, the price will not change. That sounds great, but in practice we occasionally see new work — projects that were not previously on the plate — given to the same, overworked resources. Because "resources" are human beings who need adequate rest and sleep to function well, we are concerned that the quality of our new systems will be degraded. If we are paying $X per hour for outsource resources, we expect to see new faces on any new project requiring IT staff beyond those who normally work on the account.

■ We want to avoid overly strong hooks that will keep us involuntarily tied to any particular outsourcer(s). If proprietary code from the provider becomes embedded in systems we owned outright prior to the deal, we want a way to cleanly opt out if we become dissatisfied with performance or cost. For example, assume provider X adds code to our sales software; as a result, we are able to more accurately predict which products are good cross-sell candidates. The sales software belonged to us initially and provider X merely added code on top of the package to improve its predictive capability. If we elect to completely in-source or go with another provider, it should be reasonably straightforward to remove the proprietary code.

■ The overall IT architecture should not be entirely the choice of the provider. We may not want to be tied to a particular technology suite or platform.

■ A SAS70 report showing strong data center and processing controls is essential. We do not want to outsource our applications to a provider who struggles with basic IT controls. We expect core Control Objectives for IT (CobIT) guidelines to be in place.

■ We need the right to audit the bill. If some charges are based on the performance of a particular class of server, we want some assurance that the purchase of a new server and related new price point is based on some mathematically valid formula. In other words, "twice the box" may not equate to twice the number of transactions processed. This issue is more significant in mainframe environments, where central processing unit (CPU) seconds are a major part of the pricing structure. A more powerful mainframe can do more with the same CPU second, but how much more? Where do the benchmarking statistics come from? (See Figure 8.1 for a conceptual diagram of this point.)

■ On the front end, we are concerned about the one-off expense of setting up the entire agreement. For small jobs this is not a significant issue, but for large agreements there are a plethora of expensive to do's: legal review, setting up our own structure for managing the contract, developing practical service-level agreements, and of course, the initial transitioning from our internal data center/applications to the provider's platform.

In addition to these considerations, there are the usual large vendor management issues to address. For example, in the early 1990s, as part of the Enron/EDS outsourcing deal, an initial baseline of services was established via a joint audit by both parties. EDS assumed that the current mainframe TSO (time sharing option) usage, which was relatively high, would continue into the future. Enron's practice had been to leave TSO up indefinitely. EDS consequently built TSO time as a CRU (computer resource unit) into their economic model. Unfortunately, from the EDS perspective, Enron "pulled the plug" on TSO usage by instituting a timeout after a certain number of minutes. This represented a significant contraction in EDS' anticipated revenue. Without passing judgment on either side's good or bad

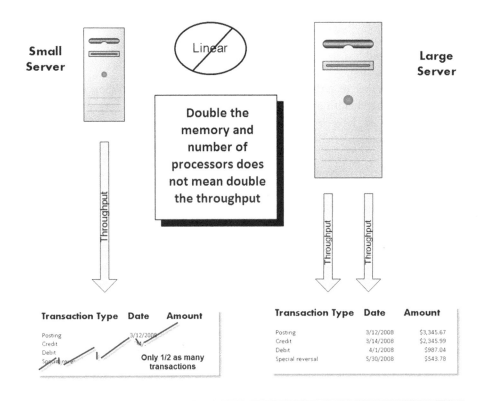

Figure 8.1 The relationship between server size and throughput cannot be assumed to be linear (twice the size may not process twice the number of transactions).

intentions, it became clear that this surprise soured the relationship initially; it took considerable management effort on both sides to reestablish a cordial relationship. The lesson here is that the bigger the deal, the more chances for friction, and the more effort required to manage the relationship. And if the relationship becomes dysfunctional, both the provider and the consumer of services suffer.

To Outsource or Not to Outsource?

It is certainly a question worthy of Hamlet. There are a myriad of factors that may influence this decision. Certainly, and increasingly, it is not an either/or decision. It is relatively easy to use salesforce.com customer relationship management (CRM) software in place of an in-house system. Payroll outsourced to ADP could be your sole outsourced application. For small- to medium-sized IT departments, some of the considerations are relatively straightforward[1]:

- If the process or application is integral to your business, you may be cautious about turning it over to a third-party provider.
- If you spend less than 8 hours a week performing some task, it is a candidate for outsourcing.
- If the number of technologies required for running your shop exceeds the learning bandwidth of your staff, outsource part of it.
- If you do not have an infrastructure upgrade road map for the next year or two, outsourcing may ease the upcoming transition.
- If you elect to outsource, do not limit your choices to the big providers in India or other international locations; particularly, if you are a small shop, a local or regional provider may be more practical.
- If you only occasionally perform some IT-related task (even though it may be a large effort), it may be easier to outsource it.

According to *CIO Insight* magazine, midmarket firms are more satisfied with their outsourcing experiences than are larger firms.[2] This may be in part because midmarket firms have simpler and easier to manage outsourcing requirements.

For traditional domestic outsourcing arrangements, the pros and cons discussed above include the most important issues. However, when off-shoring and near-shoring are put in the mix, different considerations apply. We will now outline some of these challenges and opportunities.

Xshoring

"Xshoring" (near-shore, off-shore) morphs before our eyes. India is experiencing such intense demand for skilled IT labor (particularly in the top cities) that salaries are beginning to rise; overall, India's economy is growing at 9% as of the time of this writing.[3] The cheapest work is moving to Vietnam and other growing hot spots. Even within India, work is moving to second-tier cities such as Cochin and Chennai. In the best-selling book *The World Is Flat*, Thomas Friedman outlines how many kinds of work, both heads-down transactions as well as creative design, will move to where it can be produced cheapest and best. Although there are many exceptions and caveats to this thesis, in its broad outline, the book is on target. So off-shoring is and will continue to be a standard option for IT departments.

Let us imagine we have a manufacturing system that will require thousands of man-hours to modify to suit our business requirements. What are some of the issues we face as we contemplate an offshore solution?

- How much management will the process require? Maybe we just hire a few tech writers, do some use-cases, and then send the whole package to Hyderabad for coding? Clearly, that will not work. Lots of management attention is required for any chance of success. Not just IT management — user management's earthly presence is also mandated.

■ Where are we on the outsource maturity meter? Are we like third-generation firms using offshore providers; do we have metrics, standard contracts, and strong life-cycle management tools?

■ Are there any particular advantages that accrue to the business? For example, can we take advantage of time differences to deliver a one-two punch for systems in development — coding takes place while the United States sleeps; analysis and testing are done during the U.S. business day.

■ What are our real expectations from the provider? Does the culture encourage risk taking and avoid excessive blame for small failures? The developers and managers doing the offshore work may be conditioned to hammering out a specific solution for a specific problem at a low cost. Is it reasonable to ask them to don their California-cool-dude hat and think creatively about neat stuff that could be added to a manufacturing system? Certainly they have the innate capacity to develop that mind-set, but do we want them to grow intellectually on our nickel? But, as we said earlier, IT capabilities are morphing all over the world; we can expect creative, "out of the box" solutions and deep business knowledge to flourish in all the IT hot spots eventually.

■ How will language barriers be overcome?

■ How will you hedge currency fluctuations?

■ Will you be able to protect yourself legally if something untoward happens — especially the loss of intellectual property?

The Proximity Factor

Offshore development can be hampered by the inefficiencies of communications when users and developers are separated by thousands of miles (proximity challenged). Projects developed offshore may suffer from a higher quantity of "information retransmissions" than expected. Specifications, so seemingly clear at the plant or business office, become ambiguous when seen by developers and project managers outside the context of the operations. Following are typical results when communications between business managers, project managers, and developers are poor quality, out of context, or too infrequent:

■ Convoluted and inefficient code (uncertainty results in early patches to the original concept).

■ Excessive rework that may erode many of the anticipated benefits.

■ Decisions made by the development team in a vacuum. In frustration, they simply elect to "get 'er done" by making arbitrary assumptions.

■ Late recognition of initial, incorrect assumptions.

■ Adoption of unrealistic timelines. When they are finally identified as impractical, there may be unreasonable (and uneconomic) incentives to simply pump out code, regardless of quality.

As Michael Keaton found in the movie *Multiplicity,* the third or fourth copy of anything complex is considerably degraded from the original. As specifications pass from one point to another, they become fuzzy, even if formally written with full diagrams or use-case scenarios. To some extent, the success of a project is proportional to the number of times end users can view test results in a given period of time. A lengthy turnaround process might result in multiple retransmissions, reviews, and interpretations. Time zones, culture, and physical distance dramatically slow the turnaround of results to the business (user acceptance testers). Perhaps the most important factor is business understanding. In the case of steel buildings, for example, if the developers have never seen a fabrication plant, cannot visualize the large distances under one roof or the massive size of steel coil inventory, and are unaware of the subtleties of the loading dock, then they may code sequences of events that are not practical.

So how do we speed up delivery of test results to users and also present developers with a more realistic business perspective? The answer: the proximity factor. The closer developers are to end users, the more likely they are to write systems that match the user's needs. Ideally, they are next to each other, in the same office. Proximity of business users and developers results in the following:

- *Greater accuracy of the code.* Errors are more readily apparent and are remediated earlier in the life cycle.
- *Fresh ideas from both parties.* The user knows what needs to be done. The developer knows what can be done (what is possible). The interaction typically results in slight but vital changes to system design and coding.
- *Dramatically faster results.* Users are not presented with a large number of changes all at once. Instead, they see changes daily or weekly in bite-sized chunks that can be carefully evaluated.

With developers thousands of miles away, proximity is obviously not easy to achieve. Some options to consider are videoconferencing, showing a "movie" of how the physical business environment works, or even sending a select few individuals from the outsource location to the business sites.

Keeping Xshoring and Sourcing in Perspective

If you are new to Xshoring or even to outsourcing in general, keep in mind that the provider's objective is to make money. The vast majority are hard-working firms who, in their own long-term interests, want to perform good service and garner a reputation for high-quality work. Nonetheless, they have typically been in the game much longer than you have. They know the subtleties. For example, if you ask them to develop some new applications in an environment for which they have little expertise — who pays for the training? Either way is fine, but you should be aware of the issue and nail down the deal on the front end. There are specialty firms, such as Technology Partners, Inc., based in Houston, Texas, who have been repeatedly through the hype cycles and can provide a road map. Going into an outsourcing deal without experience is much like Bessie in the 1930s play *Tobacco Road*. Raised in the backwoods, she is naïve and responds truthfully when car salesmen ask her how much money she has. Then they exclaim how coincidental it is that the new T-model Ford in the showroom costs exactly that amount. Bessie never quite understands how she has been duped. That may be an extreme example, but the principle holds true — you cannot beat the providers at their own game unless you are fully prepared.

Sourcing Is More Than IT Services

We have focused on IT in this chapter, but of course there are dozens of services, such as accounting, tax work, engineering, design, and optical scanning, which are routinely outsourced. If you go through a major IT outsource project, you may become the most experienced executive in your organization with respect to sourcing. It is a great opportunity to show your value and lead the way. Deals abound where multiple services are bundled for a lower price.

One final comment — regardless of contract terms or other factors, a sourcing arrangement that becomes negative rarely works. So although you do no-nonsense negotiating during the day, try to relax over dinner with representatives from your potential provider. Services today are too complex to negotiate every contingency and goodwill is essential. It is rare that an outsource agreement does not get modified; these modifications serve as a safety valve to ensure that the relationship does not become one-sided and therefore ineffective.

References

1. Morgan, Russell. "When to Outsource IT." *PC Magazine* (May 22, 2006): 85.
2. Alter, Allan. "'Tis a Gift to be Smaller." *CIO Insight* (March 1, 2007): 45.
3. Overby, Stephanie. "The Shape of Deals to Come." *CIO Magazine* (March 1, 2007): 44.

Chapter 9

Business Intelligence and Analytics

Now, here, you see, it takes all the running you can do, to keep in the same place. If you want to get somewhere else, you must run at least twice as fast as that.

Lewis Carroll, *Through the Looking-Glass*

Information Big Bang: The sum total of all information produced in 2008 will likely exceed the amount of information generated by humans over the past 40,000 years.

***Seed Magazine*, January 2008**

What you need in this business is more information than the other guy. Not more smarts. Not more intuition. Just more information.

Joshua Boger, President and Chief Executive Officer of Vertex Corporation

Reports that say that something hasn't happened are always interesting to me, because as we know, there are "known knowns"; there are things we know we know. We also know there are "known unknowns"; that is to say we know there are some things we do not know. But there are also "unknown unknowns" — the ones we don't know we don't know.

Donald Rumsfeld, February 2002

The demands of business today are phenomenal. Customers order a new printer from Amazon.com and expect it the next day, on their doorstep. Engineering processes must be rationalized, costs from operations minimized, and demand for your products needs to be constantly stoked, like a modern-day version of the antebellum steamboats. Compounding these demands are the short shelf life of innovations — if you are successful, your competitors will copy your product or process, bypassing development costs and undercutting your sales margins.

One answer to these challenges is the use of business intelligence (BI) and analytics throughout your organization. As we will discuss, the proper mind-set for BI is a "democratic" strategy (used by many, not just a few). Although BI provides clear benefits for senior executives, its real power comes from widespread use across the organization, particularly for your customer-facing employees. Though each front-line decision may be miniscule in impact, the summation of thousands or hundreds of thousands of them can have the same cumulative impact on profitability as a major merger/acquisition decision.

So what is BI? It is the use of software, logic, mathematics, and an up-to-date subset of your total enterprise data to provide reliable information for decision making. Following are some typical questions that will lead to decisions:

■ Do I need to add staff/change processes in Accounts Payable so that there are enough resources to ensure discounts are taken when available?
■ Should I offer the customer on the line a discounted product, based on his purchasing history?
■ Why do so many potential loan applicants get to a certain point on my Web site and then logoff before completing the application?
■ Why does my cash flow seem to lag sales more than it should?
■ Do I have any anomalies in pricing structure that may cause one or more products to be uncompetitive or unprofitable?
■ Are my raw material purchases satisfying my demand mix based on forecast and current steel prices for the next 3 months?

Getting Started — Selling Business Intelligence (BI)

Culture matters. The precursor to a successful implementation of BI is to establish the cultural value of "facts" as a guide to business. "Gut feel" works best in the context of an information-rich and visually compelling environment. In one survey, 73% of respondents from firms successfully using BI to improve operations/sales indicated that decisions were made based on facts. In contrast, 80% of respondents from firms with failed BI implementations stated that gut-feel was the most important factor in decisions.[1] Today's flat world is too complex and changes too quickly for management to rely mainly on intuition; customers, markets, regulations, tastes, and technology are not static. Some organizations are imbued with a respect and desire for real-time intelligence, but many are not — so if your organization has not yet adopted BI as a strategic tool, your challenge is to achieve enough small successes to demonstrate its value to management.

Value Proposition

The potential benefits of a BI implementation vary widely. Overstock.com used BI to reduce inventory levels from $80 million to $16 million without reducing sales, thus dramatically improving cash flow.[2] A BI project at COX Enterprises, Inc., uncovered $250,000 in uncollected revenue.[3] At our own firm, NCI Building Systems, Brad Robeson, President and Chief Operating Officer (COO) of our Metal Coaters Division identified $300,000 in missed payables discounts.

As the examples above demonstrate, BI is practical and need not include esoteric and complex modifications to operations. In fact, in some cases, the information provided is little different from that found in traditional month-end or quarter-end financial reports. What is different is *speed of delivery and presentation.* Much of the value comes from daily or even minute-by-minute information to the right people — executives, back-office personnel, and front-line employees. If you compare top executives today to those in the 1950s, their compensation in real terms is much higher, but their workload is also dramatically increased. The consequence of this change is a loss of attention span — they are simply too busy to focus on the mass of information available to them. A system to graphically present *relevant* information is at least a partial solution to this time crunch. It may take a data warehouse and a significant ETM (extract, transform, load) system to provide the underlying data to create a single screen display, but the effort usually pays off. Figure 9.1 through Figure 9.3 show example summary information presented to management and operational/financial analysts.

BI helps automate routine decisions and often enables a higher frequency of decisions. For example, in their book *Smart Enough Systems*,[4] James Taylor and Neil Raden cite the credit extending practices of a large European bank. Before the use of predictive analytics, a credit/risk calculation was made at the time of loan approval. For those approved but considered higher risk, a large loss reserve had to be maintained, thus imposing a high opportunity cost should the customer become stronger financially over time (funds were tied up in reserves). In other words, the bank was able to revisit customer metrics so they could lower their reserve. Also, the bank's various channels for offering products resulted in inconsistent risk rankings across countries and products for a given customer. After a predictive analytics capability was implemented, the risk ranking become much more accurate. Not only were all the various risk calculations for the bank's channels/products coordinated, but the risk ranking could be run repeatedly for a given customer, thus taking payment experience into consideration. The system also incorporates collateral to support multiple loans, thus minimizing expected loss.[5]

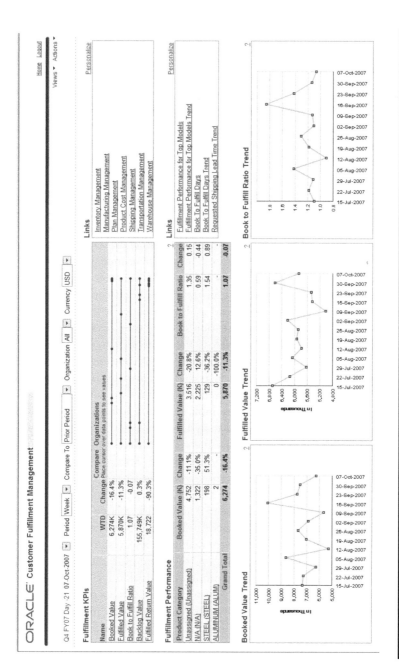

Figure 9.1   Example of a financial presentation showing key performance indicators for customer fulfillment.

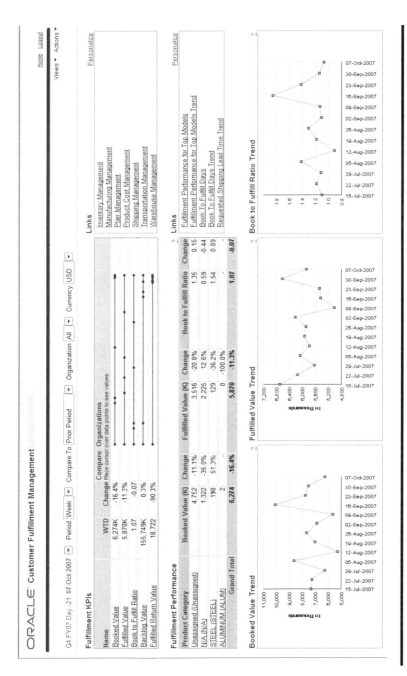

Figure 9.2 Example of a financial presentation showing key performance indicators for inventory management.

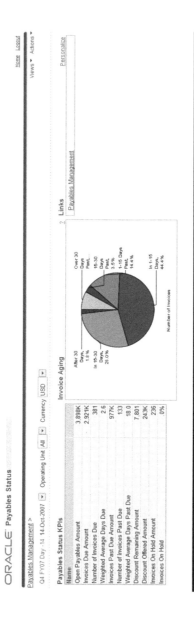

Figure 9.3 Example of a financial presentation showing key performance indicators for payables.

Another branch of BI, predictive analytics, focuses on the future and provides economic value by forecasting results. A white paper by Wayne Eckerson, director of research for the Data Warehousing Institute, lists the following predictive analytics success stories[6]:

- A Canadian bank increased campaign response rates by 600%, cut customer acquisition costs by 50%, and boosted campaign return on investment by 100%.
- A leading hospital improved its ability to classify and treat pediatric brain tumors by combining predictive and text analytics.
- An airline significantly improved its ability to estimate the number of individuals who fail to show up for a flight. The result was an increase in revenue and customer satisfaction.

Successful businesses, government agencies, and nonprofits are wringing the last drop of benefit out of assets and processes. They have to. A flat world drives production to its cheapest and best source while disproportionately rewarding innovation. Automating routine decisions is an essential part of this rationalization process. Remember John Henry, the mythical 19th century steel driver? He takes on the steam-powered hammer and wins the contest. But he dies shortly afterward — humans wear out long before machines do.

Core Components

Figure 9.4 shows the base elements of a BI system. The specific transactional databases at the start of the process will vary by need and organization, but the logical process is standard. Some organizations have developed "in-line" ETL (extract, transform, and load) processes. This inline process speeds delivery of results by sending relevant data directly to the BI application without the intermediate ETL step.

Data Warehouse

For most organizations, implementation of a data warehouse is a prudent first step. What you do not want is for your business analysts and executives, anxious to exploit the benefits of BI, to compete with workers performing operational tasks (taking orders, posting cash, etc.). Like Godot, CIOs are still waiting for the arrival of unlimited computing power; meanwhile, prudent use of resources is required. Following are the factors most organizations cite when electing to deploy a data warehouse:

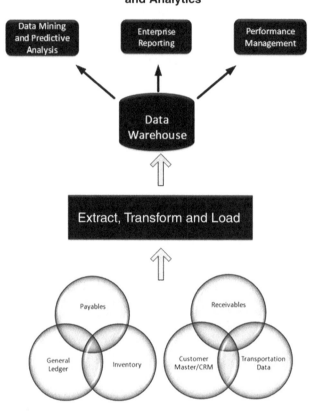

Figure 9.4 Components of a typical business intelligence system.

- *Speed and efficiency.* Most executives and others interested in BI are working during the day, which is also the time of peak server/ERP database transactional processing. A data warehouse provides a separate channel for the same information and reduces contention.
- *Preaggregated data.* By performing batch operations overnight, various totals and subtotals can be inserted into the warehouse tables so that resummarization from raw transactions need not be performed during the day.
- *Inputs from multiple sources.* Data warehouses can collect information and standardize/rationalize the format from many sources. This dramatically simplifies the analysis process.
- *Data consistency.* Using a documented model of the way all data should appear to the end user, the "extract and transform" process can clean up data variations and enable enterprise-wide analysis.

In the late 1970s and 1980s, decision support systems (DSSs) began proliferating. To feed the DSS applications, data had to be extracted from disparate systems. Eventually the number of extracts and, nearly as troublesome, the timing of extracts became a significant problem. Because all the information could not be collected in a synchronized process, the resulting reporting sometimes varied from its constituent data feeds. Based on these challenges, data warehouses were initially introduced as an IT solution and only later evolved into a more business-oriented tool.

Designing your data warehouse will require analysis and time. Loading data indiscriminately will not only tie up your servers but will present users with a confusing array of data elements. Data elements such as "Gross Sales Amount" or "Net Transportation Cost" need to be precisely defined. Differing definitions of key information across different business units reduce the value of information. Good data governance includes the often repeated question — "is this data structured only for my department or could I make changes to make it less parochial and more suitable for enterprise reporting?" If your firm flies passengers around the world, can you answer the CEO's question "how many passenger miles has our company sold this year?" Without a precise definition of the term, that answer could vary, depending on how frequent flyer trips and other revenue affecting factors are factored into the total.

A Data Warehouse Alternative

The use of a data warehouse may be driven from several directions. First, it may simply be a way to allow users to create standard, canned reports during the day without degrading the operational performance of ERPs and applications. Another use is to provide "flattened out" data for BI and analytics. However, in recent years, some vendors have begun providing an alternative data feed approach, search-based BI. Firms such as Fast, Cognos, and Endeca Technologies use efficient techniques to build sophisticated indexes on the fly (as transactions occur) to enable completely ad hoc BI-type inquiries. This adaptive and highly flexible approach would not have been possible even a few years ago — the computing horsepower was too low and the algorithms too primitive to make it practical (thanks to Google and competitors for bringing smart search algorithms to the table!).

The use of a search-based BI approach does not preclude a data warehouse, which is useful even if your firm does not use BI. A search or "in-line" approach provides some rather primo benefits, such as:

- Queries can be extremely flexible and include dozens of sources.
- BI analysts do not have to be "Karnak" or a magician to predict in advance the various data fields, time frames, and aggregations required to produce the required information. Instead of hours a day sorting through thousands or hundreds of thousands of static records, users can perform ad hoc exception reports and get the most up-to-date information.

- Linear scalability as data grows. Traditional warehouses can expand to gargantuan proportions if not culled, summarized, and constantly managed. The Web-based search approach, if properly implemented, can provide information across a much larger slice of time and transactions than is practical to implement in a static and slightly time delayed data warehouse. The need for analyzing classes of variables and transactional metadata is eliminated (or at least reduced — ultimately the meaning of data must always be understood in order to get meaningful results).

- Use of fuzzy logic and linguistic tools to group data via indexes. For example, many organizations suffer from duplicate vendor names, such as ACME Company and ACME Inc., and other variations. The built-in data-cleansing tools can combine these to provide a more accurate view of expenditures by vendor. One of us, Yarberry, was jokingly hailed as a "smart ….[epithet deleted]" when he asked for a listing of payables by vendor for a Detroit telecommunications firm and within 30 seconds found a $12,000 duplicate payment — one to AT&T and the other to A.T.T.

- Shorter learning curve. Because search-based solutions tend to use standard Web interfaces, users can more quickly make use of its capabilities.

- Minimal data latency. If your data warehouse is updated nightly, then users at the end of the business day are essentially querying yesterday's data. In contrast, search systems pull current data — most important when the BI activity deals with customer interface situations.

To achieve benefits like those mentioned above, your BI environment should have some degree of architectural integrity. The infrastructure should be consolidated so the number of tools is limited (not, for example, a dozen tools, one for each business unit). Even with search-based BI, results are improved with a reduced set of data sources (ERP, CRM, and so forth). In addition, good data governance (for example, common standards for codes) reduces the total effort required to consolidate information. Finally, change control applies to BI as well as to other applications. If each division buys its own tool and implements without regard to the rest of the organization, well, it is like surfing Waimea or Mavericks done without a leash. Once you wipe out, and you will, you are on your own and it is a long swim back to shore.

Predictive Analytics and Data Mining

How many times have bored college students, struggling in an introductory statistics class, asked "how is knowing this going to make me or my company any money?" The answer may be in predictive analysis, a mix of heavy-duty mathematics, statistics, complex algorithms, and data management. Of course, all the "quant" work is built into the software, so businesspeople need only understand its

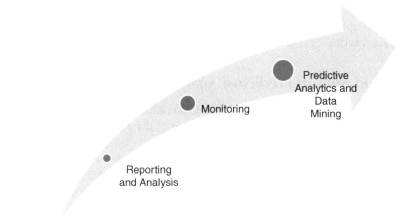

Figure 9.5   Hierarchy of business intelligence activities.

capabilities in broad terms. Predictive analytics (PA) improves business processes, helps firms understand customer behaviors, find opportunities, and sometimes presents nonobvious relationships that can lead to greater profitability. Figure 9.5 shows a hierarchy of BI activities, with predictive analytics and data mining at the top (suggesting a high level of BI maturity). Reporting and analysis represent standard query, reporting, and visualization tools. Monitoring includes daily dashboards and alerts. Predictive analysis focuses on the future and things not already known. CIOs and business executives should occasionally repeat the ancient mantra, "I don't know what I don't know" — discovery is an important element of good management.

At first glance, PA seems a bit abstract, so let us consider a practical example. Virtually all firms are interested in identifying new populations that will have a high probability of becoming customers. At the same time, they do not want to lose existing profitable customers. Any help with acquisition and retention can have a payoff. One firm, Intelligent Results, a subsidiary of First Data Corporation, uses analytical engines for credit card profitability calculations, as shown below[7]:

- Analyze business drivers and costs to create a score (using predictive analytics).
- Use the above score and First Data's pricing, loyalty, and decisioning platforms, to make decisions regarding the likely payoff of customer communications such as calling, e-mailing, letters, and so forth.
- Use results of the customer retention programs to recursively improve success over time.

Another use of PA includes analysis of past medical claims data, as well as laboratory, pharmacy, and other medical records in order to predict the future cost to an insurance company for a given applicant. Some firms improve collection of bad debts by analyzing the most cost-effective collection agencies, contract terms, and preemptive legal actions.

The Nuts and Bolts of Predictive Analytics

Predictive analytics (sometimes called modeling) has a life cycle like other projects involving software and data. Following are key steps in the process:

- Collect business requirements. What are the expected end results? What problem am I trying to solve? Maybe I do not even know what problem I am trying to solve! I do not know what I do not know (somewhat like Donald Rumsfeld's often quoted "unknown unknowns"). This is where end users need to drive the project. Ensure that objectives, time frames, costs, and specific expected results are defined.
- Develop a solid understanding of the data available and their quality. Descriptive statistics (such as standard deviations, max/min, distribution, histogram, etc.) along with data profiling tools (such as those from Infosolve, Silver Creek, and Datiris) help analysts with this process. As an aside, predictive analysts/modelers as a group are talented individuals; if your firm does a lot of work in this area, you may want to acquire a resource early on. Some of the questions answered by data profiling include:
  - Listing of numeric or alpha values allowed in a column
  - High/low restrictions on numeric fields
  - Referential integrity requirements (primary/foreign key constrains). Can a credit to a customer exist if that customer is no longer found on the primary customer table?
  - Patterns of data for any column
  - Redundancy
- Select and transform data as needed for a modeling tool. This is a time consuming but essential step. Typically, the information must be converted into a large flat file with perhaps dozens or hundreds of fields. Sometimes aggregation is performed during this step. At the end of this step, the model's input is clean and well defined.
- Develop a good model. This is usually done with vendor supplied software, although theoretically it could be done with statistical routines embedded in home-grown software or Excel. Some models can be trained with actual results and become more accurate over time. The amount of data required typically shrinks as the model becomes more sophisticated; some data have little or no predictive value and thus can be eliminated.
- Run the model, on either the entire set of relevant data or a subset.
- Review results and rerun periodically to improve accuracy, efficiency, and overall usefulness. If useful enough, models are sometimes recoded into

highly efficient programs that can be run on demand by line management or others needing continually updated information.

A very successful predictive analytics model may be embedded into an application so that it functions routinely without requiring human initiation. This may also include a transformation of the results into simpler, more understandable results. Mathematicians, engineers, and MBAs may understand "standard deviation," but many others will not; they need something that says "The computer predicts that you will lose money on this prospective customer and therefore you should decline to offer services."

Some vendors are starting to offer new features such as advanced graphical modeling/workflow, integrated workbenches, and text analytics. As we mentioned before, usability trumps features, so expect the packages to get easier to use over time.

Data Mining

Data mining is closely aligned with predictive modeling. It uses mathematical techniques to identify nonobvious trends or data relationships. It also enables customer churn analysis, security work (terrorist identification and IT security related), and analysis of product sales. In some complex business environments, neural networks[8] are used to mine data and create predictions. These models are able to create valid results, but the cross-correlations between many of the underlying variables are unknown.

Survey of Business Uses

Functional uses of BI are varied and increasing. Table 9.1 shows common business drivers, based on the results of a Gartner survey of 300 attendees at the North American and European Gartner Business Intelligence Summit in 2007.[9] Figure 9.6 from the same survey shows specific platform capability rankings.

Security and Data Quality

Information may come from either a data warehouse or, less commonly, directly from your operational databases. In either case, you may want to consider how security is enabled. For example, row-level security (a method to segregate similar data by organizational unit) provides access to data in a single table restricted by some data element, such as a business unit. Row-level security allows individuals from multiple departments to view and update data from the same database but not for a department other than their own. The alternative to row-level security, at least in some cases, is to proliferate database tables specific to a given department or organization, resulting in an increase in complexity and maintenance effort.

Table 9.1 Drivers for Business Intelligence

Driver	2007 Percentage of Respondents	2006 Percentage of Respondents
To speed up and improve the organization's decision-making ability	71.1	73.0
To respond to user needs for data on a timely basis	45.8	45.7
To better align with and track against corporate strategy and objectives	42.9	47.1
To move users toward a self-service model of informaton delivery	35.5	33.9
To decrease business costs and improve operational efficiency (e.g., supply chain)	27.2	27.0
To ensure regulatory compliance (big change year over year)	21.3	6.9
To increase the organization's revenue	20.6	23.9
To better manage a specific operational process in a more timely fashion	17.6	21.6
To share information with customers, suppliers, and partners (big change year over year)	17.3	8.9

Source: From Gartner, Inc., "Business Intelligence Platforms: Survey Drivers and Planned Investments," by Bill Hostmann, August 24, 2007.

Like the mythical Sisyphus, who was condemned by the gods to roll a heavy rock up a hill every day, only to have it roll back down, CIOs face a never-ending battle against bad data. Following are some good and bad practices that directly affect the value of the data used by your BI systems:

- Leads to Bad Data
  - Hard coding data in programs, where it is hidden from user view
  - Varying business definitions among business units
  - No defined data owner
  - Varying codes between business units (e.g., "S" in one fixed asset system and "SL" in another, both indicating straight-line depreciation)
  - Lack of inventory standardization; the same physical item has more than one part number in different divisions

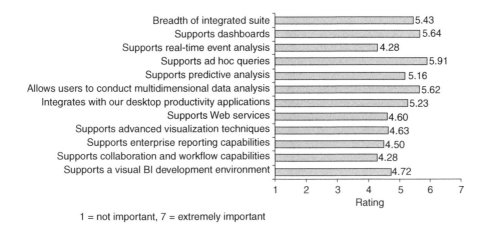

Figure 9.6 shows a horizontal bar chart with the following business capability ratings:

- Breadth of integrated suite — 5.43
- Supports dashboards — 5.64
- Supports real-time event analysis — 4.28
- Supports ad hoc queries — 5.91
- Supports predictive analysis — 5.16
- Allows users to conduct multidimensional data analysis — 5.62
- Integrates with our desktop productivity applications — 5.23
- Supports Web services — 4.60
- Supports advanced visualization techniques — 4.63
- Supports enterprise reporting capabilities — 4.50
- Supports collaboration and workflow capabilities — 4.28
- Supports a visual BI development environment — 4.72

Rating (scale 1 to 7)

1 = not important, 7 = extremely important

Figure 9.6   Business capability ratings. (From Gartner, Inc. "Business Intelligence Platforms: Survey Drivers and Planned Investments," by Bill Hostmann, August 24, 2007. With permission.)

- – Poor computer editing functions; data entry errors are not flagged even though the information is there to do so
- – Referential integrity not maintained — an extreme example would be to post a credit to a customer who is no longer in the customer master
- ■ Leads to Good Data
  - – Good data governance practices in place (e.g., ensure data integration, eliminate duplication, resolve variances, define rules for creating data elements)
  - – Common, enterprise-wide systems in place
  - – Systematic review of data quality
  - – Implementation of established data integrity system controls; turn on parameters that reject invalid data
  - – Understanding of timing requirements in place; data need to be refreshed no more or less frequently than demanded by business decisions
  - – Data retention policy upheld

Effective Implementation

Thomas Davenport, Director of Research for Babson College Executive Education, suggests the following steps for effective implementation[10]:

- ■ Bring analytical skills in-house
- ■ Improve the quality of your data
- ■ Implement analytical technology

■ Examine business strategy
■ Find an executive partner

These need not be done sequentially. In fact, the last step listed, find a sponsor, may need to be started early on. BI is best done at the enterprise level, and a senior-level supporter is needed to move the organization beyond a silo approach to an implementation across all business units.

Analytical skills include not only "top-side" analysts but also individuals with IT knowledge sufficient to create responsive and accurate systems. Specific expertise in products such as Business Objects, Cognos, and Hyperion may take some time to develop. In addition, agile development processes may be needed in order to provide the speed and flexibility required to develop BI systems. The most valuable people are those with hybrid skills — IT, business subject matter experts, and analytical orientation. Larger organizations should consider establishing a BI competency center. Continental Airlines, for example, has a fifteen-person BI competency center, including four business analysts.[11]

The market is well supplied with BI vendors. Some are restricted to a single ERP, and others cheerfully integrate disparate ERPs, data warehouses, and other data sources.

Interview with Brad Robeson, President of NCI Buildings, a Division of NCI Group, Inc.

Q: How do you use BI in your organization?

A: I typically use it, on a daily basis, as a discovery tool. For example, I review gross margin, payables, and inventory changes in order to monitor business activity and identify exceptions. We have defined key performance indicators in our Oracle Daily Business Intelligence system and use these as a scorecard.

Q: Can you give an example of operational metrics that you have or intend to implement via BI?

A: I'm looking for exceptions and trends in factory line speeds, strip widths, parts availability, service levels, compliance with aging policy, and overall inventory discipline. Metal Coaters uses FIFO (first in, first out) as its inventory accounting standard, so I'm also keeping tabs on our plant's accounting consistency over time.

Q: What other metrics do you monitor?

A: Keeping expenses down obviously drives profitability, so I'm interested in factory yields, such as utility expense per ton and man-hours per ton.

Q: What are your plans for BI going forward?

A: Let me answer that from two perspectives. For NCI as an entity, I'd like to see BI used more by all the business units so that we could extract more value from the information. My division supplies coating services to both external customers and other NCI divisions, so an enterprise-wide visibility would help us manage costs and improve profitability across the board. For Metal Coaters, BI needs to be rolled out to plant managers and even one level below that. They need to be able to see their own metrics, including revenues, expenses, and cost of sales. The ability to drill down at the expense level on a daily basis would help them avert excess costs. A side benefit to making this information more widely dispersed is the ability to more precisely reward managers with a gain sharing program. We're also looking to move toward activity-based costs (ABCs) over the next few years.

Q: So, overall, do you feel the investment of a few minutes of your time, as well as the time of your managers going forward, is worth the cost?

A: It has been a big help. For example, I was recently poking around with the numbers and noticed a problem with missed payables discounts. We are now working with the payables group to resolve the problem. There's no substitute for knowing the facts on a timely basis.

Distributing the Intelligence

If effective BI requires wider distribution, then form factors are important. Currently most reporting is through traditional channels — viewed in the office or factory, through the computer monitor. Current data are also sent out, often one-way, via Blackberry devices, pagers, and cell phones. The limitation of the one-way approach is that it is push technology, typically delivered on a fixed schedule.

Fortunately, today's telecommunications network is sufficiently robust to allow more flexible two-way data conversations, so that the information needed can be obtained on the spot and at the time needed. To provide this capability, your information architects need to design and implement technical solutions that provide the flexibility needed. Screen designs, interactive features, and security need to be part of the architecture.

High-speed, third-generation cellular networks are providing the raw bandwidth for both text and graphical display of information (one caveat: rollout of these capabilities has been faster in many international locations than in the United States). Also, younger executives and line managers are comfortable with mobile solutions, most of which are driven from the consumer market. Document sharing portals, such as Microsoft SharePoint, can be accessed via HTML enabled Web browsers. Finally, urgent BI can be "blasted" more effectively via mobile devices, because the probability of a user receiving a mobile message is relatively high compared to receipt of the information in the office.

Organizational Structure

Ideally, the BI function should have a formal structure, including a steering committee(s), guidelines, and strategy. Larger organizations may have departmental groups reporting to a central strategic group, which provides direction, allocates resources, and continually monitors business needs to ensure the BI systems remain relevant to business goals.

Roadblocks

New things, especially radically new things, are often met with suspicion. Guglielmo Marconi, inventor of the first "wireless" telegraph transmitter in the late 1800s, had difficulty initially attracting investors. Even after successful demonstrations, it was not immediately clear to the investing public that mankind's first true penetration into time and space had begun. BI may not represent a paradigm shift of that magnitude, but the psychological effects are similar. For organizations with little BI experience, time to adjust to the concepts may be required. BI goes through the same Gartner hype cycle as any other new product but suffers a bit more than other innovations because of vendor-inspired grand expectations. No matter how robust the software, salespeople (probably rightly) do not trust mere excellence to sell the product — snake oil promotion techniques are invariably used. The need for development and learning time goes unmentioned.

Based on an October 2007 survey of CIOs, *CIO Insight* magazine reports on the following pain points for BI implementations[12]:

■ 64% experience interoperability problems between systems, such as CRM and ERP
■ 57% report data quality problems that interfere with the accuracy of reporting
■ 67% say their firm continues to rely on spreadsheets

- 58% say their users simply do not understand the results of the analysis
- 61% do not have a center of excellence

As the BI tool set moves out from its traditional highly educated base and analytical base, the greater the need for selectivity of data, intuitive arrangement, and visual display. One way to speed adoption is to find a "killer application" that makes a dramatic difference in the day-to-day work of the organization. For example, Steve Canter, CIO of Berlin Packaging, found that the existing budgeting process was a source of near universal pain in his firm. By replacing the existing spreadsheet based system with BI capabilities from Microsoft SQL Server and Office PerformancePoint Server, he was able to reduce the work hours dedicated to budgeting by 50%.[13]

Spreadsheets, though obviously useful across the organization, present a special impediment to the adoption of BI. Here is what they can do easily:

- Enable dynamic links to databases (ODBC) so that the information is current from the database table accessed.
- Create sophisticated reports using logic and pivot tables. With Excel 2007, for example, up to a million rows of data can be imported and manipulated. VBA (visual basic for applications) provides additional programming capabilities if built in functions are not adequate.
- Create attractive graphical summaries of data.

The executives you look to for funding BI are aware, at least in general terms, of these capabilities. So why spend more money when we have something that works? The following should be your response — a summary of spreadsheet weaknesses as a BI tool:

- Dependence on individual effort to ensure data are properly summarized and presented. Inadequate testing and validation of data, formulas, and formats.
- Information must be obtained in a procedural manner, which is too time consuming for most executives and business managers.
- Inappropriate for real-time decisions, such as customer interaction points (offering discounts to highly profitable customers, for example).
- Inadequate collaboration/simultaneous use features.
- Lack of version control.
- Evolution of spreadsheets into a "spreadmart" — an unregulated, nonsecure datamart in the hands of users who may not backup their data and may not provide for a smooth transition should they leave the firm.[14]

To use an old analogy, when all you have is a hammer, everything looks like a nail. The very flexibility of spreadsheets makes them vulnerable to unintentional results, unless considerable quality control effort is expended. Do not allow Excel to become the default BI platform.

Having thrown rotten tomatoes at the house of Excel, it is important to keep in mind that most of the sins of Excel come from data entry mistakes and complex manipulations. A good BI system will do the heavy lifting and allow users to download the summarized and sanitized data into a spreadsheet, which can then be formatted to suit. Smart politicians know to blend technologies so that each kid gets his favorite cookie.

What Elephant?

When listening to vendor presentations on BI, it is easy to get caught up in the enthusiasm. In the area of pure logic and analytical functioning, IT professionals do tend to pull ahead of some others in the organization (though certainly not all). So as BI implementation and strategy is discussed, vendors and IT are "in sync" from a mental perspective. Both parties see clearly the analytics, ratios, exceptions, trends, neural network surprises, and a plethora of other potential BI benefits. Oops …. What about the elephant in the living room? In other words, what about the actual users, those businesspeople who do not do Sudoku puzzles in their head while driving to work but think all day about business results? Maybe they are not interested in the complexity of some of the BI packages. Maybe they simply lack the time to climb up a steep learning curve and resent poor usability/ excessive complexity in a system intended to help them make day-to-day decisions. These are most likely the same people who affect your bonus.

As you develop your BI strategy, include the true end user in planning and execution. IT personnel and advanced users obviously provide essential input, but they should not drive the project. To paraphrase an old Tennessee saying, "A huntin' dog is a fine animal but you don't give the *gun* to the dog." Usability trumps features every time. A simple system gets used by people who count.

Another danger of complexity is the potential for multiple versions of the truth. Thus, complexity contains the seeds of its own destruction — if executives are uncertain about the accuracy of the results, they may conclude that the entire system is simply not worth the effort. BI must be right. BI must be easy to use.

The Bottom Line

Analytics is a way of life, a propensity to manage based on facts and numbers. The effective CIO must support, recommend, and ease the path for this approach to business management. But business management must drive it. The reality is that BI has a relatively high failure rate, in spite of its potential power to significantly enhance profitability. The failures occur because the organization did not take "baby steps" to implementation, permitted vendors to hype products beyond plausible belief, and assumed users would take hours out of their day to understand results presented in a "propeller head" format rather than in useful business terms. BI is growing and the base of individuals who are able to use it is also growing. Your guidance and counsel will go a long way toward smoothing the organization's transition from "gut feel" to analytical management.

References

1. Howson, Cindi. *Successful Business Intelligence* (New York: McGraw-Hill, 2008), 184.
2. Hall, Mark. BI Is the Business. *Computerworld* (September 17, 2007).
3. Havenstein, Heather. Corporate BI Projects Face Skeptical Users. *Computerworld* (October 8, 2007).
4. Taylor, James and Neil Raden. *Smart Enough Systems: How to Deliver Competitive Advantage by Automating Hidden Decisions* (Boston: Pearson Education, 2007), 141.
5. Taylor, James and Neil Raden. *Smart Enough Systems* (Boston: Prentice Hall, 1007), 43.
6. Eckerson, Wayne. Predictive Analytics, Extending the Value of Your Data Warehousing Investment. www.tdwi.org (accessed January 29, 2008).
7. Customer Relationship Analytics and Business Intelligence. www.intelligentresults. com/solutions/hosted/marketing (accessed February 2, 2008).
8. According to Wikipedia.org, Artificial neural networks are made up of interconnecting artificial neurons (programming constructs that mimic the properties of biological neurons). Artificial neural networks may either be used to gain an understanding of biological neural networks, or for solving artificial intelligence problems without necessarily creating a model of a real biological system. In the artificial intelligence field, artificial neural networks have been applied successfully to speech recognition, image analysis, and adaptive control, in order to construct software agents (in computer and video games) or autonomous robots. Most of the currently employed artificial neural networks for artificial intelligence are based on statistical estimation, optimization, and control theory. (accessed May 1, 2008).
9. Hostmann, Bill. Business Intelligence Platforms: Survey of Purchase Drivers and Planned Investments. www.gartner.com (accessed January 27, 2008).
10. Davenport, Thomas. Competing on Analytics. You're no match for contenders if your business data is tied up in knots. http://www.informationweek.com/news/management/showarticle.jhtml?articleID=179101971 (accessed January 20, 2008).
11. Howson, Cindi. *Successful Business Intelligence*. (New York: McGraw-Hill, 2008), 157.
12. Dunn, Darrell. Getting Smarter, But Still Learning. *Baseline* (November, 2007).
13. Ibid.
14. Quinn, Kevin R. Worst Practices in Business Intelligence. http://www.bi-bestpractices. com/view-cases/5943 (accessed January 30, 2008).

Chapter 10

Security

IT is the digitization of the business; no more, no less. Therefore, IT security is paramount, as more and more, the assets of the company can be stolen, leaked, or damaged with little more than keystrokes on a keyboard.

Mark Radulovich, *Process Advisors,* **2008**

If we compare the evolution of info security with history, how far have we come? I believe that we're somewhere shortly after the Norman Conquest — in other words, medieval. However that's not a criticism: in fact in the 13th century they had a pretty strong grasp of security issues.

Jamie Bodley-Scott, *BCS Review,* **2007**

When a cat is at the rat hole, ten thousand rats dare not come out.

Sun Tzu, The Art of War

In writing this book, we considered embedding the topic of security within the information technology governance chapter, where it logically belongs. However, effective security is such an important part of the chief information officer's job that we broke it out in its own chapter. Here we outline some major defense components, practical guidelines for implementation, and, most importantly, how to promote a layered approach.

The Sources of Risk

According to *CIO Magazine*, 2007 marked the first year that employees were rated by surveyed firms as a greater threat than hackers.[1] Rather than reflecting a decline in moral values, this may simply be a manifestation of improved measuring tools. Employees and long-term contractors have the advantage of being *inside* the system. So, even the tiniest percentage of malicious individuals with insider access can have a disproportionate effect on losses.

Cybercrimes specifically fall into one of the following categories[2]:

- Computer intrusion
- Theft of intellectual property
- Credit card fraud
- Online extortion and Internet fraud
- Identity theft
- Money laundering

It's about the Money — Script Kiddies Persona Non Grata

Hackers have shifted focus from gaining notoriety by destruction to gaining cash from its victims. Script kiddies (those who mindlessly execute canned attacks downloaded from the Internet) are now déclassé; the serious fraudsters now predominate and, oh by the way, may still be kiddies. So, although this may result in a slight decrease in attention-grabbing worms, it means an increase in attacks specifically aimed at financial gain. Some typical schemes include:

- Renting out infected PCs, creating a "zombie network" (also called botnets) that can be used to blast targeted sites with massive traffic. This denial of service attack is continued until the target organization pays a fee to the hackers.
- Phishing scams, delivered to an increasingly targeted audience. According to San Francisco antispam provider Cloudmark, stolen credit card data sells for $100 per account.[3]
- Installation of stealth programs on clients and servers. These programs are as unobtrusive as possible and typically "call home" to transmit useful financial information. Some of these programs represent an asset to the fraudulent organization — someone with a reasonably high skill set was paid to develop the program. Every effort will be made by the attackers to make the code hard to detect.

Defense in Depth

We have all heard this term before, but what does it really mean? That we have invested heavily in one particular defense strategy? Not necessarily. Let us consider a couple of examples in history, one a failure and one a success. The Maginot line was a colossal failure; built by the French in the 1930s, it was an impressive bulwark of concrete and armaments built around previous invasion routes from Germany. In World War II, the Wehrmacht's Panzer divisions simply swept around it, moving through the low countries and into an almost unprotected France. The French bet the farm on a single defensive measure and lost. The late Roman empire provides us an example of the opposite approach. Between AD 211 and AD 284, Rome was racked by nearly continuous civil war. Before that time, the empire held undisputed military dominance on land and sea, much like the United States after the fall of the Soviet empire. However, by the time Emperor Diocletian, a strong ruler and clever military strategist, assumed control and began reversing the damage, Roman legions had been dramatically weakened. Rome's enemies were also much stronger. How did such a weakened empire survive nearly another two hundred years? By a strategy of defense in depth. Small garrisons were stationed on the borders. Shallow trenches and short walls were constructed — not to stop invaders but to slow them down. Provisions were stored in fortified buildings; sometimes the outnumbered legionnaires won by simply outlasting their starving opponents. Attackers who tried to bypass the small fortifications found they had a threatening force at their rear who might attack at an inopportune time. The strategy was, in effect, "we do not have a single defense against invaders — such as the legions in their prime — but we have many weaker defenses which, *in total*, are an effective deterrent."

The lesson for us today is clear — effective security depends on many layers of defense. Can a user security awareness campaign, by itself, stop a clever hacker? Certainly not. If a hacker renames a remote access Trojan horse so it has the same name as your Web browser, will it go through the firewall? Yes, if the firewall has been improperly configured. Nonetheless, implementing one layer of security after another will make attacks more and more difficult. Increasingly, from the hackers' perspective, the attack becomes more costly in terms of time than the value — they move on to an easier target. The same logic applies to a rogue employee or contractor. Having said that, no sensible CIO will boast *absolute* security, regardless of measures taken. Professional white hats, those individuals paid by management to attempt to benignly break IT security and report weaknesses, are almost gleeful when a CIO says "nobody can break into my network."

Tools and Defense Automation

Security tools change by the minute, so our outline here is merely suggestive. What will certainly not change is the need for more automation, more measurement, and a large variety of tools. According to *CIO Magazine*, the average organization spends 15% of its IT budget for security.[4] The dollars you spend will deviate from this, depending on the business and the environment. But almost certainly you will need to grow your security budget as the business volume grows and as your percentage of sales comes from e-business, credit cards, and other hacker-attractive activities. Following are some security tools and automation processes you may want to consider for your organization:

- *Firewalls* (both outward facing and between departments, if appropriate)
- *Antivirus, malware detection* for both servers and workstations
- *Web filtering* (some attacks can occur simply by surfing a Web site, even if nothing is clicked). Sites permitted, viewing times, and even the use of foul/hateful language can be controlled. Example packages include Websense and Zihtec Internet Control for Business.
- *Hosted solutions, if appropriate.* For example, some organizations use hosted e-mail to implement advanced e-mail filtering and quarantining, white/black list filtering, content filtering to prevent outgoing e-mails containing intellectual property, some protection from denial of service attacks, blocking of e-mails going to an excessive number of recipients, and other functions.
- *Data loss prevention systems.* For example, one tool, Reconnex, can spot outgoing e-mail containing portions of the firm's source code. It uses a previously stored code library to perform the analysis and then notifies management if a match is found.[5] The functionality is not limited to the in-house e-mail system; it looks at Yahoo, AOL, Gmail, and other external systems.
- *Backup encryption.* In the last few years, TJX, TD Ameritrade, and the Louisiana Office of Student Financial Assistance lost customer's social security numbers and other personal financial information. It is just too easy for offsite storage vendors to make a mistake, given the thousands or even millions of media backups that pass through their facilities each year. This is one area where auditors and risk analysts have a better understanding than some CIOs — out of every million events, one will occur which is highly unexpected. Do not assume 100% compliance with any agreement. To use the sanitized version of the popular expression, "stuff happens." (On that note, we highly recommend the book *Black Swan* by Nassim Nicholas Taleb[6]; it explores the unappreciated large impact of the highly improbable.)
- *Mobile device data encryption.* Laptops and small form factor devices should be encrypted if they contain sensitive data (policy should address whether such storage is really necessary in the first place; why does a Veterans Administration analyst need to take home 26.5 million records anyway?).
- *Sharing sensitive data.* In the course of business, it is sometimes necessary to transmit sensitive data to partners or customers. Centrally managed encryption suites, such as Mobile Armor's File Armor, create self-decrypting archives that can be shared with authorized partners. Before the decryption takes place, the decryption software "calls home" to a management console to ensure that the decryption has been authorized in advance. If not, the data remain scrambled.

■ *Document tools.* In some organizations, there may be a need to restrict copying, forwarding, and altering a document even though the user is authorized to view the contents. The full version of Adobe Systems Acrobat, for instance, includes these capabilities.

■ *Admission control.* You can control whether any foreign (unknown) devices hook to your network. Cisco's NAC appliance, for example, can "authenticate, authorize, evaluate, and remediate wired, wireless, and remote users and their machines prior to network access. It identifies whether networked devices such as laptops, IP phones, or game consoles are compliant with your network's security policies and repairs any vulnerabilities before permitting access to the network."[7]

■ *Remote access by mobile workers.* As part of policy enforcement, you want to control who, how, and when mobile workers can access your network. An example platform is Extend360 by Fiberlink Communications. It employs "persistent policy enforcement" to scan remote devices, check on required software installs, review registry information, and generally enforce specified policies.

■ *Combined security and operations management tools.* The best global packages combine configuration management, policy enforcement (security and otherwise), and optimization monitoring. Examples include
   – BMC's Configuration Management package, which identifies vulnerabilities, delivers policy changes to endpoints, and helps manage configuration data
   – HP's Opsware Server Automation System, which discovers servers and patch levels and also enforces policies.

Selecting security tools is somewhat like going into Home Depot looking for a hammer. There are an astounding number of choices. As you review your options keep *scalability* in mind. With growth in the number of endpoints, devices, and so forth, the management and security maintenance effort will grow as well. What you do not want is for the effort to grow proportionally. A scalable solution results in *decreased per unit cost* as the network grows.

Frameworks

Like Information Technology Infrastructure Library (ITIL) in the IT operations world, security has its own flavors of frameworks. The British developed ISO 17799 and the United States developed the National Institute of Standards and Technology (NIST) standards. Although not a framework, CERT (www.cert.org/cert/) provides many useful guidelines, including a well-organized report on governance (www.cert.org/governance/).

By way of background, ISO 17799 started life as BS 17999 and has been expanded with updates, the ISO 27000 series. The British developed computer security way ahead of the United States. Much of their security practice developed in the 1970s as a result of the IRA bombings in London. In fact, one of the things they had to deal with was the possibility of the IRA firing off a mortar with a radioactive, chemical, or biological payload into central London. If this ever happened, nobody would be able to access computers (in the case of a radioactive device, it would have to be abandoned forever). BS 17999 was therefore influenced by these terrorist threats.

Some information about the NIST:

- NIST, under the guidance of the National Security Agency (NSA), is responsible for publishing computer security standards. The division is called the CSD (Computer Security Division). Refer to http://csrc.nist.gov/.
- Their standards are called FIPS, "Federal Information Processing Standards," and are typically well researched and thought out.
- Algorithms, technologies, and procedures are included in the standards. For example, NIST developed the well-respected AES (advanced encryption standard) used throughout the world.
- The SP series (for "Special Publications") covers much of the CIO's security domain. Following are some examples:
  - Security metrics. Refer to http://csrc.nist.gov/publications/drafts/draft-sp800-80-ipd.pdf
  - PDA forensics
  - Guide for securing Windows XP (given the corporate world's hesitancy to adopt Vista, this is still relevant) (Refer to http://csrc.nist.gov/itsec/guidance_WinXP.html)

Telephone Security

We talked briefly with Mark Collier, Vice President of Technology for Secure Logix, about telecom security. As voice technology moves from the traditional "TDM" architecture to Voice over IP/IP telephony, security becomes more of a concern. Following is a summary of some of his comments:

- VoIP systems are vulnerable to denial of service attacks. This means that a determined hacker could take down *both* your data and voice systems through an effective DOS attack.
- To protect your VoIP and IP telephony systems, do the same things you would do for your other networks.
- Some of the more advanced voice capabilities (related to security) are still hard to do. For example, word spotting (e.g., sending alerts when the word "bomb" is spoken) is not as straightforward for an ordinary business as one

would think. Also, firms are bound by state and federal regulations regarding voice recording. [*Author's note*: These statements need to be put in perspective. Modern voice systems have a plethora of auditing and "call detail" functionality. Specialized hardware/software, such as those from Secure Logix, can extend these capabilities.]

- The integration of voice and data continues. Voice is merely another application.
- Traditional perimeter security is becoming less and less effective. White listing is becoming more popular as it becomes more difficult to figure out who/what to black list.
- Biometrics as a security methodology may have peaked; in general business, its use is not that widespread.
- Call center personnel need to be trained to avoid being compromised by "V" (voice) phishing. Can the caller be identified? What is the caller's intent? Analytics may help identify patterns.

A Checklist for Building Security

Maintaining effective security can be an overwhelming task. But you have a day job too, so we can think of security as something accomplished in the same manner as those odd individuals who eat elephants over a period of years — one bite at a time.

Following is a quick checklist (by no means comprehensive) to benchmark yourself on the basics of security:

- A secure infrastructure
  - Data centers
    - Secure access
    - Secure third-party management
    - Log of entry, including video and entry times
    - Redundancy
    - Hazard avoidance (earthquake zones, hurricanes, floodplains)
  - Network
    - A strong perimeter
      - Firewalls
      - Demilitarized zone (DMZ)
    - Enforce Network Access Control (NAC) to prevent unauthorized connectivity (refer to www.cisco.com/en/US/netsol/ns466/networking_solutions_package.html)
    - Secure control of network infrastructure
      - Managed switches and routers
      - Ensure only authorized people have access

- Servers and domain
  - Dual-factor authentication if security requires it
    - Reduce false alerts
    - Maximize response time for IT
    - Ensure proper configuration
    - Change management
    - Availability of spares
- Databases and applications
  - Limit access as appropriate
    - Separate development from operations
    - Prohibit developers from changing the live environment
- PCs and workstations
  - Lock them down
    - Enable access only to a white list of approved applications
    - Ensure other applications cannot be installed or run
  - Use antivirus and malware scanning
- Secure mobile devices (phones, PDA, etc.) if appropriate
  - Place on a separate network from PCs
  - Minimize access to internal applications unless there is a strong business need (SAP on a PDA?)

■ Managing the infrastructure
- Planning
  - Prioritize assets according to value (protect most valuable assets first)
  - Disaster recovery
  - Business continuity planning (BCP)
- Monitoring
  - Penetration tests (best done by outside firms)
  - Intrusion detection
    - Outsource specialty security functions (very few IT groups are big enough to have the resources to do this correctly)

Some Comments from Security Practitioners

This chapter in no way substitutes for an in-depth treatment of information security. Like stochastic calculus, nuclear physics, or brain surgery, a deep understanding of the technology, defenses, and subtleties of IT security remains in the province of the specialist. Nonetheless, the effective CIO needs to understand the big picture, the scope of the problems, and a sense of the solutions available. If you can provide adequate IT security, your firm can use information technology efficiently and grow its services without undue risk.

We conclude with two interviews, one from Joel Garmon of Florida Power & Light, covering general topics in security, and the other from Marge Muniz of NCI Building Systems, addressing the narrower topic of segregation of duties.

Interview with Joel Garmon, Director of Information Security for Florida Power & Light

Q: What do you see as the top three security threats to U.S. and international organizations?

A: The probability of threats becoming real varies somewhat by industry and organization. Based on my experience, terrorist attacks are a significant risk. States or "near states" have the resources and motivation to steal, snoop, or destroy assets. Also, true state-sponsored espionage is prevalent and has been well documented. Finally, the Russian mafia and other criminal groups are targeting any organization with financial assets. They have gone beyond virus attacks; they don't want headlines. In fact, they put pressure on their own or other hackers if any of them release an attention-grabbing virus or worm. Their goal is *long-term* theft of assets that can be monetized. To stay below the radar they change viruses frequently to avoid detection. The goal is to lay low and steal month after month. Some viruses have planned obsolescence — they talk to a mother station (another PC or workstation) for a while and then rotate to another. With perhaps two million infected PCs functioning as controllers, security groups are challenged to block all the bad sites.

As an aside, the hacker community shows the same statistical distribution of talent as any other. There are a tiny few who are truly talented and write the best of the attack tools. A second tier may not be sufficiently experienced or skilled to come up with the original code but can reverse engineer the viruses and use it for themselves. A vast third tier, "script kiddies" merely copies the attack tools from hacker Web sites and executes them with virtually no knowledge of how they work internally. To use a firearms analogy, they understand nothing of gun construction or gunpowder but know if they pull the trigger, a bullet comes out the other end.

Q: It seems there are daily reports of security breakdowns — penetrations of government agencies, stolen credit cards, and so forth. Do you believe that routine — not extraordinary — security measures would have prevented most of these breaches?

A: Routine measures will not completely stop the breaches, but they will limit the damage. For example, laptop hard drive encryption, which we instituted a year ago, will help prevent some of the most egregious disclosures of confidential information. These days you see less effort devoted to full frontal attack against a firewall (the tools have gotten better). Instead, innocuous e-mails come through with messages such as "please click here to see a valentine's card from a friend." Most of these e-mails are from spammers pursuing the usual sales objectives, but a very few contain viruses with stealth tunnels out to the mother ship. Over a period of 1 or 2 years, these embedded hacker programs gain knowledge and allow control over sensitive areas. We have implemented an e-mail rule that blocks specific text related to e-cards. Demands for ransom from the victim organizations are far more common than is reported by the media. The reason for this lack of reporting is that there is no upside for the victim to make the attack public. For example, a few years back a bank reported a loss of approximately $100 million to the authorities and to other banks. The other banks said thanks to the reporting bank and then proceeded to tout their own security in ads, explicitly mentioning the reporting bank as an example of sloppy security. Also, when you bring in law enforcement, you generally lose the ability to control the investigation and publicity.

Q: How do you help your boss, FPL's CIO, Dennis Klinger, to justify security resources when budgets are being developed?

A: We are a regulated industry and have regulated budget items. Federal, state, and regulatory bodies have specific requirements designed to protect the people of the state of Florida and other parties. So some of the security budget is nonnegotiable while the rest is discretionary. We use a cost/benefit approach in order to reduce our risk and liability. To cite a negative example of this philosophy, the Veterans Administration lost 1.8 million confidential records in 2007; this could have been easily prevented by relatively inexpensive laptop hard drive encryption.

One thing we don't use is a barrage of "FUD" (fear, uncertainty, and doubt) presentations to get resources. Crying wolf can backfire. Better to steadily inform management throughout the year so that they have a balanced and realistic picture of the threats. I keep a folder of high-level security articles that I send to the CIO for his review. He then forwards any of them he thinks appropriate to senior management.

Q: Does your group get involved in application security? For example, do you provide guidelines for segregating duties, such as separating vendor setup from vendor payment within the accounts payable function?

A: This is a focus area for us. Our most recent hire is a developer with an interest in security. She works directly with developers implementing new systems, providing them with recommended approaches and specific guidelines. We have a checklist for specific items requiring security approval. For example, any time an application uses or modifies social security numbers, credit cards, or certain other information, security approval is mandatory. We have rewritten the systems development life-cycle guidelines to integrate our security architecture into the process. Of course, education is the glue that binds all other efforts. We recently brought in Learning Tree to provide security classes for all our developers.

As a publically traded company, we are subject to Sarbanes-Oxley legislation. So we also work to constantly improve application/database security. I'll give you an example: it is tempting when developers are in a hurry to create an "application ID" that routinely accesses and modifies database tables as part of daily operations. When these get too numerous and passwords become known, security can be compromised. So now any new application ID created requires director-level approval. Because there are often ways to accomplish the access/update without creating a new ID, this control discourages the needless proliferation of IDs. In addition, my department controls the passwords for all the IDs.

But I don't want to paint a picture of perfection — with an IT staff of 800, it takes a while to get everyone on the same page. Large enterprises, like large ships, turn slowly.

Q: The hackers (at least some of them) seem to be getting smarter every day. Are you able to maintain sufficient technical expertise in-house or do you need to bring in outside specialists for penetration tests or other specialized work?

A: You always want a second set of eyes looking at security, regardless of how smart your staff is. We have a yearly budget for outside consultants and continually rotate the areas they review as well as rotate the companies that we use to insure that we have balanced reviews.

Another driver for using outsiders is the introduction of new applications, technologies, and IT services within FPL. There are specialists who focus every day on a specific software package and can develop the initial security setup more quickly and effectively than my staff, simply because of the learning curve.

Realistically, a security department does not have to be as smart as the smartest of the bad guys. We depend on vendors whose sole job is to provide tools, products, and services to counter them. For example, my staff has the expertise to look inside a virus but not necessarily to develop a defense. There is also a personality issue here. Those few individuals who are able to devote themselves almost exclusively to the most sophisticated security exploits and related remedies are not fond of some of the more tedious parts of an in-house job, such as writing policies and procedures. They and FPL are both better served in a one-off consulting arrangement.

Our users, particularly those directly involved in nuclear power generation, are intensely concerned about security. They receive ongoing training. We receive good support from executive management which also helps get the message to the individual contributors. In the most critical areas, we restrict e-mail and impose other isolation rules.

Q: We are obviously not going to ask you for specifics on your security defenses, but could you share your general thoughts on effective tools and approaches for mid- to high-level security environments?

A: The basics always come first:

- Use a multilayer defense. Isolate, to the extent possible, your most valuable assets. In years past, true "air layer" isolation was possible, but today that is not practical.
- Patch immediately or as soon as practical. Monthly is good for many systems. Tie the responsible party's bonus to effective patch management and measure its effectiveness. This is reactive rather than proactive but it keeps most malware out.
- Promote user education as your first line of defense.
- Keep up your antivirus software; it is your last line of defense. Fortunately, the vendors are getting better over time.
- Pay attention to the SANS top 20 risks. (*Author's note:* see www.sans.org/top20/.)

Q: Last question. What is the future of information security? Will we all be biometrically scanned before logon? Will artificial-intelligence–based machines be scanning our facial expressions, reviewing our thermal profile, and detecting voice stress levels, like Arnold Schwarzenegger in The Terminator? Or will it be more of the same?

A: The future will likely be in-between the two scenarios you presented. Two-factor authentication is increasingly used where medium to high security is required. Like other artifacts of information technology, security tools are increasing in capabilities and dropping in cost.

There are social issues to be considered as we develop more powerful security capabilities. For example, RFID[8] can be used to track individuals in a building, but privacy issues come into play — do organizations have the right to track bathroom breaks?

As new technologies permeate society, organizations have to make decisions about how much security is to be placed on them. Do we monitor instant messaging (IM)? Why would we pay for expensive ring down circuits for energy traders and not allow much cheaper IM for employees to ask each other quick questions?

In a past life, I worked for organizations requiring very high security; we were using biometrics 15 years ago. The old saying that "nothing is ever simple" was certainly proven true in one situation where retinal scanning was used to control access to a high-security area. The secured area included a heavily guarded inner and outer perimeter with entrance through a man-trap. There was a walk path from the outer to the inner gate and unpleasant things would happen to an individual straying away from the walk path. At the inner perimeter, the individual needing access would peer into a secure retinal scanning device and also enter a PIN. Unfortunately, the system experienced a high number of false-positives — the individual was identified by the system as unauthorized but in fact was supposed to have access. After we analyzed the results over time, we noticed a puzzling correlation between the false-positives and the sex/age of the individual identified. It turned out that younger women were overrepresented in the false-positive population. Further research revealed that pregnancy altered the retinal image enough to throw off the biometrics, at least to some extent. The bottom line of this war story is that biometrics, while useful, are not foolproof and need to be implemented with care.

That being said, I believe security is improving over time. The systems are becoming cheaper and more reliable, though some of the science fiction scenarios are a long time out in the future. Inertia applies to security systems and methods just as it does the rest of society.

Implementing Segregation of Duties (Interview with Marge Muniz, Director of Information Security and Sarbanes-Oxley Compliance for NCI Building Systems, Inc.)

Q: Pre-Sarbanes-Oxley (SOX), NCI enforced segregation of duties (SOD) informally, with no specific compliance reporting. Can you describe the process you used to implement SOD at NCI?

A: We found that the effort to implement SOD varied considerably by department. For example, Accounting was relatively straightforward and the general culture of accounting lends itself to reasonably hard and fast rules. Manufacturing and order entry, on the other hand, was more difficult because there are so many functions that are time critical. Also, at some of the smaller plants it is a real challenge to segregate duties.

Starting with a generic matrix that cross-referenced business activities with each other, we expanded that conceptual model to show conflicts based on our actual ERP responsibilities. For example, the matrix showed that an individual with the ability to create purchase orders could not also receive the goods from the supplier. It took about 3 months to develop the matrix and related exception reporting system. As NCI has acquired other firms, we've developed new matrices to accommodate their specific functions and responsibilities. Initially, some of the Oracle responsibilities had *inherent* conflicts — even if an employee had nothing but that particular (single) responsibility, he or she would have an SOD conflict. Those responsibilities had to be split up. Also, we made use of multiple business units within the same organization — even though someone should not generally create purchase orders and receive, we could relax that rule if PO creation was in one business unit and receiving in another. Many times I have wished that a tailored matrix, just for NCI, was available from some vendor. As one of the late night talk show hosts used to say "dream on, optimist breath."

Conceptually, when you move from textbook to real business life, reasonableness and practicality come into play. Except for a few areas like payroll and executive communications, we do not include "inquiry only" in our SOD reviews. We also rank each conflict from low to high risk.

Q: What are some of your day-to-day challenges in maintaining SOD across all your systems?

A: We have multiple ERPs, and new responsibilities/functions are occasionally created as a result of custom changes or from vendor upgrades. These need to be reviewed and added into the matrix. We run SOD reports at least twice a year and resolve exceptions or — worst case — develop compensating controls.

As new transactional capabilities are added, sometimes it is not always clear whether they are in conflict with existing capabilities and, if so, the level of risk. I have to work through the scenarios from an error/fraud potential perspective. Security is definitely not a pure "techie" function — you can't be effective unless you know something about the business.

If you look at textbook SOD, every employee, temporary worker, and even contractor should have one or more roles that define what he or she does. So, for example, an accountant will have certain rights and not others. It *should* be simple to assign that role to any new employee with that title. Reality, like the cold Wisconsin winter of my childhood, lets you know in a hurry that this textbook assumption is hard to achieve in practice. Employees constantly change roles and duties, sometimes without clear boundaries. There's a residual of customization and exception processing which seems to linger in spite of our best efforts to plug everyone into the right security categories.

Probably the biggest challenge is segregating duties for our smaller plants and offices. Security must always operate in an environment where customers are served and product gets out the door and at a competitive price. So, except for certain high-risk conflicts, we do not take a hard stance in those locations where there simply are not enough people to completely segregate duties. Workarounds (especially when key people are on vacation or sick) include granting temporary access and adding audit trails to be reviewed by management.

Q: Can you describe how duties are segregated within the IT group itself?

A: We segregate development, infrastructure, and production as much as possible. For example, no developer can move his or her own code into production. Database administrators do not write code (except perhaps for the occasional utility program). Historically most IT groups have done a reasonably good job of separating production from nonproduction. By nonproduction environments, I mean a pure test, development, and staging/integration. Eventually we'd like to segregate the nonproduction environments as well to prevent accidental corruption of code as it progresses from test through various stages into production.

Q: What are your top three recommendations for any organization implementing a formal segregation of duties enforcement/reporting system?

A: First, you need to educate the business units so that they understand the processes. Next, make every effort to communicate to users that any necessary restriction of computer rights is not personal and does not reflect a lack of confidence in their integrity. This is particularly important for IT personnel, who may be used to across the board access to production functions. Finally, avoid the philosophy of "completeness" — SOD is an evolutionary process and must continually adjust to fit new applications, organizational changes, and business requirements.

Q: Can you give us a specific example of a SOD tool to help you automate the reporting?

A: We have used Oracle's Logical Apps (part of the Integra product line) to help us identify conflicts. Because every organization varies in security needs, no purchased package can address all SOD requirements, but Logical Apps has been helpful for us.

References

1. Berinato, Scott. The End of Innocence. *CIO Magazine* (September 15, 2007). www.cio.com.
2. Singleton, Tommie. What Every IT Auditor Should Know about Cybercrimes. *Information Systems Control Journal* (Vol. 2, 2008): 13–14.
3. Evers, Jaris. "Hacking for Dollars." *CNET News*. www.news.com/Hacking-for-dollars/2100-7349_3-5772238.html (accessed March 21, 2008).
4. Berinato, ibid.

5. Thurman, Mathias. New Tool Pays for Itself Within Days. *Computerworld* (November 5, 2007).
6. Taleb, Nassim Nicholas. *The Black Swan* (New York: Random House, 2007).
7. Immunize Networks with Policy Enforcement. www.cisco.com/en/US/products/ps6128/ (accessed March 22, 2008).
8. According to Wikipedia (www.wikipedia.org, accessed February 16, 2008), "Radio-frequency identification (RFID) is an automatic identification method, relying on storing and remotely retrieving data using devices called RFID tags or transponders."

Chapter 11

Training

> The community value of a network grows as the square of the number of its users increase.
>
> **Robert Metcalf**

In general, people like to *know* but do not enjoy the process of *learning*. If you ask a group of people whether they would be willing to flip a switch and thereby become fluent in six languages, nearly all would enthusiastically say yes. If you asked them if they would be willing to study languages 8 hours a day for years on end to learn those six languages, virtually all would say no. In other words, the destination — having a detailed understanding of the system or application — is a great place to be, but the trip to get there is a chore. So, the information technology organization needs to create an environment where education for business users and IT staff is made available, convenient, and rewarding. It also needs to be tracked to help enforce critical training.

Often training is ad hoc and informal. Word-of-mouth and job shadowing, without supporting documentation, serve as a hit-or-miss alternative to formal training. This approach carries a number of risks:

- Resistance to implemented solutions because users do not understand the capabilities of the applications.
- Slow acclimation of new users to the subtleties of the system.
- Needless burden on the help desk (made worse if help desk personnel have not been adequately trained).
- Loss of critical skills if a key resource leaves the firm.

- Diversion of resources from skilled IT staff to resolve problems/questions that could have been addressed by users, had they sufficient knowledge of the application.
- Wasted manpower, because on-the-job training ties up two people — the newbie and the mentor.
- Potential quality defects, because there is no "standard" version of how the system should function.

One hospital neglected to train its customer-facing, data entry personnel on a new interface. In some cases the clerks chose the wrong insurance carrier because they did not understand how the pull-down menu was configured. As a result, the hospital was unable to collect on a significant number of insurance claims.

To reduce these risks, you should form a team to institutionalize training and user support. This will provide the extra nudge to enroll users in necessary training, encourage them to use online reference material and available tools for learning. The team should develop standard templates, tools, and methodology for training rollout. Key individuals, on the help desk and otherwise, should receive additional training in selected applications in order to provide a broad knowledge base. Ideally, you would run your training initiative as an IT project with milestones, responsible parties, specific goals, and a standard methodology.

IT staff training is equally important for obvious reasons: inadequately trained staff spend too much time ramping up; your best and brightest resent the omission of training and may leave; and inefficiency will slow everything from actual computer operations (for example, poorly tuned database indexes) to delivery of new technology. One problem that probably 90% of chief information officers encounter is the support of legacy/oddball/one-off-type systems. You cannot afford to devote too many resources to these systems; if the individual supporting the system leaves, it is time consuming to find another competent resource to maintain it. What is the upside for the maintenance resource? One answer is to provide a training path that at least provides the potential for advancement to more mainstream technologies.

Tools

The infrastructure for user and IT training largely overlaps with knowledge management "enablers." Tools include:

- Document/knowledge management systems
- Help desk software, which can often be integrated with your telephony system to provide greater customization and service levels
- Web conferencing
- Wikis
- Blogs
- Knowledge bases

Training and e-learning infrastructure should ideally go beyond IT and systems. For example, the certified public accountants (CPAs) in your accounting groups need to track continuing professional education credits; engineers, medical personnel, and other specialty areas also need to track courses, maintain reference material, and, in some cases, track compliance with mandatory training.

Your primary learning/tracking/repository tool should support content structured so that users and IT staff can select from predefined lists, track status, and compliance against departmental requirements, integrate with Microsoft Outlook or other calendaring systems, track certificates, and have the ability to summarize activity across the organization (to show progress and utilization). Alerts are another helpful feature, so long as they are not incessant and annoying.

User Needs Vary

For infrequent users, classroom training may be overkill. Some may want manuals but most want contextual help — just what they need when they need it. Frequent users, on the other hand, may want a variety of methods to help them learn:

- Manuals, both for training and reference
- Content in varying languages (Spanish, Kanji, etc.)
- Searchable, online help
- Context-sensitive assistance
- Interactive online training. Note that interactive training has a high retention rate. For additional examples, see www.karlkapp.com/materials/elearning-advantages.pdf
- Screencasting (video walkthroughs)
- Lunch and learn on specific topics ("quick starts")
- Targeted sessions based on responsibilities. For example, one session could be devoted to human resources (HR) and adding employees, and another session could discuss 401K and benefits processing

How Much Training Is Needed?

Training needs to have a payback. If the organization maintains metrics, it is much easier to target training needs and show results. Some of the measurement factors include:

- *Error rates*. If they are high, training is appropriate.
- *Consistency*. Are orders processed consistently? Is required information placed where it should be? Do some users perform work in a convoluted manner because they only know one way to accomplish a task?
- *Speed*. In customer-facing areas, such as call centers, response times are important. Training will affect speed which in turn will affect sales, customer goodwill, and so forth.

If your organization does not track metrics, then the question of how much training is needed cannot be easily answered. Sometimes firms overtrain and waste time. One area where training is almost never done too much is for safety. Such training has paybacks in several forms — lower insurance rates, reduced injury, lawsuit prevention, and, of course, employee morale.

Seminars or Vendor-Specific Training for IT

Education can occur in all sorts of venues. Seminars typically provide broad-based exposure to a discipline, include both positive and negative instruction on specific packages or vendors, and somewhat broader opportunities to meet peers in other firms. In addition, seminars may provide information that vendors may not want to discuss, such as problems with implementation, unresolved failure points, and unofficial workarounds.

Specific training from vendors often is essential and has immediate payback, because courses on a specific vendor's technology may not be available anywhere else (at least initially). This narrow and targeted education provides the know-how to implement packages, manage infrastructure (for example, Cisco courses), and configure user parameters. Probably a higher percentage of developers and individuals directly involved in implementation go to vendor-specific training versus broad-based seminars.

One option for training is to have managers do the training themselves for high-profile rollouts. Although it is not likely to happen in most organizations, there are some potential advantages. Because users would also be subordinates, presumably the sessions would be well attended. By preparing for the training, the managers would learn the material. Finally, having the instructor familiar with the business environment ensures a more practical focus on just what the users need to know — irrelevant materials can be quickly discarded.

The Harsh Punishment of Silo Knowledge

In general, CIOs are not individuals who hide under a barrel, bite their tongue when foolishness is being spouted, or are excessively tolerant of poor results. Sometimes these useful characteristics are held back when a critical system is understood by only one person in the organization. This is silo knowledge at its worst — "Bubba comes in late, mouths off to the user, and we have to pay another resource to do his change control tickets for him. But what choice do we have? He's the only guy who understands our cycloalkane, nonpolar solvent transportation and sales system. It is critical to our downstream business and the replacement system won't be ready for another 2 years." This is a terrible place for a CIO to be, and there is typically no quick fix. Like firing the only doctor in the world who can treat one's rare disease, the pink slip is not an option.

If we cannot get around this problem in the short run, at least we can fix it long term. Following are some recommended steps:

- *Recognize the danger.* The road to hell is paved and downhill. It certainly *seems* cost efficient on the front end to have a single resource cover a single application. The individual, being totally responsible, solves all the problems, focuses on just that application, and develops deep expertise in its capabilities and quirks. Soon other developers, even those with considerable talent, are at a distinct disadvantage working in the system — they cannot compete. However awkward it may be, you must insist that nascent silos be flattened; at least one other person must be capable of working on the system.
- *Train a backup.* Some organizations even have a mock emergency session to test the backup's knowledge.
- *Shadow the guru.* It is time consuming but sometimes just hanging around the expert provides enough of the "shadow knowledge" — the undocumented critical information —to work with the system if the guru is unavailable.
- *Pay a professional tech writer to document the system.* Most technical personnel do not like to write detailed prose but are happy to talk about their system — it becomes an ego-boosting forum. A good tech writer, even if he or she does not understand the technology, can write and organize a manual for others to follow.
- *Get the guru to provide a training session for users.* Again, another resource could help assemble the training session (PowerPoint slides, screen shots, etc.) so that the guru can focus on content.

Knowledge Management

Training is a subset of knowledge management. Both IT technical knowledge and the organization's business knowledge need to be as available as possible. There are many full-scope, sophisticated knowledge management systems such as Inxight, RightNow Technologies, and ISYS Search Software. NCI uses Microsoft SharePoint to house business and IT materials of all sorts. By establishing an enterprise-wide repository of knowledge, the CIO creates a place where all can go to get training, documentation, tips, and up-to-date information. Some benefits include:

- Training materials are centralized, reducing help desk calls.
- Manuals are online and hence are not lost.
- Business information — engineering standards, financial statistics, and so forth, are available for all.

- Organizational information, such as who is knowledgeable in a specific area, can be posted. And, of course, the usual stuff — phone directories, newsletters, employee of the month, and so forth, are also listed.
- Videos and multimedia training can be retained for those who missed live training.
- The option for course repetition. Countless studies show the value of repetition for retention of knowledge.

A culture of knowledge management takes time to develop. Cardboard boxes retain their allure as quick repositories but of course fail miserably as long-term storage for training materials and other information. But, eventually, employees begin to see the knowledge management system as a useful repository. And, as Robert Metcalf, the coinventor of Ethernet, so famously noted, the value of any network is roughly proportional to the number of users squared. So, the more the knowledge management system is used, the more it will be used.

Chapter 12

Effective Use of Consultants

Caveat emptor (let the buyer beware).

Ancient Roman Saying

Becoming a Skilled Buyer of Professional Services

Aside from budget considerations, consultant selection should be driven by business/technical skills, experience, and emotional intelligence. Some factors within these categories include the following:

- *Skills*: Do they have the mental horsepower to adapt their knowledge base to your environment? Certifications are good but pale in comparison to actual experience. Are they adaptable or have they done repetitive work for many years?
- *Experience*: Have they performed the work before or at least done similar work? Check references. And for sure, do not rely completely on firm reputation — you are getting the individual(s), not the firm, to do the work.
- *Emotional intelligence*. How effective are their relationship skills? For example, assume they are presenting a proposal for work; they launch into some PowerPoint slides describing their firm ("All about us"). You indicate a lack of interest in the details of their firm's history and ask them to move on, but they persist in sloughing through that section of their presentation. Clearly, their ego exceeds their listening skills — such behavior will probably not change

even if they get the work. For commodity-type work, lack of relationship skills *may* be tolerated but never for complex projects.

On One Side of the Table: The Consultant's Objective

To stay in business, consultants have to:

- Make money
- Hire people acceptable to potential clients
- Maintain a sufficient base of knowledge, skills, and experience to win business
- Avoid reputational damage or, worse, legal action for bungled work

Consultants may not always achieve these objectives. The most important question for you is whether your project's success is an essential part of the consultant's true set of objectives. The word "partnership" is frequently used. This is not the same as being a good provider. A good provider means that you pay $500,000 for a strategic analysis of the marketplace and how information technology can best enable the business to compete. The provider delivers an acceptable quality product. You are both satisfied, and the deal is successfully concluded. A partnership, on the other hand, means the provider has skin the game. For example, assume you have adopted a new technology. The consulting firm is willing, *at its own cost*, to train its people if you commit to a major implementation project using that technology. That is a leap of faith on the part of the consulting firm and gives you confidence that it is serious about the relationship.

On the Other Side of the Table: The CIO's Objective

Whose job is harder — the buyer's or the seller's? Buying seems easy — money provides the power. Selling seems harder because the buyer has to be convinced to buy and typically has many providers to choose from. In reality, of course, both jobs demand focus and skill. Following are some of the factors that the CIO needs to consider:

- *A well-defined scope and, if necessary, an explicit scope limitation.* It is difficult for any consultant to avoid scope creep if the boundaries are not clearly defined. For example, you may assign consultant #1 to do systems design and assign the actual development to consultant #2. The boundaries are clear, with a beginning and end for each phase and no overlap of responsibilities for the consultants.
- *A clear cost.* Sometimes a chief information officer becomes engaged in a discussion over lunch about a future project and the consultant casually mentions "yea, we did that for Acme Corp for about $2 million." That statement, completely nonbinding, nevertheless sets an "anchor" or reference point for future negotiations. There have been numerous psychological studies recently

about the effect of an anchoring statement, particularly with respect to numbers. Researchers Tversky and Kahneman split subjects into two groups, one where a wheel of fortune roll landed on 65 and a second group where the number 10 came up. He then asked both groups what percentage of nations in Africa were members of the United Nations. The median response was 45% from the first group and 25% from the second group.[1] This anchoring effect has been demonstrated repeatedly and across many cultures. Apparently it is a characteristic of human minds that under conditions of uncertainty, we unconsciously lock onto anything available to improve our odds of being correct. The point of this is to be aware of your own unconscious bias. If a rate of $300 per hour is mentioned, it sets a peg in memory around that figure, even if subsequent negotiations significantly lower the actual rate. Retailers do it all the time (for example, 50% off an inflated price). We are aware of their tricks but still fall for it. Figure 12.1 illustrates the "anchoring effect," which is an unintentional and unconscious bias arising when individuals are exposed to irrelevant facts or numbers before a decision point. In the first, scenario 1, in Figure 12.1, the mention of $2,000/hour earlier in the day makes the CIO see the consultant's rate as more reasonable than in the second scenario.

- *Carefully defined schedule.* If the schedule falls apart, the budget will follow. Also, a schedule without contingency time is suspect — no one can anticipate all events that increase risks and slow progress.
- *Knowledge transfer and inclusion.* If you value your best and brightest, do not exclude them from the most exciting projects. Also, insist that any consultants brought in freely transfer knowledge to your staff. If you hear the word "proprietary" constantly spoken by a consultant, alarms bells should go off. The intent may be to lock you in to their services.

Matching Interests

Obviously, consultants are used successfully by many organizations. In fact, consulting firms have proliferated as organizations in the United States and many other nations continue to farm out more specialty tasks in order to keep the core workforce lean. Charles Handy, for example, has written a number of books predicting the corporation will shrink to a core of essential workers and professionals, with much of the work (core or otherwise) assigned to consultants, partners, and specialty firms. So it is unlikely that the need to negotiate with contractors and consultants will go away. Following are some guidelines to help you maintain productive relationships with skilled IT providers:

- Manage expectations about current and future work.
- Avoid a focus entirely on cost. Consultants tend to win this game. The attention should be on why they are there and what they will be doing.

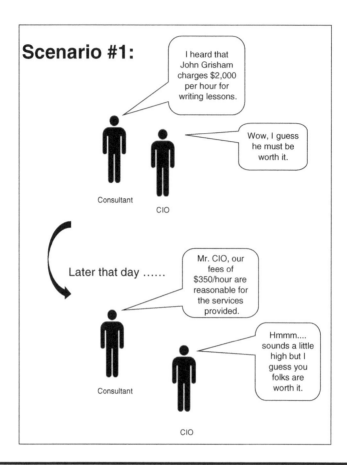

Figure 12.1 The "anchoring effect."

- Do not listen too carefully when they talk about all the areas where they can provide assistance. Concentrate on where you need them.
- Tread carefully when special interests are involved. Perhaps the consultant has a personal relationship with the chief executive officer. If the skill set offered is not adequate for the job, you could be in an uncomfortable position. To the extent possible, attempt to align with your boss' personal interests. Perhaps "phase I" could be offered to the well-connected consulting firm rather than the entire project.
- Provide nonmonetary incentives where appropriate. Good references, opportunities to apply their technology or skill in a new environment, and "goodwill" toward potential future work are all valuable but require no cash outlay.
- Subtly praise good work. Consultants are not robots, and they are sometimes ignored in the social context of the organization. After all, they are outsiders and (from the perspective of some employees) well-compensated ones at that.

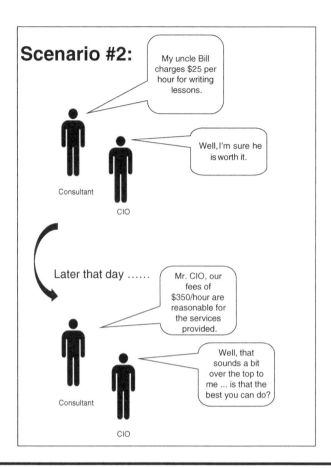

Figure 12.1   (continued)

People, including consultants, are incredibly sensitive to even the slightest praise, so just a word or two will serve. Bottom line is that you get more work and loyalty to the project for the same money.

Some Miscellaneous Defense Tactics

Most of these are basic, but are worth repeating:

- Maintain management oversight. Schedules, percentage completion, milestones, and other project management tools are essential.
- Ensure that your organization retains ownership. The consultant may be Albert Einstein, George Patton, and Mother Teresa all in one person, but he is still the *hired help*.

- Go over any contract twice yourself and then give it to your lawyers. Sometimes specialty attorneys (see the example in Chapter 3) can give you an extra edge in negotiations.
- Always build in an "out" clause so that if their work becomes unsatisfactory or something completely unanticipated happens (e.g., the subsidiary for which the project is intended gets divested), you are not financially obligated.
- Pull the plug if the consultant is negligent, emotionally unstable, disrespectful, or has clearly misrepresented his or her skill set. Do not let the fact that you brought them in distort your judgment — no one can see with perfect clarity the future behavior of individuals.
- Watch for "one-way" surprises. The best of analysis sometimes will not identify work that needs to be performed to complete a project. But if a steady stream of surprises occurs and they seem to always point to increased hours for the consulting firm (rather than discoveries that will simplify the work and reduce hours), be suspicious. If you have given them all the information they require, there should not be that many "unknown unknowns."
- If there are specific individuals who are genuine experts and are critical to the project, write those individuals into the contract. For example, an IT director at a large energy firm in Houston was assigned responsibility to benchmark the processing capabilities of two mainframes. An outside consulting firm (no longer in existence) was engaged to perform the work. Unfortunately, the expert who presented the credentials of the consulting firm never showed up for the detailed work. The "rookies" performing the work did not have the experience to realize that benchmarking an unloaded machine (i.e., one running few jobs) had no value, because the numbers are unpredictably skewed from a normal, loaded processing environment. The entire benchmarking project had to be scrapped. The inexperienced staff on the job would have done an acceptable job if the expert had been present to guide them. Beware of bait and switch.
- Key consulting resources need to be retained for the duration of the project. This point goes along with the previous comments. Not only should key resources be written in the contract, but their retention on the account should be defined (at least to the extent the consulting firm can retain an individual — when demand gets white hot, people jump).
- Project management is necessary but should not exceed what is required. It is OK to hire a "hoard" of bodies to do a specific project if you have the management bandwidth to keep them on track. Most of the time this is not the case and the consulting firm will need to supply project management. Just make sure that project management does not become an end in itself — layers of summarizers, three-dimensional (3D) graphics artists and professional orators who slather layers of cosmetics on what should be a straightforward project will run up the bill. One humorist joked that Americans love excess. If it is good to jog a mile, then it is better to run a marathon, better still to

run two marathons back-to-back, and, finally, why not run 100 miles up the Himalayas with your tax accountant on your back? Project management overhead is necessary at a certain level but can spiral out of control if not kept in check.

Knowledge Transfer

In many but certainly not all projects, knowledge transfer from your consultants to your staff or users is an important factor. Without it, you may weaken your long-term negotiating power and, more importantly, reduce the ability of your organization to use the knowledge. It is hard to be creative with a system you do not fully understand.

Knowledge transfer should be built formally into the plan, with a reasonable number of hours devoted to discussion, documentation, PowerPoint presentations, and demos. The contract should specifically state what you keep when the consultant leaves — source code, documentation, process methods, and so forth. Typically, contractors will take with them business knowledge, tools created to do the job, special-purpose databases (unless proprietary), and other information not deemed confidential.

If you bring a consulting firm in to implement a complex system that is completely new to your users, there is a human tendency to rely on the expert on the scene. You and user management will both need to pressure all in-house parties to learn and take ownership of the system. Turning a true specialist/expert into a baby-sitter and someone who doles out answers one by one is expensive. IT staff and users both have to get dirty and force the expert to teach them.

A Few Closing Comments about Consultants

They work for you. If there are five firms doing work for your firm and there is overlap of responsibilities, you may have to adjudicate territorial questions, but you should not have to endure squabbles (and worse, pay for the billable hours resulting from them). It may be best to avoid too much comingling of consultants from competing firms.

It is unlikely that you can maximize your department's effectiveness without occasionally consulting help. The key is to pick the best consultants, manage their time and direction, and know when to say "thank you for your fine effort and we'll give you a call if we have further needs."

Reference

1. Tversky, A. and D. Kahneman. 1974. Judgment under uncertainty: Heuristics and biases. *Science*, 185: 1124–1131.

Chapter 13

Operations

> Discipline is the soul of an army. It makes small numbers formidable, procures success to the weak, and esteem to all.

> **George Washington**

Tree Houses Are Great for Kids

Parents with the "let them be kids while they are kids" philosophy supply their children with boards and nails and let them start building their own tree house. It may be sloppy and ungainly, but it is an esteem-building, genuine expression of creativity. Roll forward 30 years and that same kid — you — gets a second benefit from the experience. It is the realization that anything complex built without a framework looks like a kid-built tree house — fine for a 10-year-old, but embarrassing for a chief information officer or operations director. So the first step toward excellence in operations is to establish a sound framework that informs decisions about processes, tools, staffing, and relations with the rest of the organization.

Management Frameworks

In recent years, the Information Technology Infrastructure Library (ITIL) framework has gained acceptance as a useful framework across diverse industries. The latest version, ITIL 3, includes the following:

- ■ Support-Oriented Processes
  - Help desk
  - Incident management
  - Problem management
  - Configuration management
  - Change management
  - Release management
- ■ Delivery-Oriented Processes
  - Service-level management
  - Capacity management
  - Continuity management
  - Financial management
  - Availability management

ITIL 3 then takes these processes and funnels them into an operations life-cycle approach that includes:

- ■ Strategy
- ■ Design
- ■ Transition
- ■ Operations
- ■ Continual improvement

There are other frameworks or partial frameworks. For example, CobIT, in the "DS" sections, includes many operational guidelines, many of them focused on governance. Other examples include VAL IT (relates to IT investments), Application Services Library (ASL), Business Information Services Library (BISL), Microsoft Operations Framework (FOM), and the Enterprise Computing Institute's framework. Because ITIL appears to be gaining worldwide momentum, we will use it for our discussion points.

In the following sections, we will discuss in broad outlines these processes and life-cycle phases. On the back of Harry Newton's telecom dictionary (one of the earlier editions), he had a picture of himself with the caption "the real Harry Newton is a lot older than the picture, and uglier too." We could paraphrase Newton's humor by saying "The real ITIL has about 100 times more detail than is presented here and …" — well, we will not go there.

Change, Configuration, and Release Management

Because the information technology environment incessantly changes, a large part of your framework should be devoted to the following:

- *Change management.* Ensures that changes are authorized, tested, tracked, communicated to both the IT, leadership, and user community, and planned so that risks can be identified, to the extent possible.
- *Configuration management.* The actual state of IT services or components (e.g., patches or releases) needs to match the desired state.
- *Release management.* As a specialized part of change management, this function ensures that the production environment is updated and maintained properly. For example, applications, networks, and workstations will all be updated on a schedule with a known set of programs and configurations. Huikau (haphazard), mishmashed software implementations are avoided.

Help Desk, Incident and Problem Management

These functions are more outward facing than some of the others. If done well, you can hear that rare elixir of the help desk — the absence of irritated callers. The following should be structured, managed with metrics, and supported as an essential IT function:

- *Help desk.* Get the right people, the right tools (do not forget to fully use your telephone system, even if you are a small shop), and the right information/databases. Imagine a frustrated user calling the help desk; the service representative sees a screen pop with information about the caller, including a history of calls. The user's question gets answered and an e-mail is sent containing links to a knowledge base. Or perhaps the user needs her password reset. Instead of calling a human on the help desk, she calls a special number that links her to an IVR (interactive voice response system). The IVR application asks her to say a few select phrases, matches her voice with one or more prerecorded wave files stored on the server, and then permits her password to be reset — fast, secure, and cost effective.
- *Incident management.* Track incidents to their completion and link to change management and knowledge base if the solution involves application or system changes. Reduce their frequency via follow-up and analysis.
- *Problem management.* Go beyond individual incidents to look for root causes and cross-platform issues. Look at service outages and cumulative statistics affecting delivery.

Capacity Management, Service Levels, Availability, Job Scheduling

- *Service levels.* An operations group without service levels finds itself in endless arguments with everyone from end users to IT developers within the same department. With defined (written) service-level agreements, resources can be rationally allocated to help desk activities. The trading group may say (perhaps a bit repetitively), "Two minutes of downtime at the wrong time could mean a million dollar loss." That may or may not be true, but if they are willing to pay for it, then their service level can be an order of magnitude better than that of any other group. The more service levels are defined, the easier it is to manage the overall function. Everything from the "on-boarding" process (bringing a new employee or contractor into the organization with the appropriate workstation, network access, etc.) to password resets can be set up. Service levels can be nuanced based on rank (vice presidents get priority over rank-and-file), whether the employee has a customer-facing job, or — and this gets to be interesting — who complies with the company enterprise architecture and standards. If, for example, a business unit insists on buying its own brand X PCs from Wal-Mart, then its service level may be set to "Code 10," meaning "go to the back of the line."

- *Availability.* This metric should be tracked across many services, including physical and virtual networks, servers, databases, Web sites, and applications. Outages need to be calculated with some meaningful metric. For example, telecom providers often provide uptime as a percentage of calendar time. What most businesses care about is uptime during business hours. From a user perspective, end-to-end metrics are best; they do not care what specific link in the chain went down; the service was either available or not available. Calculations of availability can include elements such as user calls, outage records, trouble tickets, component availability, and transaction response time.

- *Capacity management.* This includes the usual suspects of disk space, central processing unit (CPU) utilization, and ability to meet business transaction windows. Capacity management has a long history and a wealth of tools, based on some sophisticated mathematics, to help the practitioner see into the future. If you have the right tools, suddenly being out of capacity should be the equivalent of being run over by a moving glacier (prior to global warming that is).

- *Job scheduling.* As the age of mainframe dominance came to an end in the early 1990s, many thought job scheduling would decline in importance. That did not happen. Processing is still complex and sequenced. If a job fails, several things have to happen. The work must be immediately transferred to another server or the entire sequence cancelled and rescheduled. End-to-end execution must be monitored to ensure that policy requirements and service-level agreements are met. Intelligent schedulers go beyond simple logic — "Yes, step A completed successfully, now go to step B." They will look at performance and perhaps assign more computing resources to an essential job step that is processing slowly. This more sophisticated approach is sometimes termed "workload management."

Day-to-Day Management

A framework is essential. You start by ordering the entire set of ITIL volumes. Then you realize that it is too much to read, so you send the appropriate staff to classes, bring in a consultant, and do whatever else is necessary to get started. Unfortunately, there are many other tasks not directly addressed in a framework. Operations, for better or worse, is the "catchall" of IT, seemingly with no beginning or end. That is why it is essential to define, document, outline, and talk about scope, roles, and services, so that it is *possible* to put a gold star on the operations director's personnel file. That being said, following is a smorgasbord of functions and tools typically employed in the day-to-day operations management of IT operations:

- *Desktop administration.* A desktop administration life cycle needs to be developed — starting with the deployment of a new PC and ending with its "green" disposal. A host of services needs to be provided: purchase, inventory, standard image install, routine updates, and possibly application monitoring. Tools, such as Spiceworks, will discover desktops, identify licenses, notify of low disk space, identify printers with low ink, and even display offline stations. In addition, they may provide summary, across-the-network information that helps manage the entire desktop population. Gartner mentions one vendor, Aternity, who distributes an interesting package, Frontline Performance Intelligence Platform. This software "is enhanced by Bayesian-style learning technologies ... that provide the ability to establish performance baselines that are then referenced, in real time, to identify end-user desktop and application behavioral issues."[1]
- *Network administration.* This ranges from simple "What's Up Gold" implementations to sophisticated manager of managers (MOMs). Packages should combine the functions of network and server monitoring, alerting, and proactive analysis.
- *DataCenter administration.* Tools that monitor air temperature, airflow, humidity levels, under-floor moisture detection, and fire suppression systems should all be automated with a minimum of call home features.
- *Resource usage.* Good resource tools have the ability to collect and normalize performance data from several sources and then use mathematical algorithms to predict usage. Database administrators and application managers need these tools to help size the effect of anticipated loads or configuration changes.

Some Common-Sense Approaches to Good Operations

Smooth operations require a framework, but they also need a strong architecture to build on. If the hardware is substandard or you have an unreasonable number of delicate links between platforms, the best of operations tools will be hard pressed to solve your problems. Here are some practical steps you can take to improve your operations base:

■ Understand the general needs of the business
  – Fast growth
  – High uptime
  – Low cost
  – High flexibility
  – Regional coverage
■ Build a redundant network architecture
■ Install an easily expandable (and manageable) storage architecture
■ Implement a database and server strategy to support the core applications, data mining and data warehouse capabilities
■ Consider outsourcing some functions
  – Network monitoring
  – Call centers
  – Desktop support
  – Security (e.g., intrusion detection system [IDS])

Cloud Computing

The idea of throwing much of operations over the fence by "utility computing" has been around a long time. With changing technology, its realization seems nearer, at least for some applications. The current incarnation is termed "cloud computing" and is popularized by Nicholas Carr in his book *The Big Switch*.[2] Amazon offers S3 and EC2, storage and computing resources, respectively, metered strictly by usage. Some of the advantages include

■ Instant scalability. You write a check, and presto, you have immediate storage and a computing environment.
■ Reduction of the barriers to entry for smaller firms. If you are burning through venture capital cash, the last thing you need is a lengthy start-up time for routine infrastructure development.
■ Availability of common applications, which are typically already installed.
■ Elimination of costs when the need for the services goes away. Maybe you just needed to get a test instance up and running for a few months and after that no longer needed the resources.

Of course, there are some disadvantages, at least with the current state of the technology:

- Backup of data is not absolutely certain. You still need to backup your own data, at least occasionally.
- Platform downtime. For example, Amazon's Elastic Compute Cloud was down in the fall of 2007.
- Lack of support for your particular technology (operating system [OS] or database).

In spite of the caveats, cloud computing has significant potential, at least for some parts of the organization's requirements.

The Bottom Line — Discipline

In A.D. 61, Roman Governor Gaius Suetonius Paulinus, with 10,000 legionnaires, was attacked by a native British force of over 200,000. It was a good time to think about retirement, but instead he ordered his troops to attack and the natives were defeated. The Romans had superior armor and training but the real difference was in *discipline*. You can think of operations in the same light. The number of things that can go wrong in operations is almost overwhelming. At any moment a wire is about to pull loose, a server fan is about to go out, or a developer is poised to slip a bad piece of code into production. Your defense is the discipline to plan, develop a service-oriented organization, work within a strong framework, and constantly measure results.

References

1. Williams, David and Will Cappeli. *Cool Vendors in IT Operations, 2008*. www.gartner. com (accessed on May 12, 2008).
2. Carr, Nicholas. *The Big Switch: Rewiring the World, from Edison to Google* (New York: W. W. Norton & Company, 2008).

Chapter 14

Futures

The safety of the short term is an illusion. The hot winds of disruption swirl all around us, whether they be in the form of new competitors, business models, technologies, consumer preferences, or geopolitical forces.

John Kao, Innovation Nation

The demands of daily operations leave many chief information officers nearly exhausted. So a discussion on trends, demographics, and "what ifs" may seem like a luxury ill suited to the real world. Unfortunately, the real world is changing so rapidly that futures morph into realities even within the 5-year tenure of most CIOs. Human nature, essentially unchanged from ten thousand years ago, is excellent in assessing immediate risks and changes. Those who contemplated too long whether the figure in the dim light of the cave was a hungry lion are no longer with us (or more to the point, their offspring are not with us). Unfortunately, our formative environment did not shape us to adequately consider long-term trends. And it particularly did not enable us to easily perceive *nonlinear growth*. The Internet is a good example of how a nonlinear technology changed the world in the blink of an eye. It was a toy of military/academic specialists and was unnoticed for years by the general public. Then, suddenly, we saw Web site names on billboards. Robots will likely have the same trajectory. If you could look into the future and plot their capabilities (let us say their "IQ"), it would go something like this: for the past 30 years, their true IQ was approximately that of an intelligent rock; then over the next 3 years it reaches the level of an ant; then in 2 years it jumps to fish intelligence; within 5 more years you have the IQ of a chimp and the robot can now perform many useful tasks. Eventually, BMW sells a robot that can detail your M6 coupe as you sleep. Ray Kurzweil, a highly successful inventor and futurist calls this the "law of accelerating returns."

Following are some probable futures, starting with society and demographics, down to examples of technological changes which will certainly affect your core responsibilities.

Society and Demographics

■ *Rethinking retirement.* 76 million Americans were born between 1946 and 1964; Generation X, immediately following the baby boomer generation, supplies the workforce with only 46 million workers. By the time this book appears in print, the exodus of senior, skilled professionals will be in full progress. American business, long in favor of shedding older workers to cut costs, will find itself in the odd position of retaining and even recruiting them. As a CIO whose product is information, you need to develop work structures that blur the line between working and nonworking. Part-time work, project assignments for a limited time, and even work from home may be alternatives that appeal to your IT employees nearing potential retirement age. You are particularly vulnerable to loss of expertise in legacy systems. Young professionals typically have no interest in maintaining old code or old infrastructure. So who will maintain your essential, but dated, billing system when "ole Fred" leaves? Another, more subtle loss is the weakening of the IT governance mind-set when experienced staff leave. They know, having matriculated from the University of Hard Knocks, that things go wrong, that change control and security are not fluff, and that project management matters.

■ *Dependence of society on software.* Those of us who work with technology have a slightly distorted and sanguine perception of its prevalence. In his book *Digital Deflation*,[1] Graham Tanaka disputes the popular notion that business has automated most of the important work already. He says that only half, at best, of work in industrial nations has been automated. There is a lot more to do. So IT projects of the future will not be one more functional component added to SAP but will include completely new tasks, most of which are as yet unanticipated. Robot labor is only one example of the potential. And as this permeation of technology into society continues, the dependence will become near absolute. The shutdown of computing and networking capabilities now, if extended over months or years, would result in millions of deaths worldwide, at least from indirect causes (food, for example, requires a strong trading network to ensure that supplier, transporter, and consumer are linked). This reinforces both your responsibility to maintain availability of production systems and your personal challenge to help automate work not previously considered.

- *"Atomization" of outsourcing.* Since the early 1960s, outsourcing has made headlines because of the size of the deals. Increasing communications links between organizations of all sizes will drive outsourcing to more individually tailored and typically smaller services. For example, at www.odesk.com, individuals or firms can obtain services of developers and technical writers, on an hourly basis, from locations across the world. With less risk because of smaller scope, outsourcing of specific tasks, whether as software-as-a-service or by some other mechanism, will continue to grow.

- *Green mandate.* Assume it could be proved that human activity does not cause global warming. It would not matter. In the long run, energy efficiency and generation from alternate sources are simply cheaper than anything else. So "green" will not go away and will become an automatic consideration in any IT decision, much like you would consider the elevation above sea level when looking at a backup site. And "green" does not stop with the purchase of efficient hardware. Software is now available which can shut down a percentage of your server farm during low demand periods by shifting all the applications to designated off-peak servers.

- *Social networks.* Facebook, twitter, LinkedIn, hi5, blogs, podcasts, RSS feeds, Wikkis — the list goes on. If there is a way your organization can take advantage of the uber-connected social world facilitated by these tools, you should lead the charge. Knowledge often rides along the same conduit as personal communications. There may be opportunities to promote the business and educate customers, employees, and the public on your products and services.

Technology

- *Cloud computing.* In the book *Big Switch*,[2] Nicholas Carr outlines his vision of computing as an externally supplied utility and the revolution it will bring about. He uses the analogy of electric power plants in the late 19th and early 20th centuries. Virtually all factories and many office buildings generated their own electric power. It was a struggle for electric utilities to convince businesses that power could be supplied more reliably and cheaply by a third party. Then, after a few years of marketing and public education, everything suddenly changed. With costs dramatically lower than self-generation (as low as 1/10th the cost when all factors were considered), public utilities became accepted as a standard way of obtaining power. Similarly, with cloud computing offering every kind of environment (virtual servers and computing platforms) and on a "pay as you go" basis, traditional data centers may eventually become unnecessary or at least considerably smaller. Will the jobs of individuals who routinely build servers, manage application configurations, or perform other infrastructure duties be at risk? Most certainly they will, though the timing is not certain (not to worry — they will easily find other technical work). Amazon's EC2, elastic computing, is an early example of this service.

■ *Virtualization.* This trend will accelerate due to the profound cost savings, both in hardware and staff maintenance time. The software vendors need to ensure their pricing schemes, now based on number of central processing units (CPUs) in the box, stay competitive.

■ *High-performance equipment.* For those organizations too small to afford supercomputing, the next few years will see dramatic reductions in cost. Supercomputers were once used almost exclusively in military and research applications but now can be economically applied to mundane engineering tasks. For example, Phoenix, Arizona-based Ping, Inc., a golf club manufacturer, purchased a $100,000 Cray XD1 3 years ago to help with golf club design. The machine cut the average processing time of design simulations from 13 hours on workstations to 20 minutes.[3] These kinds of dramatic improvements drive effective CIOs to periodically challenge their own assumptions about the cost effectiveness of new technologies.

■ *Web apps as desktop apps.* Tools like Ajax, with appropriate extensions, can create applications that will run on devices not always connected to the Internet. This trend will likely accelerate so that the absolute dominance of the current desktop vendors may recede. Perhaps desktop-only applications will become rare or will be relegated to high-end applications only. General users may need nothing more than a modest network device. This is one of those trends that has come, gone, and then come back again. Originally the "network computer" was to be the thin client device of the future, but bandwidth and Web applications were limited in the 1990s. With SaaS (software as a service) and the general proliferation of robust (sometimes called "rich") Web applications, the network computer may again be a viable option.

> *Next-generation smartphones.* If people are already carrying a device with them everywhere, why not make it even more useful. With tools like Google's Android, developers may be able to break out of the proprietary cell phone model and develop more global applications for mobile devices. Making the cell phone a full application platform is a high-stakes game for all involved. For example, the following quote from an eBay executive illustrates the level of interest in expanding the technology[4]: eBay supports the Open Handset Alliance's efforts to deliver more compelling applications and content to mobile Internet users. As the future unfolds, more and more people will be accessing the Internet using their mobile devices. We see this initiative as an opportunity to get more people to experience the power of the eBay marketplace regardless of where they are or what device they are using. (Andre Haddad, SVP Products, eBay Inc.)

- *Event-driven architecture.* Real-time availability of data is growing at an exponential rate (think radio frequency identification [RFID], smart video, massive transaction databases). This growth has enabled IT systems to be far more responsive to specific, business-relevant events. This architecture ties into service-oriented architecture (SOA) because the events kick off specific, and often disparate, applications. One product, EPCenter, "allows you to create event processing solutions using data from any internet connected machines, applications or devices."[5] Practical applications range from simple monitoring of complex temperature/pressure events to real-time analysis of complex banking transactions.

- *Embedded systems.* Embedded systems are code from an outside party directly inserted into an application. For example, eBay sellers can insert shipping software from FedEx into their Web pages. Where it makes sense, this technology can provide convenience to customers, suppliers, and others.

- *Mashups.* The growth of public application interfaces on the Internet will fuel mashups of every sort imaginable. The site www.webmashup.com, for example, lists 202 mashup applications, ranging from www.bibliopage.com (combines Library of Congress with Amazon.com for book reference) to www.croatia-map.net which maps out sites of interest for Croatian tourists.

- *Three-dimensional printing.* Although the technology is developing slowly, printing in three dimensions is not that difficult to visualize. Currently, ink-jet printers deposit a layer of ink in pico-liter quantities. Machines are now being constructed which print, instead of ink, layer-upon-layer of a particular substance (it could be plastic, finely ground metal, or other materials) so that a three-dimensional object is created. For example, consider the following potential application: a customer wants to see what a building design looks like in true 3D (not a representation on a computer screen). The sales representative presses a button and the "printer" constructs a plastic model with the exact (obviously scaled down) relative dimensions of the plan. The customer gets a much better feel for the practicality of the design by looking at the model — "wow, I didn't realize that the bays would be so far apart."

We do not have the gift of prophesy. All the above are merely existing trends that we consider likely to continue in the next few years. If you look at the world as a bell curve, then most of the technologies, business trends, and innovations are in the comfortable middle. Some, however, are at the extremes. The only predictable fact about truly random developments is that they will in fact occur. What would a farmer in 1899 say if you told him that in 10 years a couple of bicycle repair guys would fly around New York City's skyscrapers in a machine? The effective CIO welcomes change and resists the urge to see the world as best when he or she was 17 years old. New technologies are arriving and will provide fabulous opportunities for personal growth and contribution. The key to success is an open mind.

References

1. Tanaka, Graham Y. *Digital Deflation: The Productivity Revolution and How It Will Ignite the Economy* (New York: McGraw-Hill, 2007).
2. Carr, Nicholas. *The Big Switch: Rewiring the World, from Edison to Google* (New York: W. W. Norton & Company, 2008).
3. Thibodeau, Patrick. Supercomputers Bulk Up on Power While Shedding Price Pounds. *Computerworld* (December 3, 2007), 14.
4. Industry Leaders Announce Open Platform for Mobile Devices. www.google.com/intl/en/press/pressrel/20071105_mobile_open.html (accessed March 8, 2008).
5. Datacomplex Epicenter. www.datacomplex.net/index.html (accessed March 9, 2008).

Chapter 15

CIO Interviews

> Men nearly always follow the tracks made by others and proceed in their affairs by imitation, even though they cannot entirely keep to the tracks of others or emulate the prowess of their models. So a prudent man should always follow in the footsteps of great men and imitate those who have been outstanding. If his own prowess fails to compare with theirs, at least it has an air of greatness about it. He should behave like those archers who, if they are skilful, when the target seems too distant, know the capabilities of their bow and aim a good deal higher than their objective, not in order to shoot so high but so that by aiming high they can reach the target.
>
> **Niccolo Machiavelli, *The Prince***

Throughout this book, we have generalized our discussion, because our readers have varied backgrounds and work in diverse organizations. But of course real chief information officers are never "average" — each one achieves success in his or her own way, using a unique set of intellectual, business, and human relations skills. For example, David Finn, CIO of Texas Children's Hospital, started his career in theater and arrived at his current position by a circuitous route. Another healthcare CIO, George Conklin, of CHRISTUS Health, majored in psychology. In the discussions below, you can see that each interviewee has a different but often penetrating perception of the job. As many in business have learned, there is a lot to be said for copying success.

Interview with David Finn, CISA, CISM, Vice President and Chief Information Officer/ Privacy and Information Security Officer, Texas Children's Hospital, Houston, Texas

Short Biography:

David Finn, CISA, CISM is Vice President and Chief Information Officer, Privacy/Information Security Officer for Texas Children's Hospital, the largest pediatric Integrated Delivery System in the United States. He is focused on using technology as an enabler of operating efficiency and deriving business value through the optimization and control of technology.

Prior to joining Texas Children's Hospital as Privacy Officer/Information Security Officer in 2001, Mr. Finn served as Executive Vice President of Healthlink, Senior Manager at PricewaterhouseCoopers, Manager of Student Accounting, Billing, and Collections at the University of Houston, and Area Manager for the Houston Apartment Housing Corporation.

Finn is a recipient of the 2007 ECRI Institute Health Devices Achievement award and 2008 Visionary award from Symantec Corporation. He volunteers his time to the needy by serving on the executive committee of Healthcare for the Homeless. In November 2007, he was elected to the Board of Directors for the Health Information Management Systems Society.

He writes and lectures frequently on topics ranging from information technology governance, business/IT alignment, management for the clinical engineering department, program management office (PMO) functions, privacy, security, and the Health Insurance Portability and Accountability Act (HIPAA).

Q: Texas Children's Hospital is a large and dynamic institution by any standard. How did your somewhat unusual educational and early professional background (at least for a CIO) contribute to your current position?

A: I guess you don't find many CIOs who majored in theater arts, served as treasurer for a theatrical production company, worked as a real estate controller, and then became the world's oldest entry-level programmer (yes, I even attended the venerable Control Data Institute). Even though I later moved through the worlds of Internal Audit, operational/systems risk consulting, and information security, I think my early experiences uniquely shaped my perspective. The theater work helped me to communicate well and the variety of jobs outside IT gave me a sense of core business requirements. For example, I worked at one point for the University of Houston, in the Bursar's Office. Even though I was part of the IT organization, my ability to communicate and discuss business issues drove me increasingly into business functions. I learned that the key to effective IT is through deep business knowledge.

Q: Your title as well as your audit, risk, and information security background suggest that you are a strong supporter of IT governance. Can you give us some examples of governance initiatives at Texas Children's Hospital?

A: Actually, even though I have always had a control orientation, in 2002 I had a gentle nudge — no, make that an outright shove — into implementation of a strong governance model. The hospital's PCs were shut down for nearly a week by what appeared to be a massive virus attack (but was later traced to a faulty API somewhere between Microsoft and Symantec). That, combined with some other IT problems resulted in a strategic review of the IT function by outside consultants. Of the IT managers before the study, I was the sole survivor after the study. The CFO [chief financial officer] asked me to accept the CIO position "only if I wanted to continue working here."

So we cranked up our "governance grinder," throwing in time, effort, management support, and a lot of jawboning. Out came many governance initiatives — an effective PMO organization, disciplined change management, an organized approach to prioritizing and rationalizing projects, a shift of the Information Management Committee to more strategic rather than tactical thinking, and a more disciplined multiyear budgeting process. I can't directly measure the effect, but just getting everyone to talk to each other, both inside and outside IT, was a major step forward. Oh, I almost forgot to mention another one of the biggies — we developed a shared governance model where various user/IT groups had specific responsibilities, such as technology standards and requirements for the research groups, clinical subcommittee, and business subcommittee. All these subcommittees report to the Information Management Executive Committee. By splitting up governance into multiple parts, we obtained focus and got more done.

Q: You have to satisfy both business and medical/scientific computing and information needs. What are some of your initiatives for the next few years?

A: Texas Children's is in a period of rapid expansion. We have two new hospitals planned as well as a plethora of research projects scheduled. So we need to coalesce our general notions of where we want to go into a well-defined vision of the future. If you're going to put major capital into new buildings, for example, you really want to get the cabling technology right. That's an example of a nuts-and-bolts-type decision that should be driven by a vision-inspired technical architecture. We've hired an outside firm to develop a vision, based on needs from all the constituents; from there we'll create an architecture serving as a blueprint/master plan for expansion.

To satisfy our growth, we have to tackle problems common to large medical organizations accumulating and generating massive volumes of data. We have 63 specialty and subspecialty areas, 600 patient-related databases (that we know about), plus many links to other hospitals and research labs. To get an idea of the data requirements, think about the implications of this — our researchers need to store genetic markers; cataloging a single 1 × 3 inch slide requires a million data points. Or consider privacy. How do you architect security to be open and closed at the same time? By that I mean we want to share data with Baylor, for example, but we can't put them as just another user group on our network. We often need a view of data but not necessarily a single database to provide that view. Finally, on top of all these technical, governance, and regulatory issues, we have to continually circle back to the doctors, nurses, research scientists, and business administration users and ask the question "are we giving you what you need to do your job?"

Q: Have you had any recent projects where you, in effect, slipped on a banana peel?

A: That's an apropos image for an ex-theater guy. We always try to balance projects in terms of our constituent's contribution to the overall success of the hospital. We don't want to cater solely to the guys with the fat checkbooks and political muscle. We initiated a project to help nurses reset their various communications links as they change shifts. As nurses come on and off a shift, the beepers and other devices that indicate patient status need to go to the right person. We ran an extensive pilot of a system that would automate some of this process. It was well received by the nurses. We only did one thing wrong. We supplied the manpower from the IT department to perform some routine data entry functions at shift change time.

When it came time to go live, the nurses balked and would not "own" the system. They have many demands on their time, and the additional steps at shift time disrupted their routine, even though it would be beneficial overall. We're going back to the drawing board on this one, but we've learned (or maybe relearned) a lesson — don't make a pilot easier than real life. If you do, it's not a real-life pilot.

Q: Just for grins, give us an example of something you have done as CIO that is off the beaten path.

A: Well, I've ordered mice breeding software for our vivarium. In fact, I'm not sure I understand all the software requests that come from some of the more esoteric research groups. But we make sure that all software purchases, even mice breeding software, goes through central IT purchasing so we can maintain licenses, maintenance contracts, and so forth.

Interview with Dennis M. Klinger, Vice President and Chief Information Officer, Florida Power & Light Company

Short Biography:

Dennis M. Klinger is Vice President and Chief Information Officer for Florida Power & Light Company (FPL). He oversees FPL's systems development efforts, computer operations, telecommunications operations, desktop computing, and advanced technology planning.

Prior to joining FPL in 1995, Klinger was Vice President and Chief Information Officer for Ryder System Inc., where he was responsible for the corporation's information systems function. Klinger's career in information management also includes working 10 years with the Florida Department of Education.

Klinger is past President of the Dade Public Education Fund and served on the United Way Campaign Cabinet. He holds a master's degree in business administration from Florida International University, and a bachelor's degree in management science from Florida Atlantic University.

Q: In the 1980s, FPL won the Deming award. Given your organizational culture, can you describe your approach to managing IT?

A: My department is driven by metrics. We review statistics on failure rates, mean time to repair, and other operational information. In general, funding follows metrics, which provide justification.

I get summary reports on hardware, software, change management, error rates, and frequency of outages. My direct reports get more detailed reports for their areas of responsibility. All these metrics are not just theory — bonuses are tied, in part, to these numbers. We have a monthly performance meeting where we focus on a broad range of issues. On our internal departmental Web site, performance information is shown with color markers of red, yellow, and green, indicating areas requiring attention or which are functioning at an acceptable level.

Performance is important enough that we maintain some six sigma black and green belts on staff. We also publish a balanced score card and perform root cause analysis where it makes sense.

Q: How do you obtain funding for your department and monitor expenses?

A: We start with a yearly business plan, with a great deal of communication with the business units. Because demand is potentially infinite, projects must be prioritized, with enough granularity to enable the decision-making process. We do not use a formal chargeback system but, based on the situation, some specific projects may be charged back. Balancing company-wide IT spending with specific needs of business units is an ongoing task if you're going to avoid suboptimization.

FPL is working on a model to assist in capital allocation, based on return on investment (ROI), market pressures, and other objective measures. We sometimes need to fund architectural projects not visible to the user (typically infrastructure projects). Whenever possible, we attach those costs to a project with payback. Otherwise, we explain the need, along with the long-term benefits.

Q: What is your approach to outsourcing, off-shoring, and so forth?

A: We use sourcing based on common sense rather than ideology. Decision factors include cost, need, and availability of talent and skill levels. One potential advantage of sourcing is that even if FPL can do "X" better than the outsource provider, FPL's resources may be better used in some other, more creative activity.

Some tasks are real commodities, such as archiving (record management), and are therefore good candidates for sourcing. One FPL employee is over the outsource staff performing scanning. In general, core functions are maintained in-house.

If you are going to do higher-level sourcing right, knowledge needs to transfer to in-house staff. In some markets, such as SAP, skills are hard to obtain. So in those cases we may use the "rifle shot" philosophy to get a specific resource. In other cases, a large project may require "bodies," and we will use an integrator. Companies have to be careful not to set up a vicious cycle, where the most interesting projects are outsourced, which causes the best people to leave, which in turn encourages more outward migration of talent, and so on.

Q: Does FPL embrace analytics as a way to improve services and reduce costs? If so, how does IT support those initiatives?

A: First, we provide a solid infrastructure for data mining and analytics. To be of value to the user community, data need to be easily accessible and standardized. Another important element in an effective analytics program is training and maintenance of the correct skills levels, within both IT and the user community.

Wal-Mart and P&G are good examples of firms who use analytics extensively. It is somewhat like Alcoholics Anonymous — first you have to admit you have a problem before rehabilitation can begin. Organizations work the same way; they have to admit they have not effectively used their available data before they can build systems to provide the value they are looking for.

It is important to avoid thinking about analytics only as a way to directly improve cash or financial assets. For example, if a giant turbine blade becomes defective, the total cost to FPL could be $50 million. So one of our goals is to use analytics to identify a problem in the blade before it happens. Another example of nonfinancial analytics is our acquisition of a firm that specializes in identifying locations and configurations to maximize wind power.

Q: As a major power producer, FPL must devote considerable resources to engineering and other "shop floor" IT activities. Do these specialty areas report to you?

A: When I first started with FPL, approximately 50% to 60% of functions that could be considered as computing activities reported to me. Now that figure is closer to 85% to 90% as centralization has been shown to be more effective than silo computing. There are some process control duties in the plants where IT functionality is embedded; the same is true for distribution lines and generation plants. We also have a trading floor with IT staff who do not report to me.

Q: What is your perspective on hiring and staff relationships?

A: I spend considerable time hiring the right individuals for my direct reports. I look at the whole person, not merely technical skills. Hiring is a hugely important activity. What is their business experience? Do they have team spirit? Can they go beyond the job at hand?

Successful performers have the option to move out to the business if the opportunity arises. We try our best to retain good people.

Q: From an IT governance perspective, how involved is Internal Audit in your development activities?

A: Internal Audit participates in new projects but as observers, not active participants. We have welcomed them to be active participants. Our life-cycle methodology has formally designated review points to ensure they have logical points to review controls.

Q: What is your strategy for integrating acquired IT groups into your organization?

A: To date, only smaller acquisitions have occurred. We generally eliminate their IT department as a separate function, as we prefer to centralize IT.

In general, if a firm's business philosophy is to "buy and sell," then the IT departments should be left alone, to simplify later sale to another party. In that case, only Sarbanes-Oxley (SOX) and internal controls need be addressed. On the other hand, if the philosophy is to "buy and hold," then the effort required to move their IT to central operations makes sense.

Q: How do you get new ideas and maintain currency with the industry?

A: I attend a few conferences each year and am on a couple of boards. A CIO obviously needs to guard his time but should stay current in order to remain excited about the possibilities.

Q: What does it take to be an effective CIO?

A: You have to nurture relationships all the time. Those relationships include senior management, your own IT staff, clients, and other constituents. Most IT failures are relationship failures — or at least relationships are the breaking point. Business conducted during a lunch hour can be more effective than a month of consultants and PowerPoint presentations. At the same time, the CIO really needs to understand what technology can do for the business.

As I mentioned earlier, hiring is critical. You have to hire people who wake up in the morning thinking how to help the business. Open relationships and a forum for staff to identify service opportunities are also helpful.

Interview with George Conklin, Senior Vice President and Chief Information Officer, CHRISTUS Health

Short Biography:

George S. Conklin is Senior Vice President for Information Management at CHRISTUS Health, the nation's fourth largest Catholic health care delivery system. He is responsible for all aspects of the delivery of information management and communications systems services, supporting CHRISTUS Health's delivery network across four states, in two countries, and in more than 300 locations. Additionally, as a member of CHRISTUS Health's senior leadership team, he participates in setting short- and long-term strategic and tactical directions for the system at large. In particular, he remains one of the core team members of CHRISTUS Health's Futures Task Force, an effort that is setting long-term system directions based on assessments of future social, technical, environmental, economic, and political factors.

Conklin was awarded the Smithsonian Institution Face of Innovation award in 1997 that recognized applications of computers to medical decision support at Integris Health in Oklahoma City, Oklahoma. These achievements have been included in the permanent research collection of the Smithsonian Institution's National Museum of American History. Additionally, CHRISTUS Health was awarded one of HHN's "Most Wireless" Awards in 2002.

Conklin writes and lectures frequently in the areas of health-care informatics, systems implementation, ROI, clinical quality, and management of complicated information systems and environments.

Q: You could probably list dozens of new demands on IT as health-care services expand in the United States and internationally. Can you give us some examples of how you have responded to the business and service requirements of your organization?

A: First, let me give you some background on the major shifts occurring in the delivery methods and technologies for health care. In the past, 80% of acute care took place in full-service hospitals, which house some of the most expensive real estate in any business environment (in terms of capital and operating costs per square foot). Now, technology is more widely diffused; for example, imaging centers and clinics can treat some patients who formerly would have gone to full scope hospitals. In addition, baby boomers want more convenience and expect more medical problems to be treated outside the hospital. Large hospitals are vital but for nonacute medicine, clinics or other less-intensive types of settings (medical spas, for example) may be a better solution for many people. Today, big hospitals are crowded, with a significant percentage of patients who are poor and uninsured and sadly very ill with diseases that could have been treated had a person had what we like to call a "medical home." We are working to satisfy that need without the high cost per square foot of a hospital. A full scope emergency room, for example, may run $700 to $1,000 per square foot, whereas the comparable per square foot cost at a clinic or another service entity could be as low as $5.

So how does this state of affairs affect IT? We are in the process of providing the technological tools so that all parts of the CHRISTUS Health system can participate in a "community" of services. Reading X-rays, imaging, patient information sharing, and other services are increasingly diffuse and not as dependent on bringing the customer to a large hospital. We are knocking down silos and standardizing as fast as we can. Using DICOM (digital imaging for medicine) standards, we can use remote services from India and other sources for 24/7 support.

Q: How has your group supported CHRISTUS' growth outside the United States?

A: We have seven hospitals and a number of clinics in Mexico with plans to expand to perhaps twenty. Health care standards, based on JCAHO (Joint Commission on Accreditation for Health Organizations), are similar to those in the United States. So we have to make the same information available to those clinics as we have in the United States. With the network we have developed working with AT&T and other telecommunications links, we can transmit large files to wherever the expertise is available in the CHRISTUS Health organization. Convergence to IP platforms helps us remotely manage equipment in the United States and Mexico — most of the updates to medical devices are now done via software, eliminating the need for physical visits by a technician. Our ability to remotely manage technology is helped by smarter software, which reduces training time. We're also moving steadily away from proprietary systems.

Q: What are some ways that you have used IT to directly help with CHRISTUS' health-care mission?

A: Suppose you've been a patient at one of our facilities and you are told to take certain vitamins. You go to our Web site, login and order the vitamins, then receive a message saying "you have an allergy to gluten." Our system will then direct you to a gluten-free alternative. Increasingly we are trying to find innovative ways to use the knowledge we have of a person's medical condition to proactively shape what we do and how we do it. Such systems and the significant standardization we have undertaken also help in research and quick transmission of best practices.

Q: Given CHRISTUS' size, how do you ensure that IT functions and operations are coordinated and rationalized with minimum duplication of effort?

A: With over 380 locations and growing, we have to standardize as much as possible, particularly for technology infrastructure. Our ATM cloud network facilitates standardization and centralization of information. That does not always mean physical centralization; our goal is to present a virtual enterprise view to the user community.

At a more strategic level, we work with a series of governance committees to ensure that IT is aligned with the organization's mission. I sit on the senior leadership team, which includes the CEO. The most directly influential forum for strategic decisions is the Information Management Oversight Committee. This committee meets six times a year and has approximately 25 participants. One of the annual meetings is face-to-face. This is where suboptimal activities, duplication, and so forth, can be discussed.

These management/governance groups are very effective. For example, in 2004 regional senior management was asked if there was any value in a single architecture. They formed a consensus and from that time we started our move to *community* (i.e., seeing information services as an enterprise function, available to all, with shared resources).

Q: Do you procure services centrally? In general, what has been your approach to cost containment?

A: Yes. Early on contracts were often negotiated locally, bringing only local volume to the bargaining table. Now we aggregate all significant contracts at the corporate level. In another case, one of our hospitals had purchased software, neglecting to budget for maintenance costs after the initial warranty ran out.

We charge back services based on direct usage of resources where we can. In some cases, allocation is required. For example, we periodically bring in outside consultants to do a white hat network penetration test — what demand-based metric do you use to recover those costs? Allocation is inexact and seems to generate considerable debate, so we try to find direct usage metrics for chargeback whenever we can. This is, however, a constantly moving target.

One of our major initiatives, which we call the "Unity Project," has been to define uniform operating structures for hospitals, home care, and even the physician's office. This strategy is bigger than IT and represents an effort to improve efficiency and service levels as well as reduce costs across our health-care system. It also leverages expertise and best practices between hospitals, clinics, and other service areas. If you have a standard set of tools, such as linked PDA devices, you capture more information faster and accumulate it in a consistent format.

Q: How important to the organization are analytics and what initiatives are in place now to take advantage of the business and clinical data available?

A: Increasingly, we are using analytics to generate real-time messages, such as glucose alerts sent to caregivers for diabetes patients; we are also looking at more complex long-term treatment protocol analysis. Certainly we have the data volume for it. Just a few years ago, we stored a several hundred gig; the data now takes 4 petabytes of storage and in 18 to 24 months I expect the total to be in the 8 petabyte range. Storage is exploding, and imaging, requiring thousands of times the capacity of text, is the primary driver.

Q: Do any engineering or technical groups outside IT report to you?

A: Biomedical engineering now falls within my group. We have been looking at process level automation and defect analysis, using statistical techniques. We benefit patients by proactively identifying equipment perturbations; with this foreknowledge, we can send out a technician before equipment fails.

Q: What are the most important personal qualities for an effective CIO?

A: Most of them are what you would expect — the ability to think strategically, provide superior service (including five 9's uptime for information access), motivate and energize staff, listen, articulate the organization's mission, define and promote vision, maintain integrity, and tell both good and bad news. The CIO needs to create standards, which are the backbone of community, support a uniform architecture, and centralize functions where it makes sense. As I mentioned earlier, centralization does not necessarily mean physical proximity but a logical/virtual place where any specific work can be accomplished most effectively.

My educational background is psychology and it has helped me understand human needs and behavior, at least to the extent that anyone can understand human beings. Given the complexity of some of our systems, I can't afford to needlessly churn staff. So we stick to our vision and keep everyone as challenged as possible.

Interview with Harold D. Bates, CPA, Executive Vice President and Chief Executive Officer, Community Resource Credit Union, Baytown, Texas

Short Biography:

Harold D. Bates is Executive Vice President and CIO of Community Resource Credit Union in Baytown, Texas. He is focused on combining in-depth business knowledge with IT resources in order to provide cost-effective and timely services to the Credit Union.

Prior to joining Community Resource Credit Union, Mr. Bates worked for Arthur Anderson & Company, Guaranty Bank in Denver, Patten & McCarthy Associates (consultants for bank mergers and acquisitions), Southwest Banking Corporation, and The Women's Bank, NA. A Vietnam veteran and graduate of Baylor and Southwest Graduate School of Banking, he has over 30 years of experience in financial management, asset-liability consulting, commercial loans, asset securitization and loan participation analysis, banking operations, major IT system conversions, and IT management. Bates says that his real expertise is in tearing down walls between IT and the operating units.

Q: Management consulting firms typically say that important things can be counted on one hand. What is the handful of traits or characteristics that make a good CIO?

A: First, the CIO must have a willingness to thoroughly learn the organization's business model. I couldn't function as CIO if I didn't appreciate every component of the business, from making loans to running check processing. Second, the ability to communicate up and down the line is essential. To be useful, you have to understand business needs and match those with what IT can deliver. Third, every CIO needs a strong service orientation. Our help desk personnel are required to pick up calls immediately. I personally review each help desk request that comes in. It helps me monitor whether we are effectively executing our plan and responding to business needs.

Q: Have you seen examples of IT organizations that have lost business focus?

A: Certainly. Some credit unions run their own ATM network. It's crazy to do that … it might be fun for the techies but is clearly not operationally effective or rational from a cost management perspective.

We make every effort to tear down walls between IT and the operating units. We look for business skills and orientation when we hire and don't make the mistake of "techies hiring techies." That doesn't mean we don't appreciate technical skill, but the business has to come first.

Q: What is the breakdown of work for your group?

A: We devote 25% of effort to user assistance through the help desk, 50% toward projects, and 25% for all other activities. We generally purchase solutions rather than make them, so most of our projects revolve around either implementation or enhancement of vendor-supplied systems.

Q: How did you start working with credit unions to begin with?

A: Although my career has always centered around accounting, finance, and banking, my entry into the credit union business was one of those chance events that seem to shape so much of professional life — I responded to a *Wall Street Journal* ad for a chief financial officer (CFO) position at a Los Alamos credit union near Santa Fe.

Working for Community Resource has been fun. I also manage a $100 million investment portfolio along with my IT duties. My background is not deeply technical but by working in so many areas of the business and by hiring a strong VP of IT, I've been able to meet and exceed expectations.

Interview with "X," Chief Information Officer of a West Coast Utility ("X" Requested Anonymity Indicating a Preference to Stay out of the Limelight)

Q: XYZ Utility has gone through mergers/acquisitions in the past. For many organizations, combining two IT groups is a challenge. What is your approach at XYZ Utility?

A: First, let me talk about the phrase "merger and acquisition." It's a standard business term you hear all the time. However, in my experience, only acquisitions are successful. This doesn't imply lack of appreciation for the acquired firm but a recognition that someone has to be boss, set the standards, and provide the definitive vision for where the merged organization is headed.

Due diligence takes a lot of work and is hard to get right. Is their data structure a good fit with your existing databases? What about historical data conversion? Where are the synergies between the two organizations? Can you take a peek under the hood and look for structure, documentation, and the discipline/governance that are usually associated with a higher value asset? How much effort will it take to move them to your standard footprint?

Our philosophy is to listen, learn, and select a standard way to do things. If an acquired IT shop has a better widget than we do, then one of two things will happen: (a) we will make them use our widget in the interests of economies of scale and rationalization of management effort or (b) we'll all use *their* widget. In either case, there will be ONE way of performing a particular function. Duplication across the enterprise saps energy and increases costs dramatically.

With respect to the people — we tell them relatively quickly what their fate will be. To some we say "you are gone" so they can find another job and get on with their life. Others will be told we need them for a specific time period and the rest will be retained as ongoing resources. It is important to have a defined timeline and avoid a cloud of uncertainty. And that timeline typically includes about 2 to 4 weeks to size up the management team. One last point on acquisitions — it's critical to retain the business knowledge. The technical know-how is much more fungible.

Q: Can you give us an example of a key business initiative where IT is directly involved and is a major player in executing the strategy?

A: One of the best examples I can give is the "intelligent grid." Although we are not there yet, this system, which requires both IT and operations development, will lead to an amazing array of benefits. Once all the components of this architecture are in place, we can acquire customer meter reads at 15 minute intervals and provide information to the consumer to allow them to better manage their electricity usage during the day. For example, as utilities move to time-of-day pricing, consumers can save money by running their laundry during times of non-peak electricity demand. Had this system been in place during some recent weather disruptions, restoration of services would have been hours rather than days. IT systems will be able to have embedded algorithms controlling demand, providing new remote control features, Web information for the customer, and other services. By providing information to consumers and helping them load balance the electrical grid, we may delay or even eliminate the need to build another power plant.

Q: Do you report on key performance indicators to your internal customers?

A: We are just beginning to report IT's contribution to the business in terms of their key performance indicators (KPIs). An example of this is the consolidation of the performance of the 120 IT components relating to the efficiency of a call center agent's response to a phone call into one metric for the call center manager. Dashboards help us present the results of operations in business terms — the specific metrics of highest interest to management.

We also try to proactively anticipate information that may be useful to the business. For example, we recently provided our electric company president with statistics about meter reads after she had mentioned a concern with the number of reads being estimated. We gave her detailed information about the number of estimated meter reads by routes which enabled her to improve the meter reading process. That's an example of IT as a strategic resource versus IT as an order taker. Bringing a practical business idea to the table is far more effective than a discussion about new systems or tools.

Q: You have a large number of IT projects in place and a demanding schedule, yet manage to keep staff turnover down to 3%. How do you manage the people side of your business?

A: It has always been clear to me that people don't leave a company, they leave people. So, all the things that need to be in place to keep employees happy in their work and productive must be administered by managers who can properly balance the needs of the employee and the company.

To stay in touch, I use the "MBWA" approach — management by walking around, talking to managers and staff, staying in touch with the day-to-day. Compensation is not an issue, as we pay at or above market for our area. Training is important. Some of the new initiatives rely on service-oriented architecture (SOA) and we are an SAP shop, so education is vital. For those who have spent years working on legacy systems, we encourage them to retool themselves so that they have a continued career path with XYZ Utility. Some of our legacy people, close to retirement, may not want to retool and can productively spend their time in maintenance activities. The challenge is to always provide a career path that fits the talent of the individual.

Appendix A

Examples of Key IT General Controls

General Control Category	Example General Control
Acceptable Use Policy	All employees are required to read and sign the Acceptable Use Policy that includes company policy against unlicensed or unauthorized software installation.
Backup/ Operations	At minimum, "incremental backups" are performed nightly and "full backups" are performed on at least a monthly basis. These backups are rotated offsite to a well-protected storage site. The term "incremental backups" applies to redo logs and any other method that permits files to be reconstructed from an original base file plus records that will bring it up to current state.
Backup/ Operations	Procedures exist and are followed to semiannually test the effectiveness of the restoration process and the quality of backup media.
Backup/ Operations	Backup media (tapes, disks, etc.) are rotated to an offsite storage facility. The backup includes operating system and application databases. Logs showing the rotation and presence of backup media should be maintained.

General Control Category	Example General Control
Change Control	System software changes are approved, tested, and recorded based on documented change management procedures.
Change Control	Production (executable and source code) libraries are protected from unauthorized access or modification.
Change Control	Source code changes to programs should be captured so that between successive moves to production, the modifications to code can be identified.
Change Control	Changes are tested by users in a separate test environment prior to use in production. In the case of infrastructure, testing may be performed by the same individual who performed the work.
Change Control	Change request forms, manual or electronic, are completed by the Programmer/Tech/Admin/App Support, and include ticket number, requestor's contact information, change description (reason, back out procedures, etc.), change priority, and change category. Both program changes and data changes are included in this control.
Change Control	All change control requests are approved by user management (with the exception of infrastructure-only changes). This approval is verified by the help desk using a management approved "requestor/approver" listing. Only requestor/approvers or alternates can approve changes. Designated requestors can approve low-risk changes; medium- and high-risk changes must be approved by an approver. Both program changes and data changes are included in this control.
Change control	UNIT testing (by developer) and user acceptance testing "UAT" is performed to assess that user requirements are met, that changes function properly, and that changes do not negatively impact other systems. Both program changes and data changes are included in this control.
Change Control	Emergency changes are logged in Incident Monitor and approved in advance by a responsible IT manager and user. If the emergency change cannot be approved in advance, it is approved after the fact within 48 business hours. Pure infrastructure changes are not approved by a user.

General Control Category	Example General Control
Information Security	An information security policy exists and has been approved by an appropriate level of executive management.
Information Security	Security requirements, objectives, policies, standards, and procedures are identified, documented, and published in the Information Security and Computer Use Policy.
Information Security	Systems and information are protected via user authentication mechanisms, user ID, and password, to prevent unauthorized access or use.
Information Security	The granting of access, changes to existing access rights, and removal of access is authorized by the appropriate system owner taking into account least privilege, segregation of duties, and the level of access required.
Information Security	Access rights are reviewed semiannually by the Information Security Administrator and/or the appropriate level of user management to confirm they are still as granted and that they correspond to the user's and the organization's needs.
Information Security	Automated controls are in place to suspend network IDs and passwords after a period of inactivity more than 90 days.
Information Security	At the network/Windows level, users are forced to change their password upon initial login.
Information Security	Confidential information, such as salary, social security number (SSN), and sensitive financial calculations, should be restricted at the network level to authorized personnel.
Information Security	Within 24 business hours, network access for a terminated employee or contractor is removed.
Information Security	At the network level, the user ID is locked out after three login failures and contact with the help desk is required for reinstatement.
Information Security	Computer security is based on strictly limited access to the underlying operating systems and databases. All users sign on to applications and the applications access databases and operating systems, as required. Only a few carefully designated administrators have direct access to the operating system or databases.

General Control Category	*Example General Control*
Information Security	Firewall is configured to restrict viewing of IP addresses of all internal addresses from the Internet.
Information Security	Separate access to the data/network center within the headquarters location is maintained, including electronic locks, alarms, an audit trail of entrance/exit events, and a restricted list of individuals with access, on a business need basis.
Information Security	Where appropriate, functions within the enterprise resource planning (ERP) should be restricted by location or organizational unit. This control does not apply to inquiry-only functions or functions that are intentionally set up for enterprise-wide operations (e.g., vendor setup for payables).
Operations Controls	Scheduled jobs that must run in proper sequence and depend on the success of prior steps are monitored either through visual inspection of run logs or via automated controls, such as Oracle's "Request Set, abort on error" setting. Simple one-step, user submitted reports are not in the scope of this key control.
Physical Security	Environmental protections are in effect, including fire protection, alarms, and humidity control.
Physical Security	Uninterruptible power is available for critical applications. There should be protection against voltage flux. Duration of the auxiliary power should be sufficient to continue operations for a reasonable period.
Segregation of Duties	A segregation of duties (SOD) matrix showing incompatible duties is maintained and updated annually.
Segregation of Duties	Using the SOD matrix, a SOD report is created showing exceptions. These exceptions are resolved (either by security changes or management acceptance of risk) semiannually.
Systems Development	For system projects classified as medium or high risk, business requirements must be specified in sufficient detail to enable technical/function design to be completed. In addition, formal signoff by the appropriate level of user management (or IT management in the case of infrastructure) must be documented.

General Control Category	Example General Control
Systems Development	For system projects classified as medium or high risk, technical and functional design specifications are required. Signoff by IT management is required (paper or electronic signature).
Systems Development	For all changes or projects, user acceptance testing (performed in the test environment, not production) is required. UAT must be accompanied by user management signoff (paper or electronic signature).
Systems Development	For system projects classified as medium or high risk, technical/functional design specifications are developed to ensure that security, availability, and processing integrity are included in the project.

Appendix B

Examples of Key IT Application Controls

Application Control Category	Example Application Control
Accounts Payable	The Oracle application system uses edit and validation checks to reject invoices submitted for processing that do not have all required fields.
Accounts Payable	To prevent duplicate payments to a valid invoice, the Oracle system application flags a previously paid invoice as paid.
Accounts Payable	A Voucher Numbering system within Oracle AP assigns a voucher number to every single invoice entered for payment processing.
Accounts Payable	The Oracle systems define what invoices should be paid during the weekly payment run, in accordance to payment terms set up in the system for each vendor.
Accounts Payable	Disbursements can only be made to vendors that have been set up in the Oracle systems through the vendor set-up process.
Accounts Payable	The Oracle system applications require that vendors must be set up in the system prior to payments being made.

Application Control Category	Example Application Control
Accounts Payable	The Oracle systems do not allow the creation of duplicate vendor names in the vendor master file.
Accounts Payable	An automated three-way matching procedure is in place in the Oracle accounts payable system. Invoices are matched to related receiving data in the system and approved purchase order prior to payment processing.
Accounts Payable	The Oracle application system uses edit and validation checks to reject invoices submitted for processing that do not have all required fields entered.
Accounts Payable	The Oracle application prevents duplicate entry of an invoice number previously processed for payment for the same vendor.
Fixed Assets	The Oracle systems automatically calculate depreciation on subledger assets.
Fixed Assets	The Oracle systems do not overdepreciate assets in subledger.
Fixed Assets	The Oracle systems automatically post the entries for the remaining net book value (NBV) when a disposal is made.
General Accounting	The accounting systems will not permit an entry to be posted to an invalid account number.
General Accounting	Only authorized employees can create and establish new accounts. These accounts are authorized by management prior to being established through this limited access capability.
General Accounting	The accounting systems will not allow an out-of-balance journal entry to be posted.
General Accounting	If an Oracle system entry fails to post, an error message is sent to the process owner alerting him/her of the problem. They then can correct the problem, allowing the system entry to post. This system control gives confidence that all system journal entries have been posted.

Application Control Category	Example Application Control
Inventory	The system is configured to automatically track inventory movement by moving material placed in production into work-in-process (WIP), finished goods, and finally to cost of goods sold.
Inventory	System is configured to ensure cost of sales is recorded for each ship confirm.
Inventory	System is designed to automatically identify and post variances to the proper accounts.
Inventory	The system is designed to automatically calculate the book-to-physical adjustment.
Inventory	System is designed to automatically calculate COS (cost of sales) and inventory values based on predefined standards.
Payroll	A system application control prevents further payroll checks from being generated to terminated employees.
Payroll	The XYZ payroll module is automatically updated with all changes to standing personnel data, including pay rate changes entered into the XYZ HR module; hence, no manual intervention by payroll personnel takes place.
Payroll	An automatic system notification is generated when a termination has not been marked as "complete." An exception report ("Outstanding XYZ report") is issued to all XYZ mail groups including PR.
Payroll	System validation setups within the timekeeping system include employee status verifications, valid organization setup, hour thresholds that flag excessive employee hours incurred, and other timekeeping system validations.
Purchasing	Oracle systems do not allow purchasing to issue duplicate purchase order numbers.
Purchasing	Oracle systems do not allow purchases from vendors not set up in the Vendor Master File.
Purchasing	Oracle system controls do not permit a buyer to issue a purchase order (PO) if the total amount of the PO is above his/her approval level.

Application Control Category	Example Application Control
Purchasing	The workflow within the Oracle system defines spending limits and authorization procedures for purchase orders. The workflow and spending limits are documented in the Approval Hierarchy System.
Purchasing	Edit and validation checks exist in the Oracle system to verify key data fields (i.e., PO#, supplier, amount, coding, and approval) for purchase requisitions and orders.
Purchasing	The workflow within the Oracle system defines spending limits and authorization procedures for purchase orders. The workflow and spending limits are documented in the Approval Hierarchy System.
Revenue	The Oracle systems applications perform validation tests of key information prior to allowing the entry/posting of key information.
Revenue	The Oracle systems applications are configured to require a valid sales order before an order can be processed.
Revenue	The Oracle systems applications are configured to require approval of sales orders.
Revenue	The Oracle systems applications automatically record a sales entry when a sales invoice is created.
Revenue	The Oracle system automatically generates an invoice when shipment is recorded.
Revenue	The Oracle systems applications are configured not to allow manual overrides of key customer, product, or sales information.
Revenue	The Oracle application is configured so the system date is the default date.
Revenue	The Oracle systems applications are configured to post an invoice number only once.
Revenue	The Oracle system application does not allow different invoice/shipment dates.

Application Control Category	*Example Application Control*
Revenue	The Oracle application is configured to automatically update the General Ledger and subledger upon shipment.
Revenue	The Oracle systems applications are configured to age accounts receivable invoices correctly.
Revenue	The Oracle systems applications are configured to create shipping documents from information contained in the sales order and customer master files.
Revenue	The Oracle systems applications are configured to verify customer and sales accounts before processing sales orders.
Revenue	The XYZ System Application looks at the amount shipped and the current AR balance and puts the shipment on credit hold if the shipment exceeds the available customer credit limit.

Appendix C

Project Management Artifact Examples

Project Charter:

Project Charter
XYZ Corp
Project Name

Author: Author Name
Creation Date: May 16, 2007
Last Updated: July 28, 2008
Version: 1

Approvals:

Approver 1   _____

Approver 2   _____

Approver 3   _____

Contents

Project Charter
    Project Overview
    Project Scope
    Project Organization
    Summary Schedule
    Constraints and Assumptions

Purpose

The purpose of a Project Charter is to formally authorize the start of a new project. Specifically, the charter is intended to authorize the project manager to apply organizational resources to project activities and requires the approval signature of the Project Sponsor.

This charter authorizes the **<Project Name>** project which will… <state the purpose of the project in a brief sentence>.

Project Overview

The Project Overview should provide the following information:

- Background information about the company, division, or business situation that requires this project
- The specific problem this project will solve or new function it will provide
- The purpose of this project stated in clear, concise terms

Project Objectives

<Project Objectives should be listed in numerical or bullet point order and follow the SMART logic (Specific, Measurable, Agreed Upon, Realistic, Time-Constrained).>

1.
2.
3.
4.
5.

Project Scope

<The Project Scope should list the products and services that will be provided by this project.>

<As part of the Project Scope, the key deliverables of the project should be outlined below in the Deliverables section.>

Deliverables

This **<Project Name>** project will produce the following deliverables:

1.
2.
3.
4.
5.

Project Organization

<The Project Organization section should provide details on the project teams and project team members. The section contains generic information about the Steering Committee, Project Core Team, and Advisory Team, but these sections can be modified as needed for the specific project.>

Steering Committee

The purpose of the Steering Committee is to provide the financial resources for the project. Specifically, the steering committee's roles and responsibilities are to:

- Commit financial and human resources to the activities of the project.
- Empower and support the project team in achieving the project objectives.
- Assist with resolving issues that cannot be resolved by the project team.
- Review and respond to project recommendations.

Steering Committee members are senior-level managers from the departments/divisions most impacted by the project and consist of the following:

- Steering Committee member #1
- Steering Committee member #2
- Steering Committee member #3
- Steering Committee member #4
- Additional members as needed

Project Core Team

The purpose of the Core Team is to represent a department or division and share with other team members the unique requirements of the department/division they represent. The Core Team will be the most engaged with the project and may contribute up to 50% of their time to this project. Specifically, the roles and responsibilities of the Core Team are to:

- Answer questionnaires and conduct site visits.
- Gather business requirements.
- Provide sample data and analyze it.
- Prepare recommendations for global design and present the findings.

The Core Team consists of:

- Project Core Team member #1
- Project Core Team member #2
- Project Core Team member #3
- Project Core Team member #4

Advisory Team

The purpose of the Advisory Team is to periodically provide historical perspectives and guidance. The Advisory Team will be included on project correspondence but will not participate in all site visits and requirements gathering exercises. Advisory Team members will provide industry, technological, accounting, or historical perspectives to the project. The Advisory Team consists of:

- Advisory Team member #1
- Advisory Team member #2
- Advisory Team member #3
- Advisory Team member #4

Summary Schedule

<The Summary Schedule section should be used to provide a high-level summary of the project schedule showing major milestones, stage gates, or phase completion dates.>

Constraints and Assumptions

<The Constraints and Assumptions section should provide information on both constraints and assumptions that can affect the scope of the project. A constraint is any restriction (time, resource, cost) that affects how an activity can be scheduled. An assumption is a factor that is considered to be true or certain.>

Constraints

1.
2.
3.
4.
5.

Assumptions

1.
2.
3.
4.
5.

Requirements Document

Requirements Document
{Document Title}
XYZ Corp

Author: {name}
Creation Date: {date}
Last Updated: {date}
Version: 1.0

Approvals:

_____

_____

Document Control
Change Record

Date	Author	Version	Change Reference
3/24/07	Ginny R. Thrall	1.0	Initial version
5/1/07	Harry Vikington	1.1	Includes tax modifications for enterprise zone

Distribution

Name	Company	Position

Contents

Document Control
Business Requirements Overview
      Introduction/Business Case
      Solution Proposal
      Existing Processes
      Required Processes
Functional Detail
      Definitions and Acronyms
      Business Process
      User Community
      Functional Requirements
      Usability Requirements
      Documentation Requirements
      Examples
      Constraints and Assumptions
      Acceptance Criteria
Technical Detail
      Technical Requirements
      Data Requirements
      Performance Requirements
      Security Requirements
      Scalability Requirements
Open and Closed Issues for this Deliverable
      Open Issues
      Closed Issues

Business Requirements Overview

Introduction/Business Case

Solution Proposal

Existing Processes

Required Processes

Functional Detail

Definitions and Acronyms

Business Process

Business Process Flowchart

Business Process Definition

User Community

Functional Requirements

Usability Requirements

Documentation Requirements

Examples

Constraints and Assumptions

Acceptance Criteria

Technical Detail

Technical Requirements

Data Requirements

Performance Requirements

Security Requirements

Scalability Requirements

Open and Closed Issues for this Deliverable

Open Issues

ID	Issue	Resolution	Responsibility	Target Date	Impact Date

Closed Issues

ID	Issue	Resolution	Responsibility	Target Date	Impact Date

Appendix D

IT Risk Assessment Checklist

How Much Structural Impact?

Area of Risk	Risk Factors	Impact
Changes to Organizational Structure	The changes to the organizational structure are: • None or completed • Planned • Not considered	___ Zero to low ___ Medium ___ High
Impact — Computer Operations	The effect of the enhanced/modified system on computer operations of the organization: • Little change • Moderate change • Severe change	___ Zero to low ___ Medium ___ High
Changes to Procedures	Procedural changes required to support the enhanced/modified system • Small change • Moderate change • Large change	___ Zero to low ___ Medium ___ High

How Complex Is the Existing System?

Area of Risk	Scenario	Impact
Requirements for System Availability	The system should be available: • 95% • 99% • Greater than 99%	___ Zero to low ___ Medium ___ High
Links between Systems	The number of existing systems with which the enhanced/modified system must interface: • 0 • 1 to 4 • Over 4	___ Zero to low ___ Medium ___ High
Type of Processing	The system requires: • Primarily batch processing • Simple online query and update • Complex processing (e.g., distributed system)	___ Zero to low ___ Medium ___ High
Response Time	The system requires online response time of: • Greater than 6 seconds 95% of time • 3 to 6 seconds 90% of time • 2 seconds of less 90% of time	___ Zero to low ___ Medium ___ High
Data Quality	The quality of data for the conversion process: • Simple to convert • Average complexity or of fair quality • Complex or of poor quality	___ Zero to low ___ Medium ___ High
Data Complexity	The level of complexity of the data used by the current system (by the number of entities and the relationships between them): • Not complex • Moderately complex • Very complex	___ Zero to low ___ Medium ___ High

Database Complexity	The level of complexity of the database used by the current system (by the degree of denormalization) is:	
	• Not complex	___ Zero to low
	• Moderately complex	___ Medium
	• Very complex	___ High

How Much of the Existing System Is Documented?

Area of Risk	Scenario	Impact
Availability of Documentation	The status of the documentation of existing systems and procedures in the user areas is:	
	• Complete and current	___ Zero to low
	• More than 80% complete and current	___ Medium
	• Nonexistent, less than 80% complete, or outdated	___ High
Availability of Technical Documentation	The status of the documentation of existing systems and procedures in the development area is:	
	• Complete and current	___ Zero to low
	• More than 75% complete and current	___ Medium
	• Nonexistent, less than 75% complete, or outdated	___ High
Subject Matter Expertise	People involved know enough to support their role and responsibilities:	
	• Participants are fully knowledgeable	___ Zero to low
	• Participants are somewhat knowledgeable	___ Medium
	• Participants are not knowledgeable	___ High
User Know-How	Personnel responsible for providing application knowledge on the project are:	
	• Knowledgeable in both user and IT areas	___ Zero to low
	• Knowledgeable in user area only	___ Medium
	• Lacking adequate knowledge of user area	___ High

Business Knowledge of Project Team	Project team members who are highly knowledgeable about or experienced in the business area: • All • Half • None	___ Zero to low ___ Medium ___ High
Team's Experience with Application	The number of times that team members have implemented this application system: • More than once • Only once • No knowledge or experience with the system	___ Zero to low ___ Medium ___ High
Skills with Development Technology	All team members have sound knowledge of the technology they will use, and they have adequate practical experience: • All team members have practical experience of the technology they will be using • There is experience in each technology, but some team members have no training • There are some technologies in which no team member has practical experience	___ Zero to low ___ Medium ___ High

Is the Project Well Defined?

Area of Risk	Scenario	Impact
Project Scope	The project scope is: • Well defined • Defined, but at a high level • Fuzzy	___ Zero to low ___ Medium ___ High
Logical Project Scope	The logical scope of the project includes: • A single application only • Between one and three applications • More than three applications	___ Zero to low ___ Medium ___ High

Complexity of Enhancement/ Modification Needs	The requirements of the enhancement/modification are: • Straightforward and understandable • Somewhat known, but complex • Fuzzy and complex	___ Zero to low ___ Medium ___ High
Benefits of the Enhancements/ Modifications	The benefits of the existing system enhancement/modified are: • Well defined or quantified or of strategic importance • Defined in general, not quantified • Not defined or unclear	___ Zero to low ___ Medium ___ High
Project Deliverables	The project deliverables are: • Well defined • Defined, but at a high level • Vague	___ Zero to low ___ Medium ___ High
Dependence on Other Projects	The number of other projects on which this project is dependent: • 0 • 2 • 3 or more	___ Zero to low ___ Medium ___ High
Dependence of Other Projects on This Project	The number of projects that are dependent on this project: • 0 • 2 • 3 or more	___ Zero to low ___ Medium ___ High
Facts/ Knowledge to Be Shared	Knowledge coordination needs are: • Simple • Moderate • Complex	___ Zero to low ___ Medium ___ High

How Effective Is the Project Management Structure?

Area of Risk	Scenario	Impact
Scope Management Procedures	The scope management procedures for the project are: • Well defined and accepted • Established but unclear • Nonexistent	___ Zero to low ___ Medium ___ High
Knowledge Coordination Process	The knowledge coordination processes for this project are: • Well defined and accepted • Established but unclear • Fail to exist	___ Zero to low ___ Medium ___ High
Use of Methodology	The methodology and other standards to be used on the project: • Use of a formal methodology • Use of informal practices and standards • No methodology/seat-of-pants	___ Zero to low ___ Medium ___ High
Methodology Background of Participants	The experience of the organization with the methodology: • Full life-cycle experience with the methodology • Single phase or partial life-cycle experience with the methodology • First time to use the methodology	___ Zero to low ___ Medium ___ High
Quality Management Procedures	The quality management procedures for the project are: • Well defined and accepted • Established but unclear • Nonexistent	___ Zero to low ___ Medium ___ High

What Is the Project Size and Necessary Resources to Bring It to Completion?

Area of Risk	Scenario	Impact
Hours of Effort	The total estimated hours of effort for the project: • 900 or less • 901 to 1,900 • Over 1,900	___ Zero to low ___ Medium ___ High
Calendar Time	The estimated calendar time for project completion: • 2 months or less • 3 to 5 months • Over 5 months	___ Zero to low ___ Medium ___ High
Places	The number of different physical locations that will use the production system: • 1 site • 1 to 3 • Over 3	___ Zero to low ___ Medium ___ High
Team Size	The project team size will max out at: • 3 or fewer members • 4 to 6 members • Over 6 members	___ Zero to low ___ Medium ___ High
Project Manager Experience	The project manager experience level: • 3 or more prior projects of similar scope • 1 or 2 prior projects of similar scope • No prior projects of similar scope	___ Zero to low ___ Medium ___ High
Experience as a Team	The experience of team members as a team: • All have worked together before • Some have worked together before • Team members are strangers	___ Zero to low ___ Medium ___ High

Team Location	The physical location of the team:	
	• Team is located together	___ Zero to low
	• Most of the team is located together	___ Medium
	• Team is located at several sites	___ High
Percent of Time Devoted to Project by Key Project Members	Allocation of key project participants to the project:	
	• All key participants are sufficiently allocated to the project	___ Zero to low
	• Key participants are partially allocated to the project	___ Medium
	• Key participants are insufficiently allocated to the project	___ High
Good Testing Environment Is Available	Availability of hardware for development and testing:	
	• Guaranteed availability	___ Zero to low
	• Reasonable assurance of availability	___ Medium
	• No assurance of availability	___ High

How Well Is the System Supported by the Sponsor(s)?

Area of Risk	*Scenario*	*Impact*
Number of Project Sponsors	The project has:	
	• One project sponsor	___ Zero to low
	• Two project sponsors	___ Medium
	• More than two project sponsors	___ High
Project Sponsorship	The sponsor is:	
	• Identified, enthusiastic, and strong user influence	___ Zero to low
	• Identified but passive	___ Medium
	• Unknown	___ High
Project Scope is within Project Sponsor's Span-of-Control	The project scope is:	
	• Completely within the project sponsor's direct span-of-control	___ Zero to low
	• Partially outside the project sponsor's direct span-of-control	___ Medium
	• Outside the project sponsor's direct span-of-control	___ High

Commitment of User Management	Management: • Understands value of and supports the project • Is reluctant • Is highly skeptical or resistant	___ Zero to low ___ Medium ___ High
Commitment of User Organizations	The organizations: • Understand the value of and support the project • Are reluctant • Are skeptical or resistant	___ Zero to low ___ Medium ___ High

How Vulnerable Is the Organization to a System Failure? How Visible Is the System to Outsiders?

Area of Risk	Scenario	Impact
System Visible Outside of the Organization	The number of organizations outside the enterprise potentially impacted by a change is: • Zero or near zero • Manageable • Very large	 ___ Zero to low ___ Medium ___ High
Security and Internal Control	The information processed by the system is: • Basically protected • Normally protected • Sensitive or classified	 ___ Zero to low ___ Medium ___ High
Importance of the Information Processed	The level of importance of the information processed by the system to be changed is: • Not vital for the enterprise • Importance for the enterprise • Vital for the enterprise	 ___ Zero to low ___ Medium ___ High

Appendix E

Due Diligence Checklist for Mergers and Acquisitions (Business)

The following information should be provided by the acquired entity in order to fully assess the value of the acquisition as well as to estimate the level of effort required for integration into the enterprise. This list is intended to be comprehensive and covers important business concerns. The term "Company" refers to the acquired or to-be-merged firm. See Chapter 7 and the last section of this appendix for specific information technology-related topics.

Although much of this checklist will be of primary interest to your accounting and legal staff, you should review the topics to ensure that you have addressed any IT-related concerns.

1.0 Operations

    1.01   Accounts Receivable and Payable:

        a. Current Aged Accounts Receivable.

        b. Current Aged Accounts Payable.

    1.02   Budgets and Growth:

        a. Any budget prepared for the current year.

        b. Last 3 years detailed financial statements.

        c. Monthly revenue, gross profit, and operating income before goodwill.

        d. Most recent month ended balance sheet.

        e. Any special internal statistics used by management to operate the business.

    1.03 Safety and Risk Management:
- a. Copy of latest workers' compensation statement showing experience modifier and rates.
- b. Workers' compensation payments by job classification over the valuation period.
- c. Latest vehicle insurance statement and vehicle insurance expense over valuation period.
- d. Complete listing of all vehicles, type of vehicle, trade, type of coverage, and insurance premium.

    1.04 Employee Handbook and Policies:
- a. Copy of employee handbook.
- b. Copy of bonus or contractual agreements with employees.

    1.05 Uniforms:
- a. Copy of any uniform contract.
- b. Valuation period uniform expense and number of uniformed employees.

    1.06 Hospital Insurance — Copy of most recent health-care and dental statement showing employees covered and premiums.

    1.07 Sales and Marketing:
- a. Copies of all promotional materials and recent articles on the Company.
- b. A list of top 10 customers in 2006, 2007, and 2008 year to date, including type of product, quantity, and dollar amount of each product type purchased.
- c. Total 2006, 2007, and 2008 year-to-date sales itemized by product.
- d. Any projections, forecasts, analyses, or reports of sales for year 2008 and/or future years.
- e. Any projections, forecasts, analyses, or reports of sales by product for year 2008 and/or future years.

    1.08 Vendors:
- a. A list of top 10 vendors of supplies, equipment, accessories, or other materials, including a description of types and quantities of each item purchased from such vendors in 2006, 2007, and 2008 year to date.
- b. Total purchases of top three raw materials by product, quantity, dollar amount, and vendor for 2006, 2007, and 2008 year to date.

2.0 Finance/Accounting

    2.01 Full asset listing.

    2.02 Any projects or forecasts for earnings, earnings before interest and tax (EBIT), earnings before interest, taxes, depreciation, and amortization (EBITDA), or earnings per share (EPS) for year 2008 or future years.

2.03 Current 5-year budget and all existing business plans, projections, financial forecasts, and capital budgets.

2.04 Past 5 years and year-to-date financial statements for the Company.

2.05 Copy of auditors' letters to management regarding internal accounting controls and compliance with Foreign Corrupt Practices Act, for 3 years, including auditor inquiry letters and responses thereto.

2.06 Copy of all client-prepared audit schedules.

2.07 Year-end intercompany balance elimination schedule.

2.08 Balance Sheet Review (accountant's schedules where available).

2.09 Profit and loss analysis by month-actual and budget for 3 years: Variance explanations.

2.10 Review accounting system:
    a. Job profitability
    b. Product line profitability
    c. Services profitability

2.11 Copy of accounting manual and chart of accounts.

2.12 Summary income statement by facility for last 3 years.

2.13 Schedule of bank accounts detailing bank, account number, American Bankers Association (ABA) number, account purpose, signatories, signature limits, and restrictions.

2.14 Review cash management system and internal controls.

2.15 Schedule of debt detailing holder, amount, rate, term, payment schedule, security, significant disputed payables, any principal amounts that cannot be repaid at closing.

2.16 Review Letters of Credit, escrow accounts, and all financial assurance instruments.

2.17 Review debt schedules and related liens, if any.

2.18 Required bonds for any licenses or permits relating to trade.

2.19 Tax returns for last 5 years (federal and state).

2.20 Communications between the Company, the Internal Revenue Service (IRS), and state and local taxing authorities, including
    a. Audit and revenue agents' reports (federal, state, and local);
    b. Settlement and consent documents and correspondence;
    c. Agreements waiving statute of limitations or extending time.

2.21 Copies of documents relating to federal, state, or local tax proceedings, deficiencies assessed, or audits commenced.

2.22 Copies of capitalized leases and guarantees.

2.23 Name of person responsible for cash management.

3.0 Risk Management/Insurance

3.01 Copy of insurance policies (Workers' Compensation, Automobile Liability, General Liability, Property, Equipment Floater, Environmental,

Umbrella, Fiduciary, and Fidelity) for each of the last 3 years (including current year) showing the following items:

a. Limits of Liability

b. Deductibles or Self-Insured Retention amounts

c. Annual Premium

d. Are policies subject to audit, retrospective adjustments, or dividend plan?

e. Payrolls and payroll classifications (Workers' Compensation)

f. Identities of additional insureds

3.02 Current loss runs for each line of coverage listed in item #1 above showing both open and closed claims with the type of occurrence, date of accident, amounts paid for property damage, bodily injury, medical indemnity, expense, and the pending reserves.

3.03 The aggregate total of all the losses within the deductibles and/or retentions should agree with the reserves on your company's general ledger; otherwise, please provide a reconciliation.

3.04 List all open or pending lawsuits and claims that are insurance related in excess of $25,000.

3.05 Claims service contracts and arrangements, if any.

3.06 Identify letters of credit and any other security held by any insurance companies regarding your insurance programs.

3.07 All surety performance bonds using the following format: Name of Obligee/Bond #/Bond Amount/Premium/Expiration/Type of Bond/State.

3.08 All certificates of insurance issued for past year.

4.0 Human Resources

4.01 Copy of employee handbooks and policy and procedure manuals.

4.02 Copies of all labor union contracts and collective bargaining arrangements.

4.03 Copies of all employment or consulting agreements and of all confidentiality, noncompete, severance, or indemnity agreements. Written summaries of oral agreements, if any.

4.04 Copy of recent benefit plan billings and end claims run for past 2 years.

4.05 Copy of organizational charts (total company and facility).

4.06 Personnel list with date of hire, title or job description, and compensation.

4.07 Screening, interviewing, and hiring procedures.

4.08 Longevity and turnover history.

4.09 Compensation and performance appraisal policies and procedures.

4.10 Policies regarding bonuses, salary review, severance pay, moving expenses, any tuition programs, loans, advances, vacations, holidays, sick leaves, and other benefits.

4.11 Review any labor unrest situations, arbitration or grievance proceedings, and any ending or threatened labor strikes.

4.12 Review the current status of all unfair labor practices complaints arising during the past 3 years.

4.13 Documents relating to workers' compensation or disability policies, and any material claims with respect thereto.

4.14 Safety and other training manuals.

4.15 Occupational Safety and Health Administration (OSHA) logs.

4.16 Name of any Consolidated Omnibus Budget Reconciliation Act (COBRA) participants and their effective dates.

4.17 Name of any disabled (not actively at work) employee and brief description of his or her disability.

4.18 List any catastrophic claims — name, diagnosis of any participant with annual claims in excess of $20,000 (aggregate) for past 3 years.

4.19 Documents relating to any participation in any active or terminated multiemployer plans including withdrawal liability and funding status.

4.20 Employee Benefit Plans. For *each* funded or unfounded pension, retirement, savings, thrift, or other similar deferred compensation plan, program, policy, or arrangement and *each* welfare and fringe benefit plan, program, policy, or arrangement (including any such plan, program, policy, or arrangement for which the Company continues to have any financial, administrative, or other liability or obligation) furnish the following data, as applicable:

    a. Name of plan, plan sponsor, and each participating employer, along with a description of type of benefit(s) provided and funding medium utilized (e.g., insured, trusteed, combination, etc.).

    b. A copy of the formal plan document and, if applicable, related trust document, including all amendments. A copy of any third-party administrative and record-keeping service contracts. If the plan is not set forth in a formal document, a detailed description should be furnished.

    c. For any multiemployer plan, an estimate of withdrawal liability from such plan (or, for any multiemployer plan from which the Company has withdrawn, provide the amount of withdrawal liability imposed, together with any amount that remains unpaid).

    d. A copy of the summary of plan description (or any other similar plan booklet issued to employees), summary of material modifications (if any), and summary annual report (for the last 3 years) required by Employee Retirement Income Security Act (ERISA).

    e. An estimate of annual contributions to the plan and, for nonqualified plans, a statement of liabilities for deferred compensation plans reflected on the plan sponsor's most recent financial statements.

f. A copy of the last 3 years' most recent annual report/return (Form 5500 series) filed with the IRS together with all attachments, including, but not limited to, any related audited financial statements and reports.

g. A copy of the last 3 years' actuarial valuation reports for defined benefit plans, and summaries of account balances by investment funds for defined contribution plans.

h. A copy of the last 3 years' reports, analyses, and testing reports relating to demonstrating compliance of the plan with all applicable Code and ERISA requirements. A copy of any compliance audit reports with respect to the plan.

i. If the plan is intended to be tax-qualified, a copy of the most recent IRS determination letter, along with a complete copy of the IRS submission package and a copy of any pending IRS submission package.

j. A copy of the last 5 years' PBGC-1 annual premium report.

k. A copy of any Notice of Reportable Event that has been filed with the Pension Benefit Guaranty Corporation.

l. A copy of the most recently available analysis of plan asset investment portfolio issued by plan trustee, custodian, investment manager, or other investment advisor.

m. A financial report describing any special asset dedication arrangements, and any other "special" investment arrangements requiring special attention (e.g., impaired or illiquid investments).

n. A copy of any insurance company funding contracts (e.g., group annuity contracts, life insurance contracts, guaranteed investment contracts, etc.).

o. Information regarding any outstanding issues with the IRS, Department of Labor or Pension Benefit Guaranty Corporation, including copies of all correspondence with any such governmental entities concerning such issues. A copy of any closing agreements, compliance statements, no action/no change letters, or evidence of similar administrative actions taken by a governmental entity resolving any prior issue with respect to the plan.

p. A copy of any applicable insurance policies, third-party administrative services contracts, managed care agreements, or other similar contracts with respect to the plan, including all amendments or endorsements.

q. Name of any applicable insurance carrier, health maintenance organization, managed care provider, and/or third-party claims administrator, along with the identifying policy (or contract) number, name of policy (or contract) holder, policy (or contract) anniversary, and expiration date.

    r. An explanation of the financial arrangement with insurance carrier, health maintenance organization, managed care provider, and third-party claims administrator (i.e., straight premium, minimum premium with retrospective agreement, premium lag, standby letter of credit, etc.).

    s. A copy of the latest available periodic premium (or other similar billing) statement, along with an estimate of the total annual cost of the plan.

5.0 Legal/Corporate

5.01 Copy of certificate or articles of incorporation or other charter documents of the Company.

5.02 Copy of by-laws of the Company.

5.03 Minute books of the Company.

5.04 Stock books and stock transfer ledgers of the Company.

5.05 List of states in which the company currently does business or has done business in the past 5 years, and corresponding evidence of qualification as a foreign corporation, where required.

5.06 List of all trade names of Company and the states in which such trade names are registered.

5.07 List of all names under which the Company and its predecessors have done business in past 5 years and a copy of all assumed name certificates and related filings.

5.08 Copies of joint venture or partnership agreements to which Company is a party.

5.09 Statement of outstanding and treasury shares of common stock, preferred stock, and any other securities of the Company and each subsidiary.

5.10 List of officers and directors with applicable term of appointment, as applicable.

5.11 Copies of any immigration/visa documentation relating to any employee of the Company.

5.12 List of stockholders of the Company owning 1% or more of any class of issued and outstanding stock in the Company and percentage owned.

5.13 List of all entities affiliated with the Company.

5.14 Copies of all stock option agreements, stock option plans and warrants, any agreements, written or oral, to give or sell an interest in the Company.

5.15 Copies of all stockholder agreements and any and all other agreements with respect to securities of the Company or its subsidiaries or giving any shareholders or management any rights in the event of an acquisition or merger.

5.16   Copies of any agreement restricting transfer of the Company's capital stock or assets.

5.17   Copies of agreements granting to the Company any right of first refusal to acquire any business or assets, or pursuant to which the Company has granted any such rights.

5.18   Copies of registration rights or preemptive rights agreements.

5.19   List of all leases of personal property involving annual expenditures in excess of $10,000 (aggregate) to which the Company is a party.

5.20   Schedule of outstanding debt as of May 1, 2004, and copies of all loan agreements, debt instruments, liens, and other financing instruments and all related material documentation.

5.21   Copies of all mortgages, liens, pledges, security interests, zoning restrictions, or other encumbrances to which any personal property of the Company is subject and any related material documentation.

5.22   List any consignment purchase arrangements with copies of documentation.

5.23   All appraisals of any material property of the Company.

5.24   Copies of all capitalized leases.

5.25   Copies of all guarantees and other contingent obligations.

5.26   Copies of any power of attorney granted to any person to act on behalf of the Company.

5.27   Copies of all confidentiality, noncompetition, or similar agreements entered into by Company employees or other third parties.

5.28   Licensing agreements, trade secret agreements, or merchandising agreements.

5.29   Form of warranty agreements or service warranties of the Company.

5.30   Copies of all standard forms, including without limitation, terms and conditions of sale, sales orders, purchase orders, acknowledgments, and invoices.

5.31   All agreements with service vendors, suppliers, and manufacturers, which are for 12 months or longer and cannot be terminated with less than 30 days notice without penalty or have an aggregate value in excess of $25,000.

5.32   All material agreements and arrangements with customers, distributors, dealers, or sales agents, which are for 12 months or longer and cannot be terminated with less than 30 days notice without penalty or have an aggregate value in excess of $25,000.

5.33   Copies of all franchise agreements.

5.34   Copies of all agreements involving the payment of commissions.

5.35   List all trade or industry associations of which the Company is a member. Copies of any contracts relating to the Company's membership in trade or industry associations.

5.36 Copies of any contracts restricting the ability of the Company to compete in any line of business with any person or entity, restricting the Company from operating in any geographical area, committing the Company to continue in any line of business, or granting a preferential right of purchase.

5.37 Copies of any trust agreements or other documents pursuant to which any shares of capital stock of the Company or any of its subsidiaries is held in a fiduciary capacity.

5.38 List of all employee contracts (including any terms or at-will arrangements).

5.39 Copies of any government contracts (federal, municipal, and state).

5.40 Copies of all contracts, agreements, commitments, or understandings pursuant to which the Company has assumed or agreed to be responsible for or provided indemnification against uninsured liabilities to third parties or liabilities for consequential damages.

5.41 List of directorships and other significant relationships held by directors or senior management of the Company with unaffiliated entities.

5.42 List of all current material transactions between Company and officers, directors, stockholders, employees, or equity holders of the Company, including indebtedness or other obligations owed to the Company, or assets used by the Company and owned by a Company stockholder or employee and documents in support of such transactions.

5.43 All other agreements pursuant to which the Company has acquired securities or has issued or may be obligated to issue securities.

5.44 All private placement memoranda, prospectuses, or other documentation relating to an offering of securities by Company.

5.45 All reports to, documents filed with, and correspondence with any state or federal securities commission.

5.46 Copies of all agreements and plans entered into by the Company relating to the acquisition or sale of a business.

5.47 Governmental permits, licenses, and approvals held by the Company or its subsidiaries or their employees.

5.48 All correspondence, reports, and notices relating to laws and regulations administered by any governmental agency for the past 5 years.

5.49 Copies of material filings with governmental agencies.

5.50 Contracts containing termination or other provisions triggered by a change of control or disposition of assets of the Company and contracts requiring the consent of any third party in the event of a sale of the Company or of assets of the Company.

5.51 Copies of all information and material received in connection with due diligence requests made by other third parties.

5.52 Copies of any contracts that impose confidentiality or nondisclosure obligation on the Company.

6.0 Legal/Real Estate

6.01   List of real estate owned, leased, or used by the Company, stating whether owned, leased (whether as lessor or lessee), or otherwise used. Furnish copies of deeds, leases appurtenant easements, and licenses, as applicable.

6.02   Copies of all notes, mortgages, liens, pledges, security interests, restrictions (zoning and otherwise), easements, licenses, and other encumbrances to which any real or personal property of the Company is subject, and any related material documentation.

6.03   Copies of title insurance policies for all real property, whether owned or leased.

6.04   Copies of all surveys, site plans, architectural drawings, plans and specifications, certificates of occupancy, environmental reports, warranties, zoning and rezoning applications and approvals, variances and other governmental applications and approvals, and any other documentation relevant to any real property of the Company.

6.05   Copies of all contracts and letters of intent for the purchase, sale, or lease of any real property.

7.0 Legal/Litigation

7.01   List and brief description of all outstanding judgments, decrees, or orders to which the Company is subject or is a party.

7.02   Copy of last 3 years' response to auditors' request for information about litigation and or contingent liabilities of the Company.

7.03   Summaries regarding all threatened, pending, and concluded litigation and arbitration proceedings to which the Company, its officers, or its directors is or was a party since January 1, 2008, containing the following information: parties, description of claim or threatened claim, nature of proceeding, date and method commenced, amount of damages or other relief sought, and, if applicable, paid or granted.

7.04   To the extent available, summaries or memoranda regarding all governmental and administration investigations, proceedings, and arbitrations, whether pending, threatened, or concluded since January 1, 2008.

7.05   Opinions or other assessments (other than audit response letters) of the Company's counsel as to any pending or threatened litigation.

8.0 Legal/Environmental

As used with this request, "Company facility" shall mean any and all properties at any time owned or operated (including leased) by Company, its subsidiaries, affiliates, or their respective predecessors in interest.

A. General Documents

8.01   A list of all Company and Company facility properties and copies of documents imposing restrictions, limitations, or conditions on the use of these properties, including without limitation, leases, deeds, recording certificates, trusts, liens, leases, easements, and zoning notices or variances.

8.02   Copies of title insurance policies for all properties previously owned by Company, or to be owned by Company on or before proposed closing date.

8.03   A list of and copies of all environmental permits held or previously held by Company or any Company facility, including but not limited to those for air emissions, wastewater discharges, and solid and hazardous waste disposal.

8.04   Any geological and hydrogeological studies, maps, surveys, photographs, and other documents related to any Company facility.

8.05   Any aerial photos of each Company facility.

8.06   A drawing showing the layout of each Company facility.

8.07   All environmental audits, facility inspections, or other reports prepared by outside consultants or Company or Company facility personnel relating to environmental or health and safety matters at any Company facility, regardless of the date of the report.

8.08   Any and all health and safety or loss prevention reports of any Company facilities prepared by or for benefit of insurance companies.

8.09   A copy of all Company facility document retention policies, if any.

8.10   A list of the executives, officers, and other personnel of Company or its facilities who have been primarily responsible for the Company facilities' compliance with federal, state, and local environmental statutes, regulations, ordinances, rules, and permits.

8.11   A list of any federal, state, or local environmental enforcement authority requirement or anticipated requirement of which Company or any of its facilities knows may require it to expend $10,000 or more to achieve compliance, or which will effect the ability of any Company facility to produce, market, distribute, transport, or sell products currently produced at any Company facility.

8.12   A copy of all environmental compliance plans required of or used by any Company facility, including, without limitation, any Spill Prevention Control and Countermeasure (SPCC) plans and emergency preparedness plans.

8.13   The results of any radon assessment effort conducted at any Company facility.

8.14   All insurance policies and any agreement, waiver, or indemnification relating to actual or potential environmental claims against Company or any Company facility and documents related thereto.

8.15 A list of all chemical substances used by the Company facilities in their manufacturing processes, or present in products, which are considered by any governmental agency to pose a risk to human health.

8.16 A list of any violations of environmental statutes, regulations, ordinances, or permits that have been committed by or at Company or at any Company facility whether or not reported to governmental authority.

8.17 All material safety data sheets (MSDSs) for each Company facility.

8.18 A description of any testing program for health or environmental effects implemented at any Company facility.

8.19 All correspondence between any units of government (federal, state, and local) responsible for the enforcement of environmental statutes, regulations, rules, or ordinances and Company or any of its facilities including, without limitation, all notifications, certifications, reports, notices, applications, manifests, and submissions filed by Company or its facilities pursuant to the Comprehensive Environmental Response, Compensation and Liability Act (CERCLA), as amended, the Resource Conservation and Recovery Act (RCRA), as amended, the Federal Water Pollution Control Act, as amended, the Toxic Substance Control Act (TSCA), as amended, the Emergency Planning and Community Right to Know Act (EPCRA), the Federal Insecticide, Fungicide and Rodenticide Act (FIFRA), as amended, or other similar state statutes including, without limitation, any state statutes enacted pursuant to or under the authority of the above federal laws.

8.20 All Company or Company facility cost estimates or budgets relating to future capital or operating expenditures for environmental matters.

8.21 All contracts imposing responsibility on Company or any Company facility for accrued or contingent environmental liabilities, claims, or other expenditures.

B. Judicial and Administrative Actions

8.22 A list and description of any and all lawsuits and administrative or other proceedings in which Company or any Company facility are or have been involved, relating to environmental matters including, without limitation, those concerning exposure to hazardous materials, and all documents relating thereto.

8.23 A list of each and every consent decree, administrative order, or compliance schedule, or any other agreement or informal understanding with any governmental authority that any Company facility is subject to concerning compliance with environmental statutes, regulations, ordinances, rules or permits, and copies thereof.

8.24 A list and brief description of any complaints, oral or written, to any governmental authority or to other party, including any Company facility, from any private party, including adjacent landowners, regarding any Company facility and copies of any memoranda, reports, studies, or correspondence related thereto.

8.25 All pleadings and other papers filed in any lawsuit or administrative proceeding to which Company or any of its facilities is, or has been, a party relating to any environmental, health, or safety matter.

C. CERCLA

8.26 Any correspondence between any Company facility and any other party including the United States or any state involving possible, threatened, or actual claims relating to the environment or relating to the use, generation, transportation, or disposal of chemicals, hazardous wastes, hazardous substances, or hazardous materials at any Company facility, including, without limitation, any notice letters, information requests, or demands concerning a Company facility's status as a Potentially Responsible Party (PRP), and all documents related thereto.

8.27 Documents that pertain to any Company facility's relationship to any site listed either on the CERCLA National Priorities List (NPL) or on a comparable state list of hazardous contamination sites — including HRS scoring, and inclusion on the CERCLIS list of potential Superfund sites.

8.28 A list of each person, firm, or other entity that has transported waste of any kind from each of the Company facilities during the existence of that facility and documents related thereto.

8.29 A list of prior owners or operators of each of the Company facilities.

8.30 A brief description of how the Company facilities were used or operated by any prior owners or operators.

8.31 A list and description of the location quantity and chemical composition of any and all solid or hazardous wastes, hazardous substances, or hazardous materials, disposed of by, or for, any Company facility since that facility's commencement of business and on property the Company does not own.

8.32 A list of the location, quantity, and chemical composition of all solid or hazardous wastes, hazardous substances, or hazardous materials disposed of at any Company facility, including any disposal by the Company facility, its lessees or sublessees, or any other party.

8.33 A list of all contracts each Company facility has entered into regarding the disposal or other handling of solid or hazardous waste, hazardous substances, or hazardous materials.

D. RCRA

8.34 Any permit applications or permits or notices (including interim status) for the operation of any hazardous waste treatment, storage, or disposal unit at any of the Company facilities and any monitoring or inspection reports or memoranda, contingency plans, annual reports, and financial responsibility documents relating to those permits.

8.35　All manifests, bills of lading, contracts, and other documents relating to the transportation or disposal of any solid or hazardous wastes generated by each Company facility dating back to the earliest such records maintained by Company or its facilities.

8.36　A list and description of all manifests, bills of lading, contracts, and other documents relating to any hazardous or solid waste, hazardous substance, or hazardous material not generated by any Company facility but which Company or the Company facility transported or arranged for the disposal of at any location.

8.37　A description of each waste stream generated at each of the Company facilities and analytical results for each waste stream described.

8.38　Any and all solid waste disposal permits currently or previously held by each Company facility and any monitoring or inspection reports or memoranda relating to those permits.

8.39　A list of all underground storage tanks currently or previously located on any Company facility, including a description of the material stored in those tanks at any period during their lifetime.

8.40　All Company facility notices to federal, state, or local environmental enforcement agencies advising of the existence, removal, or upgrading of underground storage tanks located at the Company facilities.

8.41　All memoranda, correspondence, or reports relating to any underground storage tanks at the Company facilities.

8.42　If underground storage tanks have been removed or tightness tested at any Company facility, all memoranda, correspondence, reports, and photographs documenting or otherwise commenting on the removal or tightness testing, and any leak or contamination assessment conducted in connection with the removal or tightness testing.

E. TSCA

8.43　A list of all raw materials, chemicals, intermediates, or products used, stored, or manufactured at any Company facility which are subject to regulation under TSCA, FIFRA, the Federal Food, Drug and Cosmetic Act, or other federal, state, or local laws, or foreign premanufacturing or premarketing laws imposing requirements on the use, storage, or manufacturing of such raw materials, chemicals, intermediates, or products, and documents relating thereto.

8.44　Documents relating to the installation, maintenance, removal, or notification of polychlorinated biphenyl (PCB)–containing transformers and/or any other PCB-containing electrical equipment located at any time at any Company facility, and any contamination resulting therefrom.

F. Asbestos

8.45 Records regarding the survey or assessment existence, abatement, encapsulation, and/or removal of asbestos at any of the Company facilities, including reports and analysis results.

8.46 Any blueprints or specifications showing building materials used at the Company facilities at the time of original construction and at the time of each subsequent addition or modification.

8.47 All violation or spill reports filed by Company or any Company facility under the Clean Water Act (CWA), as amended, or similar state laws, including, without limitation, any under Section 311 of the CWA or state law counterpart.

8.48 National Pollutant Discharge Elimination System (NPDES) permits and related documents, currently or previously held by each Company facility and monitoring reports relating to those permits.

8.49 Discharge monitoring reports (DMRs) and any other reports or similar documents submitted by Company or any Company facility to any federal, state, or local governmental agency.

8.50 Any agreements or permits with local sewer authorities for any Company facility dischargers to any city or county sewer systems, and any monitoring reports relating to such discharges.

8.51 Documents concerning the compliance status of any Company facility under the Clean Water Act and/or similar state laws.

G. Clean Air Act (CAA)

8.52 All air quality/air emission permits/applications for such permits currently or previously held by each Company facility and monitoring reports relating to such permits.

8.53 Documents concerning the compliance status of any Company facility under the CAA and/or similar state laws.

H. OSHA

8.54 A copy of each Company facility Hazard Communication Program.

8.55 Any and all documents relating to Federal Occupational Safety and Health Act (OSHA) inspections at the Company facilities.

8.56 All workers' compensation claim records for each Company facility for the last 5 years.

8.57 Reports, logs, or other documents of occupational injuries or illnesses sustained (or allegedly sustained) at any Company facility by Company employees or by employees of any other employer.

8.58 A description and copy of any program utilized at Company facilities for estimating or measuring the occupational exposure (i.e., personal monitoring data) of its employees to chemicals (such as those listed in 29 C.F.R. § 1910.1000), or physical stresses such as noise or radiation.

8.59 A list of regulated carcinogens (29 C.F.R. § 1910.1001 to § 1910.1045, such as asbestos and vinyl chloride) that have been or are currently being used in any Company facility process.

8.60 Documents pertaining to compliance status of any Company facility under OSHA, and/or similar state law, including, but not limited to, employee complaints, OSHA citations, abatement letters, variances, and "no citation but concern" letters.

I. Community Right to Know

8.61 All Emergency Preparedness and Community Right to Know Act (EPCRA) Tier 1 and Tier 2 reports, or similar reports required under state laws, submitted to local and state emergency planning commissions or other entities by any Company facility.

8.62 All EPCRA EPA Form R annual toxic emission inventory forms submitted to EPA by any Company facility.

8.63 All notifications submitted by Company or any of its facilities to EPA under EPCRA Section 302 and Section 304 or similar state laws.

8.64 Any community relations plans prepared by any Company facility with respect to federal, state, or local law.

8.65 All written complaints concerning any Company facility's compliance with EPCRA requirements and/or similar state or local statutes, rules, or ordinances.

J. Petroleum Product Use and Storage

8.66 A description of the use and storage (i.e., aboveground tank or underground tank) of petroleum products, including but not limited to fuel oil, gasoline, and solvents, at each Company facility.

8.67 A description of any spills, leaks, or releases of petroleum products at any Company facility whether or not reported to federal, state, or local authorities.

8.68 Any Company or Company facility written reports or confirmations of spills, leaks, or releases of any petroleum product at or from Company facility.

9.0 Tax

A. General

9.01 Provide organizational charts of the Company for last 3 years.

9.02 Provide a list of all states in which the Company and each of its subsidiaries is domiciled or qualified to do business.

9.03 Provide a list of the states in which the Company files any income, franchise, sales and use, or property tax returns.

9.04 Provide an analysis of the Company's sales of finished product by state.

9.05 Provide copies of all tax sharing agreements by which any entity of the Company is a party.

9.06   Provide an organization chart showing relationship of the Company's tax department personnel.

9.07   Describe any tax-related matters that are handled outside of the Company.

9.08   Provide copies of the records of the tax basis of subsidiaries, accumulated earnings and profits and base period research and development expenditures and gross receipts.

B. Sales and Use/Property

9.09   Provide copies of property tax returns for last 3 years for each of the Company's locations.

9.10   Provide a listing of any Company employees who do not reside in a state in which the Company files income or franchise tax returns and the activities of any such employee.

9.11   Provide a listing of agents or individual contractors who provide services to the Company in states in which the Company does not file income or franchise tax returns.

9.12   Provide copies of state employment tax filings for last 3 years.

9.13   Provide copies of all sales tax registration filings.

9.14   Provide a listing of all interests in general or limited partnerships or limited liability companies owned by the Company.

9.15   Provide a listing of all minority interests or shareholdings in corporations.

9.16   Provide a listing of all filings in "Geoffrey" states.

9.17   Provide a listing of business license filings.

9.18   Provide an analysis with accompanying documentation of the sales and use tax history of the Company for the last 3 years.

9.19   Make available all audit files with respect to sales and use tax returns for last 3 years.

9.20   Provide a listing of all sales and use tax refund claims.

9.21   Provide a listing of any state in which open statute waivers (sales and use taxes) have been granted and a copy of such waivers.

9.22   Provide copies of any direct pay permits or any other special filing agreements.

9.23   List and describe all sales and purchases that are made over the Internet.

9.24   Describe the procedure by which any appropriate sales and use taxes are collected and remitted for Internet sales and purchases.

9.25   Provide an explanation as to how the Company records transactions that take place over the Internet.

9.26   Provide all state sales and use tax correspondence, including any rulings, for the last 3 years.

9.27   Provide an analysis of all unused sales and use tax credits available to the Company.

9.28 Provide an analysis and documentation of any federal net operating loss carryover, capital loss carryover, and/or credit carryovers.

9.29 Provide an explanation as to how the Company maintains sales and use tax exemption and resale certificates.

C. Federal/State; Income/Franchise Tax

9.30 Provide copies of federal income tax returns for all open years and, in any event, for the last 5 years.

9.31 Provide detailed work papers of book/tax differences (Schedule M-1) for the last 5 years.

9.32 Provide copies of all state income or franchise tax returns for all open years and, in any event, for the last 5 years.

9.33 Provide copies of all supporting schedules and work papers for computation of property, payroll, and sales/receipts factors for apportionment formulas.

9.34 Provide an analysis of sales throwback information.

9.35 Provide a listing of all income/franchise tax liabilities by state and/or local jurisdiction.

9.36 Provide an analysis of any net operating loss and credit carryforward by state.

9.37 Provide an analysis of separate accounting policies used in any state.

9.38 Provide a list of any open income or franchise tax audits, including federal, state, or local jurisdictions. Include identification of tax jurisdiction, audit periods involved, issues involved, status, and any and all interest or penalty amounts.

9.39 Provide a list of all open federal, state, or local income or franchise tax refund claims.

9.40 Provide copies of all federal, state, or local jurisdiction waivers of the statute of limitations.

9.41 Provide copies of income or franchise state tax calendars.

9.42 Provide a listing of the states in which the Company files a unitary tax return.

9.43 With respect to such unitary returns, provide a list of companies included in each unitary group.

9.44 With respect to such unitary returns, provide a list of the states that mandate worldwide filing.

9.45 Provide copies of federal and state Private Letter Rulings.

9.46 Provide a list of any existing deferred intercompany transactions, as defined under the federal consolidated return provisions.

9.47 Provide an analysis of any current federal, state, or local jurisdiction income or franchise tax audits, appeals, and refund claims.

9.48 Provide any communications between the IRS or state or local taxing authorities with respect to open audit issues, including any Revenue Agent's Report.

9.49 Provide documentation of the reporting of all federal adjustments to the appropriate state.

9.50 List any expenditures related to prior acquisitions that were treated as deductible expenses.

9.51 Provide copies of any federal, state, or local jurisdiction's Revenue Agent's Report, settlement, or consent documents for the last 3 years.

9.52 Provide a list of all penalties imposed on the Company by any taxing jurisdiction within the last 3 years.

9.53 Provide copies of all documentation relating to any federal, state, or local tax proceedings, deficiencies, assessments, or audits currently open.

9.54 Provide a list of all states in which fee-in-lieu or similar arrangements have been negotiated with state authorities regarding property tax matters, including copies of such arrangements.

9.55 Provide copies of all property tax protests for the last 3 years.

9.56 Provide copies of all documentation of tax or economic incentives received by or available to the Company.

D. Financial Reporting

9.57 Provide a copy of the accrual review work papers, including any reserve analysis.

9.58 Provide copies of cumulative temporary difference work papers including reconciliation of book and tax basis of assets and liabilities.

9.59 Provide a detailed analysis of any amounts deemed "permanently reinvested" under generally accepted accounting principles (GAAP).

9.60 Provide a detailed reconciliation of the Company's effective tax rate for the past 3 years.

E. Payroll Taxes

9.61 Provide copies of all 941s and 940s for the past 2 years.

9.62 Provide documentation that all withheld taxes were deposited in a timely manner for the past 3 years.

9.63 Provide an analysis of all independent contractor relationships.

F. Unclaimed Property

9.64 Provide copies of reports filed with any state in the last 3 years.

G. Foreign Matters

9.65 Provide copies of all reports filed regarding foreign bank accounts.

9.66 Provide copies of any governmental authority's review of the Company's transfer pricing policies.

9.67 Provide a list of expatriates and copies of the Company's expatriate equalization policy.

9.68 Provide a list of amounts of all unremitted earnings of the Company's foreign entities.

9.69 Provide copies of 1120-FSC.

10.0 Intellectual Property

10.01 List of directors, officers, employees, and third persons, formerly and presently employed, whose assignment, contract, job duty, or actual performance involves the invention, creation, authorship, development, exploitation, protection, or litigation of intellectual property, including any offshore personnel.

10.02 List of directors, officers, employees, and/or third persons who will be available to provide documents and information during the due diligence period, including acquisition strategy processes (ASPs) and escrow entities.

10.03 List of the countries and territories worldwide ("Jurisdictions") in which the Company owns intellectual property and a description of the type of intellectual property owned.

10.04 List and copies of all loan and/or financing agreements and all other documents granting Company intellectual property as collateral, security, or cap contribution.

10.05 List and copies of all issued, pending, and abandoned patents in all Jurisdictions, including any reissues, continuations, continuations-in-part, revisions, extensions, and reexaminations thereof ("Patents"), and a list and description of all discoveries, inventions, concepts, ideas, and improvements the Company believes may be patentable or otherwise protectable, or which it considers proprietary ("Inventions").

10.06 The entire "file wrapper" (prosecution history) of all Patents, including official correspondence (office actions, amendments, etc.) to and from, and notes of telephone conversations with, any patent authority regarding such patents.

10.07 List and copies of all invention disclosures received by Company from employees and from third parties, including employee invention disclosures and unsolicited third-party invention disclosures.

10.08 Description and copies of invention disclosure policies and forms.

10.09 List and copies of validity, patentability, and infringement searches and opinions pertaining to Company's Patents and Inventions, or to third-party Patents and Inventions, which pertain to Company's business.

10.10 List and copies of validity, patentability, and infringement searches and opinions requested by Company pertaining to any third-party Patents and Inventions and otherwise pertaining to the business.

10.11 List of all publications and public speeches by employees and third parties on behalf of the Company; including employee or third-party name(s), date, location, and technical/intellectual property subject of publication/speech; and copies of each.

10.12 List and copies of all agreements granting Company rights under third-party Patents and/or Inventions; including copies of the subject Patent(s) and/or Invention(s), and the date of such agreement(s).

10.13 List and copies of all agreements granting third parties rights under Company's Patent(s) and/or Invention(s); including copies of the subject Patent(s) and/or Invention(s), and the date of such agreement(s).

10.14 All documents pertaining to disputes involving Company and/or third-party Patents and/or Inventions that pertain to the business, including the identification of the Patent(s) and/or Inventions involved, plaintiff party(ies), adverse party(ies), dates, situs, and disposition or resolution of dispute.

10.15 List and copies of all trademarks and service marks (including logos, designs, and slogans), (collectively referred to as "Mark(s)") and trade names owned, used, or planned to be owned or used by Company in all jurisdictions, and all registrations and applications therefor; the information to include a description of the Mark, the jurisdiction, the application and/or registration numbers, the date(s) of application and registration, the international and local classes (as applicable), and descriptions of the goods and/or services provided under such Marks.

10.16 Copies of promotional and marketing materials, including all print and audiovisual advertisements, brochures, Internet, intranet, and extranet Web sites, and other marketing materials and promotional documents used by Company.

10.17 Copies of all Mark registrations, validity, and/or infringement searches opinions obtained by Company in connection with third-party Marks and trade names that relate to the business.

10.18 Copies of all Mark registrations, validity, and/or infringement searches opinions requested by Company pertaining to Company Marks and trade names or otherwise pertaining to the business.

10.19 Evidence of date of first use and of continuous use of all Marks and trade names, and, if applicable, dates of lapse in use of Mark and explanation for such lapse.

10.20 List and copies of all Agreements granting Company rights under third-party Marks and trade names; information regarding each, including specification of subject Mark(s) or trade name(s), and date of such agreement(s).

10.21 List and copies of all agreements granting third parties rights under Company's Mark(s) and/or trade name(s); information regarding each, including specification of subject Mark(s) and/or trade name(s), and date of such agreement(s).

10.22 All documents pertaining to disputes involving Company or third-party Mark(s) and trade names that pertain to the business, including the identification of the Mark(s) and/or trade name(s) involved, plaintiff party(ies), adverse party(ies), dates, situs, and disposition or resolution of dispute.

10.23 List of all domain names, owned, used, and planned to be owned or used by Company in each jurisdiction, and a list of all registrations and applications therfor; and including information, in applicable, to any top-level, secondary, and further higher domains to which the domain name(s) relate(s), date(s) of application, and registration.

10.24 Copies of promotional and marketing material, referencing each such domain name. Copies of all domain name registrability, validity, and/or infringement opinions pertaining to Company's domain name(s).

10.25 Copies of all domain name registrability, validity, and/or infringement opinions requested by Company pertaining to third-party domain names.

10.26 Evidence of date of first use and of continuous use of each domain name(s) and, if applicable, dates of lapse in use of domain name(s) and explanation for such lapse.

10.27 All documents pertaining to the domain name registration authority for each such domain name.

10.28 List and copies of all agreements granting Company rights under third-party domain names, and information regarding each, including specification of subject domain name, and date of such agreement(s).

10.29 List and copies of all agreements granting third party(ies) rights under Company's domain names; information regarding each, including specification of subject domain name, and date of such agreement(s).

10.30 All documents pertaining to disputes involving Company and/or third-party domain names, including domain name involved, plaintiff party(ies), adverse party(ies), dates, situs, and disposition and/or resolution of dispute.

10.31 List, description, and copies of all works of authorship (including, without limitation, literary, audio, audiovisual, pictorial, and musical works, and including software, whether on premises, in escrow, off-site, or offshore and Internet, intranet, and extranet Web site content), which is owned, used, or planned to be owned or used by Company; and a list of all copyright registrations and applications for copyright registration.

10.32 List, description, and copies of all derivative works (including modifications, translations, and adaptations), and compilations and collections of the works of authorship specified above.

10.33 List, description, and copies of all prior software and other works of authorship on which all such works specified above are based.

10.34 Copies of all work of registrability, validity, and/or infringement opinions pertaining to Company's software and other works or authorship.

10.35 Copies of all registrability, validity, and/or infringement opinions requested by Company pertaining to third-party software and other works of authorship.

10.36 List and copies of all agreements granting Company rights under third-party software and other works of authorship, information regarding each, including specification of subject work(s) of authorship, and date of such agreement(s).

10.37 List and copies of all agreements granting third party(ies) rights under Company's software and other works of authorship; information regarding each, including specification of subject software and other work(s) of authorship, and date of such agreement(s).

10.38 All documents pertaining to disputes involving Company and/or third-party software and other work(s) of authorship, including software and other works of authorship involved, plaintiff party(ies), adverse party(ies), dates, situs, and disposition and/or resolution of dispute.

10.39 List, description, and copies of all databases (table, index, stored procedure, triggers, etc.) and files of types (including, without limitation, ASP, js, Java, class, html, jpg, gif, etc.); all registrations and applications therefor owned, used, or planned to be owned or used by Company; the information to include a description of the database, the author(s), date of creation of database, and date and country of first publication of the database.

10.40 List, description, and copies of all derivatives databases (including modifications, translations, adaptations), and compilations and collections of the databases specified above.

10.41 List, description, and copies of all prior databases on which any such databases are based.

10.42 Copies of all registrability, validity, and/or infringement opinions pertaining to Company's databases.

10.43 Copies of all registrability, validity, and/or infringement opinions requested by Company pertaining to third-party database(s).

10.44 List and copies of all agreements pertaining to Company's exploitation of third-party data and/or databases; information regarding each, including specification of subject data and/or database(s), and date of such agreement(s).

10.45 List and copies of all agreements pertaining to third-party ownership or exploitation of Company's data and/or databases; information regarding each, including specification of subject data and/or databases, and date of such agreement(s).

10.46 All documents pertaining to disputes involving Company or third-party data and/or databases, including data and/or databases involved, plaintiff party(ies), adverse party(ies), dates, situs, and disposition and/or resolution of dispute.

10.47 Description and copies of technical drawings, specifications, and other documents describing trade secrets and proprietary information that is owned by Company, and which is identified by Company as being material, or planned to be material, to the conduct of the business.

10.48 Description of and copies of all documents pertaining to Company policies and procedures regarding confidentiality protection of trade secrets (nondisclosure documents, access to facility policies, facility and information system security measures).

10.49 Copies of all registrability, validity, and/or infringement opinions pertaining to Company's trade secret(s).

10.50 Copies of all registrability, validity, and/or infringement opinions requested by Company pertaining to third-party trade secret(s).

10.51 Copies of all secrecy, confidentiality, and nondisclosure agreements between Company and third parties pertaining to Company trade secrets and/or third-party trade secrets.

10.52 List and copies of all agreements granting Company rights under third-party trade secret(s) and/or proprietary information, including the description or specification of the subject trade secret(s), and the date of such agreement(s).

10.53 List and copies of all agreements granting third party(ies) rights under Company's trade secret(s), including the description or specification of the subject trade secret(s), and the date of such agreement(s).

10.54 All documents pertaining to disputes involving Company and/or third-party trade secrets, including trade secret(s) involved, plaintiff party(ies), adverse party(ies), dates, situs, and disposition and/or resolution of dispute.

10.55 Any batch processing scheduled for interfacing suppliers feedback or integrating with accounting system.

Appendix F

Due Diligence Checklist for Mergers and Acquisitions — IT

I. Application architecture
   a. Overview of the entire application environment, including physical and logical diagrams for all environments (production, preproduction, disaster recovery, etc.)
   b. List of all purchased and licensed software, including version number; describe the functions of the software
   c. List of all languages and tools used in the environment
   d. Documentation of the coding standards and practices used in the development of software
   e. Documentation of all databases used

II. Platforms
   a. Types and versions of operating systems
   b. List of servers and purpose of each server
   c. Hardware configuration of each server, including model numbers, processor speed, memory, and disk space
   d. Documentation for supporting software such as (but not limited to) anti-virus software, monitoring tools (including network), backup software, and deployment software used on the servers

  e. A list and description of any security tools used, such as (but not limited to) logging tools, event management tools, or vulnerability assessment

  f. For any commercial Web sites used, description of the scaling model, which includes number of concurrent users supported and number of users supported

  g. Documentation on the use of any load balancing products

  h. Description of any specific modules or links relating to regulations or any other rules or standards of external controlling bodies that influence the structure or processing of the system

III. Operational components

  a. Documentation of the organization's disaster recovery capability (not merely the plan) — include the results from the last disaster recovery plan test

  b. Documentation of backup procedures

  c. Documentation of deployment processes and procedures

  d. Listing of all monitoring tools used (e.g., CA Unicenter, Opsware)

  e. Documentation of operational direction and 1- to 3-year plans (e.g., virtualization of servers)

IV. Governance capabilities

  a. Description of change management procedures

  b. Diagrams and documentation on the systems development life-cycle process

  c. Description of unit, user acceptance, and regression testing procedures

  d. Description of overall quality assurance process

V. Skill levels of staff

  a. For each enterprise resource planning (ERP) listing of number of individuals with application expertise in key areas, such as general ledger, inventory, sales, and so forth

  b. Number of individuals with expertise in database administration

  c. Numbers of help desk staff with 1 to 3, 3 to 5, and more than 5 years of experience

  d. Numbers of infrastructure staff with experience in networking, server administration, and operating systems (Solaris, Unix, Windows, etc.)

  e. Summary of IT-related certifications (Cisco Certified Internetworking Expert [CCIE], etc.)

VI. Security

  a. Listing and description of any security tools used

  b. Documentation of security models for internal, external, and ad hoc (contractor/temp) access to corporate information

  c. Description of how duties are segregated within the user and IT groups

  d. Description of firewalls, intrusion detection, and other means of preventing unauthorized access from external parties

e. Listing of logs, audit trails, or other similar records for the last 6 months, showing
   i. Number of known security breaches
   ii. Incidents of unscheduled downtime and the reasons and duration of each such incident
   iii. Incidents reported by customers

Appendix G

Example IT Policies and Direction for "XYZ Corp"

IT Architecture

Policy and Direction

a. Software, hardware, and configurations of IT systems are expected to conform to standards established by corporate IT.

b. Standards are set in order to meet the following objectives for computer systems: reliability; ability for enterprise-wide exchange of data; reasonable cost and opportunity for volume discounts; security; high parts availability; and ease of maintenance.

c. Corporate IT will govern the software, hardware, and protocols that have access to the network.

d. Standards are established from a "middle of the road" technology perspective. Generally, XYZ CORP has no business reason to bear the cost of truly leading-edge technology. However, XYZ CORP will maintain currency in technology (avoid obsolescence and related risks) and continually evaluate alternatives to ensure business needs are met.

e. Newly acquired business entities may require some time to integrate with XYZ CORP's existing centralized infrastructure. However, all business units are expected to eventually conform to XYZ CORP's overall architecture. "Islands of computing" are expensive to maintain and often create both processing errors and efficiency bottlenecks.

Technological Direction

XYZ CORP is committed to technology standardization for both infrastructure and applications. Common platforms and standards-based architectures have been repeatedly shown to reduce the total cost of providing IT to the organization. However, to quote a well-known television commercial, "wait, there's more!" Common architectures enable enterprise-wide analysis of trends, customer purchase patterns, exceptions, and other analytics that are otherwise impossible. The ability to easily exchange data between different units of XYZ CORP is a strategic direction that will provide superior information for both operations and management decision making. XYZ CORP is also moving toward a SOA (service-oriented architecture) direction, although specific timetables have not yet been developed.

Infrastructure

It was only in the 18th century that newly constructed English roads began to exceed the quality of their ancient Roman counterparts. The secret to the Roman roads was a solid and carefully planned bedrock — infrastructure in today's terminology. Similarly, XYZ CORP has a serious commitment to sound technology infrastructure. The hardware, software, and design features support an expanding, centralized computing network. The following are directions and key expectations for infrastructure deployment over the next 12 to 36 months:

- Standardize hardware
  - Windows (HP) servers
  - Unix (Sun) servers
  - Blade server technology at the Dallas hot site
- Reduce reliance on human monitoring and intervention
  - Lights out data center — Seabrook
  - Lights out data centers — remotes
  - Ability to remotely reboot and control devices
  - Improved environmental monitoring
- Substitute bandwidth for server infrastructure, where possible
- Standardize desktop
  - Laptops (light and standard)
  - Desktops (light and standard)
  - Workstations
  - Standard build — master image
- Enhance remote access
  - Virtual private network (VPN) as basic communication path, using broadband and Citrix portal

- Improve imaging
  - Use of Image1 as a standard with a more "knowledge management"-oriented architecture
  - Enhanced unified messaging, fax server, and other business tools (future development)
- Better quantification of service levels to business units
  - Improve telecommunications delivery via service-level agreements with new vendor(s) selected as a result of the telecom request for proposal (RFP)
  - Develop a practical service-level agreement (SLA) format for internal reporting to business units
- Expand the Seabrook NOC (network operating center) monitoring hours and capability
  - Move toward 24/7 full scope monitoring of operations
  - Extend the number of computing elements covered by the Computer Associates tool (CA Unicenter)
  - Extend the utilization of security alarms
  - Shift focus more toward end-to-end performance tuning
- Involve infrastructure personnel earlier in the systems development life cycle (SDLC) to ensure that production deployments are not plagued with bottlenecks and inefficiencies
- Continue focus on total cost of ownership (TCO)
  - Eliminate "Wal-Mart infrastructure" hardware purchases — inexpensive on front end but significantly greater TCO. Hardware and software must meet standard requirements.
  - Enforce minimum standards for hardware, software, and design
  - Increase control and monitoring of vendors — more rigorous specifications
- Take the Help Desk function to the "next level"
  - Provide a much broader scope of desktop support to the user community — Excel, Word, and so forth
  - Train resources to be more interchangeable so that users are not tied to specific help desk individuals
  - Develop levels of service. For example, executives may be served by 1:1 Platinum level instruction
  - Provide broad-based training based on brown bag luncheons and other techniques
  - Development of an Event Tracker-1 knowledge base to improve response time to user questions and provide newer help desk representatives with answers to common questions
- Implement a robust, cost-effective, high-availability voice and data network across all XYZ CORP business units

Change Management
Policy and Direction

a. All requests for changes to applications, systems, and vendor hardware/software are standardized and subject to change management processes. For example, change requests are submitted to user management then to IT management for review; direct requests for changes from users to developers are not acceptable.

b. Changes are categorized and prioritized based on both business need and implementation risk.

c. All changes to XYZ CORP's IT systems go through the Event Tracker-1 change/problem management system, regardless of their physical location or previous history of local maintenance. Medium- and high-risk changes/projects are typically documented as part of the Program Management Office (PMO) function, stored in Sharepoint and cross-referenced to Event Tracker-1.

d. Urgent/emergency changes have specific procedures to ensure that the integrity and security of the process remains intact and the process is responsive to business needs. See flowchart.

e. Data changes to production data go through the same process as program changes. However, in some cases, these changes cannot be tested in a test environment and must be verified after being implemented in production.

f. Changes are approved by user management, with the exception of infrastructure-only changes. Authorized requestors and approvers are maintained on a list kept by the help desk. Change requestors are appropriately updated on the status of their request and the date/time when the move to production has occurred.

g. High-risk changes are accompanied by an impact statement/backout plan. These plans may be terse and need contain only sufficient information as required to reduce the risk.

h. Testing plans are prepared and executed prior to implementation of the change. The only exceptions to this policy are emergency fixes that may have to be implemented "on the fly" as well as certain infrastructure changes that cannot be technically tested prior to implementation.

i. A detailed conversion plan is required when data or system elements are converted from an older to a newer system. As part of the plan, old and new data should be reconciled (i.e., compare record counts and dollars before and after) and quality checks of the data incorporated into the effort.

j. Changes are documented (at both the macro and micro level if appropriate)

    k. User-related changes (i.e., everything except technical infrastructure changes) are tested by the user in a test environment (user acceptance test [UAT]).

    l. Changes to software are governed by a standard software release policy — signoff, packaging, regression testing (if appropriate), handover to users, and so forth.

    m. Software is updated and distributed in a timely manner, with appropriate audit trails.

    n. All parties affected by change are notified by management prior to migration into the production environment.

    o. A schedule for the change is documented with clear assignment of responsibilities to developers, quality assurance/testers, and others.

    p. Separate program/module libraries are set up for test, staging, and production. In some cases, a staging library may not be in use. However, in all cases, a minimum of test and production libraries are used to separate development from production. Each of these libraries has a separate set of access controls.

    q. Individuals included on the requestor/approver list must be approved by senior-level management.

    r. An audit trail exists for all changes to the production environment.

Security Administration

Policy and Direction

    a. Corporate IT is responsible for safeguarding the information in its possession.

    b. IT security administration is centrally administered by Corporate IT.

    c. Access to XYZ CORP's computer systems and databases requires review and signoff by the employee's or contractor's supervisor, based on business need.

    d. In addition to supervisory approval, the Director of Information Security or a designee must approve requests for access. Authorization and management review of any access request are based on business need rather than a "blanket security" approach.

    e. The logical access to and use of IT resources is restricted by the implementation of adequate identification, authentication, and authorization mechanism, linking users and resources with access rules. Only authorized personnel have the ability to manage user accounts. Such privileges are limited to a small number of individuals with a clear need for the authority granted.

    f. A list of incompatible duties is maintained and used to ensure that any new or revised security access request does not result in a segregation of duties (SOD) conflict. This functions as a preventative control.

    g. A process is in place for maintenance of the SOD tables, which is then applied to extracts of application security across XYZ CORP's ERPs). Exceptions are resolved with appropriate levels of management. This follow-up process is intended to catch any SOD conflicts not identified in the initial request for access.

h. A formal system of communication (electronic) is established between human resources (HR) and IT security for prompt notification regarding terminated personnel.

i. Access rights, terminations, and reassignments will be reviewed *semiannually* by both Corporate IT and appropriate user groups in order to maintain all security tables current.

j. Access to the resources on the network is controlled to prevent unauthorized access to all computing and information systems. Access is denied unless explicitly authorized.

Procedures exist to ensure timely action relating to requesting, establishing, issuing, suspending, and closing user accounts. These actions are recorded permanently in the Event Tracker-1 database.

k. Contractors and others with need for temporary access are given IDs with expiration dates such that they are granted access for 90 days at a time. This policy is true for ERP#1 applications as well as overall network access.

l. New account IDs and passwords are monitored to determine if they are used; if they are not, the accounts are disabled within 14 days of creation. This policy is true for ERP#1 applications as well as network access.

m. Users are provided access based on the individual's demonstrated need to view, add, change, or delete data.

n. System access for any terminated employee or contractor is removed within 72 hours of notification received by IT. User management is responsible for providing prompt notification of employee or contractor termination.

o. A periodic review of IT user accounts is performed by management and appropriate IT personnel. Accounts are disabled and removed in a timely manner, based on the results of the review.

p. Systems are configured so that users are forced to change the password on new accounts upon initial login.

q. Access rights and identification of users is centralized to obtain consistency and efficiency of enterprise-wide access control.

r. Access requests are stored in the Monitor 24/7 system database that maintains the document requests, grants, modifications, and deletions.

s. Corporate IT maintains a centralized platform that can support incident management; this ensures an appropriate and timely response to security violations.

t. Any trusted relationships with outside parties are secured with appropriate tools such as trusted exchange of passwords, tokens, or cryptographic keys. EDI is an example of a secured system linking XYZ CORP with suppliers.

Additional policies include:

a. Controls are in place to provide authenticity of transactions and establish the validity of a user's claimed identity to the system.

b. Password and ID sharing are prohibited except where explicitly permitted (e.g., an inquiry-only application open to all employees).

c. Where applicable, controls are in place so that transactions cannot be denied by either party (nonrepudiation). For example, time stamps and digital signatures may be used.

d. Highly sensitive data are transported only over a trusted path.

e. Controls are in place to prevent, detect, and correct malicious software, such as computer viruses or Trojan horses.

f. Downloads of software from the Internet (or via removable media) are prohibited; such practices expose XYZ CORP to viruses and other destructive code, potential software licensing violations, and unnecessary consumption of communications bandwidth.

g. XYZ CORP's acceptable use policy must be signed by employees; it prohibits the installation of unlicensed/unauthorized software. All connections with public networks are defended with security hardware and software to protect XYZ CORP from attacks or disclosure of confidential information.

h. XYZ CORP strictly prohibits the use of unlicensed (pirated) software. XYZ CORP will comply with all licensing and other contractual obligations for software use and will maintain appropriate controls over the number of copies used where volume agreements are in place. "Shareware" is licensed software; its use must be approved by Corporate IT and payment made to the appropriate party on a timely basis. Any use of "freeware" must also be approved in advance by Corporate IT.

i. XYZ CORP performs an annual review of software licenses to ensure compliance with contractual obligations to providers.

j. Virus protection is centrally administered and up to date. Except for servers, virus protection resides on the desktop.

k. Business units designate information owners who grant/deny access to information. Those information owners should designate a backup person to act on their behalf if they are unavailable. Information owners are defined on the "Requestor/Approver" list which is used for change control

l. All work done by XYZ CORP's users or contractors, unless specifically designated otherwise, is XYZ CORP's property. For example, a program that is written by a member of Corporate IT while at XYZ CORP becomes the property of XYZ CORP. Nondisclosure agreements (NDAs) are required for independent contractors working for XYZ CORP.

m. Management's security expectations are communicated to the user community on a regular basis. This includes IT policies and procedures (on the intranet) as well as summary e-mails sent out at least annually.

n. Access to systems and infrastructure is logged and monitored regularly. Formal signoff of review occurs at least annually for infrastructure (e.g., router password change) and by schedule for applications.

o. Compliance by all employees and contractors is required. A single exception could result in serious damage to the entire firm, shareholders, employees, and customers.

Segregation of Duties

The partition of rights among users is critical to maintenance of application controls. For example, if an individual can cut a purchase order, receive the goods, and pay the invoice — then perpetrating a fraud would be relatively easy, without requiring collusion. XYZ CORP's manufacturing processes require the critical cross-check of separated transaction capabilities (rights) so that erroneous and/or unauthorized activities will be prevented or at least detected.

Semiannually, XYZ CORP runs a complete segregation of duties (SOD) analysis, based on a predefined SOD template and existing computer access records. In addition, the IT managers and security director review critical security requests for SOD conflicts prior to the granting of those rights.

Database Security and Administration
Policy and Direction

Security is established for XYZ CORP's application databases at a granular level. Users and administrators are given no more authority to access or update database information than is needed to accomplish their assigned tasks.

Patches and upgrades for systems no longer supported by the vendor are implemented only if essential. XYZ CORP will be moving, in the long run, toward a uniform ERP#1 platform. When this occurs, software will be maintained as current as is practical to implement. Until that time, stability of current database implementation has priority over any optional enhancements.

XYZ CORP is moving, over time, to a single ERP system, based on ERP#1.

Corporate IT's direction is to provide maximum service to the business units by stressing the following general principles. Any changes are implemented within a framework of long-term management and ability to easily upgrade as new versions are received from the vendor.

Per XYZ CORP senior management, ERP and other purchased package systems should receive minimal modifications. This greatly reduces the long-term maintenance costs of the application. "Core" code is modified only as a last resort; any such changes are approved in advance by IT management and are well documented.

Documentation and procedures are such that XYZ CORP is not reliant on any specific individual to make future changes. Practices such as table-driven design are used to facilitate development and reduce the cost of changes. For example, data are not hard coded into applications.

Referential integrity, while not strictly enforced due to performance concerns, is considered where practical. Data relationships are maintained at a high level of quality.

Changes to production database structures go through the standard change management process (see change management section). Authorization, testing, approval, and independent move to production are required.

Good technical practices are consistently used, for example, naming conventions are established for forms, tables, queries, and variables; code is logical and well formatted; and errors are trapped and logged.

Real-time monitoring is used to notify Corporate IT staff when runaway processes or other disruptive events occur.

Network Operating System (OS) Parameters

Policy and Direction

XYZ CORP's networking operating systems provide the foundation for processing all XYZ CORP's business applications. Compliance with these policies ensures that the base infrastructure supporting XYZ CORP's applications is robust, secure, auditable, and efficient.

a. Network OSs are protected with physical and logical security to ensure continuity of operations, prevention of unauthorized access, and accuracy of processing and retention of necessary business information.

b. Password controls are enforced by both administrative policy and automated enforcement methods.

c. Users and groups are segregated according to business units and job function. Access (read, write, update) is based on business need and remains in force only as long as is necessary for the individual to perform the job.

d. Profiles of access rights are set up based on user functional requirements. These profiles improve the efficiency of administration and reduce the likelihood that an individual will be inadvertently given excessive authority.

e. The underlying file structures and partitions are configured to provide maximum security (e.g., NTFS for NT).

    f. Relevant activities are logged so that audit trails are available for review.

    g. Both servers are workstations that are monitored and secured by physical and logical safeguards.

Firewalls, Intrusion Detection, and Routers

Purpose

To prevent unauthorized parties from accessing the data and other resources on XYZ CORP's computers attached to the network. The firewall also allows XYZ CORP to control the resources on its computers that can be accessed by those outside its local network.

Policy and Direction

    a. XYZ CORP uses a versatile, industry standard firewall.

    b. XYZ CORP's network is shielded from direct connection to the Internet by a firewall. The internal XYZ CORP network is subdivided by the firewall into two sections: an extranet and an intranet. Each of these sections contains a secure area for confidential data and transactions.

    c. Connections from off-site locations to XYZ CORP's network are enabled by secure VPN connections and are passed through the firewall.

    d. XYZ CORP's objective is to have only one link to the Internet, which permits the firewall and IDS systems to analyze all inbound and outbound traffic. At some point during the next few years, the only allowed connection to the Internet will be through the corporate data center at Seabrook.

    e. Traffic traveling over XYZ CORP's network is restricted to approved services, hosts, protocols, and network configurations. These services must satisfy a business need in order to be on the network. The need and validity of these services are reviewed quarterly.

    f. Firewall services are allowed or denied based on business requirements and security needs

    g. Firewall, IDS, and related equipment are located in physically secure areas on XYZ CORP's premises.

    h. The need for additional firewalls to protect specific "zones" is continually reviewed. Corporate IT recognizes that a single, monolithic firewall defense will not scale as the organization grows.

    i. The firewall architecture defends itself from direct attack (e.g., through active monitoring of traffic and pattern recognition technology).

    j. Traffic is exchanged through the firewall at the application layer only.

    k. The firewall is intentionally configured to allow detection/rejection of any unauthorized use of the Internet, such as viewing/communicating with porn sites, hate groups, and hacking groups. Use of XYZ CORP's communications facilities for such purposes is strictly prohibited. Employees and contractors working on behalf of XYZ CORP have no right of privacy regarding communications using XYZ CORP's Internet and computer facilities.

l. Firewalls, IDS equipment/software, and other IT security-related elements are purchased and configured solely by the central IT group. Centralization of this function is de rigueur, given the complexity of network security.

m. Only appropriate services are allowed to pass through the Internet.

n. Strong authentication is required to administer the firewall. The firewall can be configured remotely only via the VPN, using a strong password.

Physical Security

a The computer room is secured via an outside security agency.

b. Routers, switches, storage area networks (SANs), firewalls, and other computer equipment are housed in the computer room, which has restricted access.

c. Alarms are sent to the Director of Operations and other IT infrastructure personnel as a result of unauthorized physical entry, fire, smoke, temperature outside defined limits, water, and very loud noises.

d. Videotapes are used to monitor activities in the computer room (from vendors or in-house personnel).

e. The Director of Operations manages the physical access controlled by the electronic access system. The access list is reviewed at least twice per year and individuals who no longer need access are removed from the list.

f. An audit trail of entrance to each room or series of rooms protected by an electronic lock is available for review.

Project Management

XYZ CORP has established a PMO (Program Management Office) function within the IT Group. The PMO's mission is to provide oversight and control for medium- to large-scale IT projects. Benefits include the following:

- Project management and oversight using Project Management Institute (PMI) principles
- Proactive scope management
- Risk identification and mitigation
- Improved accuracy of project estimates
- Reduction in hours expended, calendar execution time, and lifetime cost of the delivered product
- Improved quality of deliverables

Tools and Methodologies

The PMO uses tools and techniques supported by the PMI to accomplish its goals. MS Project is used for detailed tracking of projects. Reporting and working documents include the following:

- Project charter
- Scope statement
- WBS (work breakdown structure)
- Project plan
- Weekly status reports

Direction and Goals

The PMO maintains oversight for IT standards compliance, documentation requirements, and XYZ CORP's SDLC.

By providing mid- to senior-level management with accurate and timely reporting, the PMO enhances the quality of information needed for decision making. For example, reports include

- Actual versus budgeted expenditures by project
- Quarterly accomplishments and items that require management attention
- Informal communication of potential risks

Help Desk

XYZ CORP maintains an IT help desk to provide application, infrastructure, and telecom-related assistance to all users. In addition, help desk personnel serve as the focal point for access approvals, problem management, change management, and escalation of incidents.

The Help Desk serves to enforce IT policy. For example, requested changes and approval for those changes are authorized based on authorizations by specific individuals maintained in a "requestor/approver" table. The Help Desk updates this table periodically.

Problem Management

XYZ CORP uses the Event Tracker-1 software package to manage reported problems and requests for assistance.

Help desk tickets are tracked from beginning to end by Event Tracker-1.

Emergency procedures are defined, documented, approved by IT management, and executed as needed. XYZ CORP maintains a separate Help Desk procedure manual, which includes problem management.

Systems Development Life Cycle

XYZ CORP uses an SDLC to develop new products and maintain purchased software. The benefits include decreased total cost of ownership; fewer coding and implementation errors; better documentation; and improved compliance with Sarbanes-Oxley and other regulations.

SDLC can be considered as the "meat" inside a change control sandwich. Change control encloses SDLC on both sides, ensuring that the change or development is properly evaluated/approved on the front end and reviewed/approved on the back end, just before its move to production. In the middle is an industry standard approach to development, user involvement, testing, documentation, and business review.

The life cycle specifically addresses security, availability, and processing integrity.

XYZ CORP reviews its SDLC methodology and related artifacts on at least an annual basis. Changes are made as required. Users are appropriately involved in the design of applications, selection of packaged software, and testing to ensure a reliable environment. Training needs are assessed for each project. Both users and IT staff are trained on software and business processes as needed.

Manage Third-Party Services

XYZ CORP monitors all third-party interfaces to ensure that proper information security is maintained.

IT managers and directors serve as the relationship manager for third-party suppliers. When possible, XYZ CORP requires service-level reporting to ensure an adequate level of performance. Vendors are evaluated on an informal basis; nonperforming or below par providers are eliminated as circumstances permit.

The XYZ CORP legal department reviews vendor contracts before they are signed. This ensures that all necessary terms and conditions are included in the proposed contract.

For large purchases or service contracts, IT management qualifies suppliers. Qualification is based on financial stability, ability to deliver the goods and services at the required level of quality, and other operational factors.

Manage Performance and Capacity

XYZ CORP uses industry standard infrastructure tools to monitor performance and capacity for the network, network devices, and servers.

Infrastructure Standards

Location of Documentation and Standards

XYZ CORP's direction for IT documentation and project management is to use the Microsoft Sharepoint application. Until that implementation is completed, infrastructure documentation and other reference material will be stored in the following location:

```
XYZ_file99\groups
```

Folders are logically named: desktop, exchange, Image-1, self-testing, network, projects, server, and others.

High-Level Policies for Infrastructure Installation and Maintenance

- The acquisition of systems hardware/software is based on known or estimated business requirements. For example, an understanding of required response time drives the calculation of WAN bandwidth.
- Preventive maintenance is scheduled.
- Infrastructure changes are implemented using standard XYZ CORP change management processes.
- Only trained and fully qualified infrastructure personnel are permitted to install and maintain system-level software.
- System software utilities are restricted to authorized administrators only.
- Performance tools are used to identify failure points — proactively if possible but certainly after the fact if a breakdown occurs.
- Standard approval and acquisition processes are used to acquire infrastructure equipment and software; all such software and hardware are approved by appropriate management. Typically the Director of Operations approves infrastructure purchases.

Manage Telecommunications

Telecommunications Service Levels

XYZ CORP's goal for critical applications is processed centrally at the Seabrook location (or the Kansas hot site if Seabrook is disabled). Accordingly, the voice and data communications lines are critical for business continuity.

XYZ CORP requires the service levels listed below from its network transport provider.

Network Reliability

a. Availability: the core network infrastructure must be available 99.999% of the time.

b. Access to Public Switched Telecommunication Network (PSTN): Access link connecting the vendor's point of presence (POP) to the PSTN must have a guarantee of 99.999% uptime.

c. Redundant POPs: XYZ CORP requires all national POPs to be fully redundant with multiple routes to the Telco and the core network.

d. Transport Level: The network must provide seamless connectivity for all XYZ CORP users at transport level. The crossing of technology platforms, geographic areas, or carrier networks must be transparent to the protocols being used.

e. Local End Infrastructure: Local end infrastructure (i.e., cabling, telephone exchange, and POP infrastructure supporting the primary and secondary core locations) must be fully redundant through network diversity and alternative routing. At no point should alternative cable and routing provisions have a single point of failure exposure.

f. Vendor Equipment: All vendor equipment, including network terminating equipment at the primary and secondary locations, must be fully redundant, powered by UPS system with a minimum 8-hour battery reserve, or a standby generator, and have an on-site critical spares kit provided for all nonredundant components.

Network Management

a. Redundancy and Location: The Primary Network Management system must have backup locations and the ability to manage the entire network from multiple locations. Coordination of trouble reporting, monitoring, and repair with all organizations involved in the provisioning of services to XYZ CORP must be guaranteed.

b. Operation Hours: XYZ CORP requires 24-hour support, 7-days/week in a fully staffed Network Control Center (NCC).

c. Online Access to NCC: XYZ CORP's goal requires online access to obtain network status information.

d. Fault Management: The fault management system has the ability to perform diagnostics and testing of the hardware, channels, and circuits, remotely from single or multiple NCCs for the data network only.

e. Pro-Active Fault Resolution Management: XYZ CORP's goal requires notification of faults on a proactive basis by the NCC. This includes both outages and degraded performance.

Network Performance Reporting

a. Service-Level Agreements: SLAs are a key component in the management of a network. XYZ CORP requires from its provider(s) a 99.999% core network availability, and 99.995% end-to-end service standard. This is the same goal for our Telecom Network as well.

b. Monthly Performance Reports: XYZ CORP's goal requires a monthly report on the health and performance of the network. The following information must be provided within the agreed timescales as agreed with NCI:

- Monthly performance graphs of service availability
- Service uptime
- Number of trouble tickets by location
- Duration of downtime, if any
- Grid thresholds reports
- Network utilization

c. Detailed trouble tickets: XYZ CORP's Goal requires they include short descriptions, organized by circuit identification and type, time ticket opened, time ticket closed, duration of issue, and resolution. Some of these are in place and being used to date.

Connectivity Standards

All locations on the XYZ CORP network should connect using technology that conforms to the following standards:

a. Local loop — primary rate interfact (PRI) for the premises link from the central office (CO) where available and feasible based on need and costs.

b. Local loop — plain old telephone service (POTS) lines for any site where primary rate interface (PRI) circuits are not available or are not feasible based on need and costs.

Messaging

Policy and Direction

a. XYZ CORP email is to be used primarily for business purposes. Any personal use is of short duration and limited. Any use for personal business ventures is prohibited. Use for charitable purposes, beyond an occasional e-mail, must be approved by appropriate business unit management.

b. Personal IDs and passwords are not shared with others.

c. No offensive materials whatsoever will be permitted in any e-mails, whether incoming or outgoing, whether business related or personal. Should such e-mails be received unsolicited, they are to be immediately deleted. XYZ CORP employees and contractors are to use common sense in the use of e-mail; for example, materials that are sexually explicit, contain hate group/ racist comments, or excite readers to extreme/illegal behaviors are strictly prohibited.

d. Employees and contractors using XYZ CORP's computers for e-mail are not to consider such e-mail, whether incoming or outgoing, to be private. Do not write things in e-mails that you do not want others to see.

e. XYZ CORP requires e-mail etiquette. For example, harsh or obscene language; defamatory statements regarding employees or contractors; and extremely negative statements regarding individuals or groups within NCI, are all prohibited.

f. All outgoing e-mail will contain the following disclaimer statement:

Information contained in this transmission is intended for the use of the individual or entity named above and may contain legally privileged and/or confidential information. If the reader of this message is not the intended recipient, you are hereby notified that any dissemination, distribution or copy of this communication is strictly prohibited. If you have received this communication in error, please permanently delete this message and immediately notify us by telephone at (555) 777-2222.

g. Instant messaging is not considered a corporate vehicle for business communications and is not supported. Retention of instant messaging logs (e.g., as a text file) is prohibited.

h. Mass mailings are prohibited unless approved by appropriate business unit management as well as Corporate IT.

i. E-mail IDs (directories) are the property of XYZ CORP and are not to be distributed to outsiders, such as marketing organizations.

E-mail System

MS Outlook/MS Exchange Server

a. Only the e-mail system hosted by Corporate IT is acceptable for communications. Others, such as Hotmail, are not secure or backed up. In addition, such e-mail systems are outside XYZ CORP's network and hence beyond policy enforcement.

b. Standard disclaimer.

c. Each outgoing e-mail will include the text shown above within the body of the message.

Acceptable Use Specifics

a. E-mail is primarily for XYZ CORP business purposes.

b. Personal use is permitted as an employee benefit if it is occasional and discrete.

c. No employee or contractor should have an expectation of privacy when using XYZ CORP's e-mail system.

d. No communications to the press, stock analysts, or others with potential to affect XYZ CORP's public standing are permitted without appropriate senior management approval (in some cases legal review will be required).

e. E-mail is not to be used to communicate confidential or sensitive information to individuals who do not have a specific need to know.

f. Encryption is recommended where transmission of sensitive information to authorized parties outside XYZ CORP's network is required. Although password protection for standard MS Office attachments (Word, Excel, etc.) is better than plain text, stronger encryption, such as PGP, is recommended for the most confidential materials. Corporate IT will research simple encryption alternatives.

g. USE OF E-MAIL FOR PURPOSES OF SEXUAL HARASSMENT, ETHNIC/RELIGIOUS INTOLERANCE, DISCRIMINATION, OR ILLEGAL ACTIVITIES IS STRICTLY PROHIBITED. SEXUAL HARASSMENT INCLUDES, BUT IS NOT LIMITED TO, THE TRANSMISSION OF "OFF COLOR" JOKES AND PORNOGRAPHIC IMAGES.

h. The use of e-mail to transmit materials and facts that could potentially be classified as "insider trading" information is prohibited.

i. Any violations of the above acceptable use provisions may result in sanctions, up to and including discharge from employment.

j. See data retention policy for e-mail retention.

Disaster Recovery and Business Continuity

Policy and Direction

a. XYZ CORP recognizes the potential for financial, operational, and reputational loss arising from unforeseen events affecting IT services, such as hurricanes, chemical spills, or even a highly destructive security breach.

b. Provisions for electrical power backup, fire suppression in the computer room, humidity control, alarms, and other physical security capabilities are kept up to date. Critical files are backed up and routinely rotated to a site physically separate from the Seabrook location. The rotation occurs at least weekly.

c. A disaster recovery plan has been developed.

d. A hot site is available for temporary resumption of IT services.

e. Although XYZ CORP has not yet developed a complete business continuity plan, the following general goals are recognized:

- The full range of resources must be included in the final plan. For example, personnel, communications links, computing, workspace, voice communications, and documents are essential for a complete recovery from a major disruption.
- The effect of downtime must be quantified, based on XYZ CORP's business environment. This will drive the architecture of the plan, because factors such as restoration time and completeness directly affect the cost and scope of the recovery effort.
- Employee responsibility. XYZ CORP employees are expected to take reasonable steps to protect XYZ CORP's assets. However, if health-threatening events occur (fire, smoke, fire suppression discharge, etc.), employees should secure their own safety and avoid dangerous "hero" efforts.
- An approved list of personnel authorized to have access to backup tapes is maintained.
- Formal restoration tests from backup tapes to servers are performed at least semiannually. Note that this testing is independent of any incidental restores that must be completed as part of routine operations (e.g., due to a hard drive crash on a server).

Disaster Recovery Planning and Capability

XYZ CORP has developed a comprehensive disaster recovery plan. Due to its size and level of detail, only highlights are included here (see IT management for a copy of the plan).

Key Objectives

a. Recovery time objective is 72 hours from disaster declaration
b. Data recovery point objective is 24 hours prior to outage
c. Recovery site will be a single-purpose facility for XYZ CORP and will not be utilized for testing or development
d. Replication will be accomplished utilizing Coritas Volume Replicator on a dedicated circuit
e. Circuit capacity will be sufficient to replicate all required data changes in production with a lag time less than 12 hours
f. Changes to the production environment need to be tracked and applied in disaster recovery site in a timely manner, no greater than 24 hours, in order to meet the RTO
g. IT change management process must include the disaster recovery (DR) environment

h. Frequent testing is required to validate DR readiness because application synchronization has manual processes dependent on an effective change management process

i. The following applications have been deemed Mission Critical and hence are to be recovered at the disaster recovery site:

- ERP#1 12.9
- ERP#1 15t
- PR#1 PR/HR
- Image-1
- JT#1
- ERP#2
- ERP#4
- MS Exchange 2003

Application Recovery Process

The application recovery process described in this document details the steps required to recover the Mission Critical applications, the sequence in which they will be recovered, and the time necessary to get the applications operating as required in the new disaster recovery Data Center. This will include the detailed applications recovery tests that will be necessary to validate that the systems at the DR Data Center are ready to act as the primary production environment.

An organization's Application Recovery strategy is a balance between the cost of risk reduction measures and recovery options to support the recovery of critical business processes within agreed timescales. Typically, the more risk reduction and the shorter the timeframe to recovery, the more expensive the solution. Three general categories of Application Recovery and risk reduction are described below.

Gradual Recovery

This option (sometimes referred to as "cold standby") is applicable to organizations that do not need immediate restoration of business processes and can function for a period of 7 to 30 days, or longer, without a reestablishment of full IT facilities. This may include the provision of an empty accommodation fully equipped with power, environmental controls, and local network cabling infrastructure, telecommunications connections, and available in a disaster situation for an organization to install its own computer equipment.

Intermediate Recovery

This option (sometimes referred to as "warm standby") is selected by organizations that need to recover IT facilities within a predetermined time to prevent impacts to the business process. This typically involves the reestablishment of the critical systems and services within a 3- to 7-day period.

Most common is the use of commercial facilities, which are offered by third-party recovery organizations to a number of subscribers, spreading the cost across those subscribers. Commercial facilities often include operation, system management, and technical support. The cost varies depending on the facilities requested, such as processors, peripherals, and communications, and how quickly the services must be restored (invocation timescale).

The advantage of this service is that the customer can have virtually instantaneous access to a site, housed in a secure building, in the event of disaster. It must be understood, however, that the restoration of services at the site may take some time as delays may be encountered while the site is reconfigured for the organization that invokes the service, and the organization's applications and data will need to be restored from backups.

Immediate Recovery

This option (sometimes referred to as "hot standby") provides for immediate restoration of services and is usually provided as an extension to the intermediate recovery provided by a third-party recovery provider. The immediate recovery is supported by the recovery of mission critical business and support areas during the first 72 hours following a service disruption. This again is an expensive option but may be justified for a certain business process where nonavailability for a short period could result in a significant impact. The facility needs to be located separately and far enough away from the home site that it will not be affected by a disaster affecting that location.

For highly critical business processes, a mirrored service can be established at an alternative location, which is kept up to date with the live service, either by data transfers at regular intervals, or by replications from the live service. Such a service could be used merely as a backup service, but it might also be used for enquiry access (such as reporting) without affecting the live processing performance. This is also useful if there are legal or legislative obligations to safeguard the completeness and integrity of all financial records. As this is essentially spare capacity, under normal circumstances this spare capacity can be used for development, training, or testing, but could be made available immediately when a service continuity situation demands it.

Selected Options — Immediate Recovery

XYZ CORP has decided to utilize an immediate recovery approach for the defined Mission Critical application in a standby Data Center. The data in the Seabrook Data Center will be synchronized on a predetermined schedule. Automatic synchronization is accomplished by using Util_3 for Wintel applications, Guard_ IT for ERP#1 applications, and Util-6 for ERP#2 applications.

Data Retention and Management

Purpose

    a. To provide timely and accurate access to XYZ CORP's data and messages for those who have a legitimate business need

    b. To ensure that data are available even if business interruption occurs

    c. To efficiently manage current information storage and delete obsolete and no longer relevant data

Policy

    a. XYZ CORP will retain electronic data and source documents in accordance with all appropriate legal, regulatory, and certification requirements, such as those from the IRS, OSHA, and ISO9000 governing bodies. This retention is based on a formal archiving/deletion schedule.

    b. Critical ERP data are not purged; for example, warranty information is maintained indefinitely. Operational data in ERP#1 12.9 are archived using a separate schema; designated key users can directly access archived data, on a read-only basis. ERP#1 12.9 data older than October 2002 have been moved to the archive system, which is still online and also backed up for off-site storage. ERP#1 15t does not yet have enough old information to require archiving. Separate monthly, quarterly, and yearly "snapshots" of databases are not kept. DB-Control#1 is used to archive the ERP#1 data. ERP#2 databases are backed up using the *Util-6* backup software.

    c. For all production data, the minimum backup schedule includes a daily incremental and weekly full backup. Most data are backed up more frequently than the minimum required.

    d. Documentation of backup/recovery procedures and schedule is embedded within the Coritas backup and recovery software as well as ZMUN for ERP#1.

    e. XYZ CORP has a business need to eliminate unnecessary and duplicative electronic documents as well as e-mails and voicemails. Hence, data will not be permanently retained on XYZ CORP's computer systems, except where specific business requirements apply, such as the major ERP systems.

    f. An inventory is maintained for electronic storage media housing production data. Off-site storage is included in this inventory, along with a rotation and physical movement schedule.

g. Backup procedures for IT-related media include the proper storage of the data files, software, and related documentation, both on-site and off-site.

h. Daily logs of backup and evidence of review (to ensure failed jobs are timely corrected) are maintained. For ERP#1, special scripts have been written to send the results of backups to an e-mail inbox. If backups fail, an e-mail is sent to the DBA's Blackberry.

i. Planned, formal restore testing occurs at least quarterly. Documentation of results and signoff are retained.

j. Key data are backed up based on a documented schedule; the usability and integrity of the backups are regularly verified.

k. XYZ CORP data are confidential; employees and contractors are prohibited from copying XYZ CORP data onto removable media (such as USB drives) for transport outside XYZ CORP's premises.

l. All important business data are stored in a controlled, backed-up infrastructure. For example, key consolidation spreadsheets are not maintained on local hard drives; instead, they are maintained on an appropriate backed-up and monitored SAN.

m. Corporate IT does not back up data stored on local drives unless the "my documents" personal folder has been set to the "z:" drive, located on a backed-up network drive. All important XYZ CORP information should be stored on the network, where it is regularly backed up.

n. IT will follow XYZ CORP's standard retention policy as defined by the Legal department. See Appendix G.

o. Special folders or storage areas are available for privileged documents and files. To comply with Sarbanes-Oxley requirements, "critical spreadsheets" are part of these special folders.

p. E-mail and voicemail are not considered as a long-term storage medium.

Procedures and Description

a. XYZ CORP uses the Coritas backup and recovery software to create backups of ERP databases, sequential files, and system data. All XYZ CORP backups use this package with the exception of the soon-to-be-retired Data General platform. Other backup/synchronization software includes Util_3 for Wintel applications, Guard_IT for ERP#1 applications, and Util-6 for ERP#2 applications.

b. To improve efficiency, ZMUN is used to consolidate individual ERP#1 database files prior to backup on "virtual tape" (a separate hard drive) and traditional tape media. Scripts have been written to kick off backup jobs. Coritas initiates a ZMUN job and then writes the consolidated files to tape.

c. Full backups of ERP#1 and other systems are created every business day. The current (most immediate) backup tape is rotated off-site. This provides for a current backup in the event of a disaster at the building. If a restore needs to be run due to database or disk drive corruption, the data can usually be retrieved from the virtual tape, without resorting to a physical delivery from the off-site storage vendor (TrueVal — not related to Coritas).

d. Restore times for ERPs vary. From a good backup tape, ERP#1 12.9 could be restored in 4 to 6 hours; ERP#1 15t (at the time of this writing) can be restored in roughly an hour.

Job Scheduling

Although diminished in importance from the batch-processing era, job scheduling must nonetheless be properly implemented and monitored. Financial close and other specific applications have processes that must be executed in the correct sequence and at the right time.

Except for backups and routine system-level maintenance activities, job scheduling parameters are defined within the application.

Uninterruptible Power Source

a. Corporate IT recognizes that the easiest way to address disruption is to avoid it in the first place. Accordingly, servers and key computing equipment are located in a locked, air-conditioned, FM200 protected room on the second floor at Seabrook (high enough to protect the equipment from flood damage). A backup generator provides auxiliary power.

b. The backup generator is a Serial 1 Diesel Spectrum 230 Kilowatt system; it holds 156 gallons of fuel and will run approximately 11 hours under full load. It is tested for 50 minutes every Tuesday. Parts are serviced by State Line Diesel Maintenance. Critical equipment, including routers, servers, firewalls, and other devices, is stored in the computer room, which is physically secure.

c. There are two UPS batteries serving the computer room; current is filtered through the batteries

d. A standard 200 ton AC chiller is used to cool the building; an auxiliary 30 ton pony chiller further cools the computer room (only). The pony chiller runs only if the main chiller fails or Seabrook is running on diesel generator power.

e. Fire alarms and smoke detection devices are deployed throughout the building.

f. The computer room uses an FM200 (FM200 derivative) to deplete the oxygen and almost instantly put out any fire. Within a few seconds, 600 pounds of FM200 are discharged. If two detectors recognize smoke in the computer room, the FM200 is released within 10 seconds (there is an abort button).

g. Stony Brook Fire Company, located a few miles from Seabrook, responds to any fire/smoke alarms.

Backup of Data, Programs, and Operating Systems

Infrastructure

Backup Packages

Coritas S1 Backup is XYZ CORP's direction for backup. XYZ CORP currently uses two packages for backup, both from Coritas:

- Backup Exec version 9.1
- S1 Backup 5.1

Backup Exec is an older backup software for the Windows environment only. S1 Backup 5.1, intended for data centers, is newer software and is able to backup a large variety of data formats, not merely those structured in Windows friendly format. By 2008, XYZ CORP expects to perform all backups using S1 Backup.

In order to increase efficiency and speed, backups are written to a virtual tape library (hard drive) that is later copied to tape media for off-site storage.

Backups

XYZ CORP's IT department performs weekly full and daily differential/incremental backups of all business critical servers. The method and frequency of each server's backup are determined by its volume of data, how often the data changes, and the criticality of its data.

All backups are stored on industry standard backup devices located and stored in a secure location with restricted access.

The Seabrook Corporate location uses a VTL (Virtual Tape Library). The data center computers consider the VTL to be a tape library, but it is actually a sophisticated disk array system. The benefit is that the VTL backs up and restores data faster than a physical (traditional) tape library.

Restore Testing

Quarterly — Random Sampling

Backup media containing key production files and databases must be tested periodically to ensure they contain expected data and are properly indexed by XYZ CORP's backup management systems, such as Coritas. The failure of even a single "find" on backup media for a major application, database, or OS file indicates a flaw in the backup process.

The restoration of randomly selected files from backup media provides a strong indicator of the backup system's health. To ensure timely monitoring of the process, XYZ CORP tests each ERP and major system on a quarterly schedule.

Annual — Full System Restore

Although the monthly sample restores provide some assurance that the backup systems are functioning correctly, only a full restore provides 100% assurance that every necessary system component (raw data, executables, scripts, etc.) has been correctly captured and can be restored in the correct sequence.

Accordingly, XYZ CORP performs a full system restore for each major ERP/application annually. After the restore is complete, key control totals are obtained and verified by user management to ensure a faithful reproduction of the production environment. For example, a general ledger balance sheet may be used to verify balances. Verification by user management is recorded and stored in the Event Tracker-1 system.

IT Governance

XYZ CORP will engage a well-known external audit firm, such as Smart & Smart, to perform annual independent audit of the financial statements as well as compliance with SOX 302 and 404 requirements.

In addition, Internal Audit serves to review and promote internal controls within the organization and provide year-to-year continuity with the external auditors. Management periodically engages contractors to provide testing and documentation support for SOX and any other required compliance activities.

Monitor and Evaluate Internal Control

The XYZ CORP IT group performs quarterly self-testing for selected key controls. In addition, internal control related reports are retained at the network level. Key IT controls are stored on the Internal Audit and IT "Intranet" Sharepoint sites.

Insurance

XYZ CORP's insurance group maintains replacement cost business personal property insurance. Accounting develops replacement cost estimates for equipment and contents (tax values are used). These estimates form the basis for recovery in the event of a loss due to fire and water damage among other events. Note that the damage from certain specified events, such as civil disturbance, is excluded from coverage.

Business interruption insurance covers events that would prevent XYZ CORP from conducting normal business. Estimates of daily loss are prepared by the Accounting group and used by XYZ CORP's insurance carrier (Logos) as a basis for coverage.

Deductibles, for both business interruption and business personal property, are maintained at relatively high levels to reduce insurance costs. Coinsurance provisions have been removed.

Leased equipment (e.g., servers or other infrastructure devices) is covered by obtaining a certificate of insurance. Since XYZ CORP is responsible for coils maintained on its premises (but not purchased or leased), a certificate of insurance is obtained to mitigate the risk of housing these items as well.

Hardware and Software Purchase Policy

Policy and Direction

a. All hardware and software purchases will be reviewed for compliance to XYZ CORP's technical architecture prior to purchase.
b. Any deviations from the approved software and hardware list must be approved by the chief information officer (CIO) or her designee.
c. XYZ CORP maintains a Standard Hardware/Software List.
d. No software will be acquired without the requisite license/proof of right to use.
e. No software or hardware is to be acquired outside the standard purchase process.
f. Hardware and software purchases will be centralized in order to provide greater standardization, lower maintenance costs, and increased purchasing power.
g. Implementation of major hardware or software purchases will be planned and sufficient notice given to affected parties.
h. Records (licenses) will be maintained such that a review by an outside party, such as the Business Software Alliance, will demonstrate XYZ CORP's compliance with all applicable agreements and legal regulations.

Peripheral hardware, such as a PDA, is included in this policy if it attaches to the network. If purchased individually, it must nonetheless conform to XYZ CORP's technical architecture before linking to the network.

Capital expenditures will conform to XYZ CORP's capital appropriation policy.

Software

General

a. All software and hardware must be purchased via Corporate IT.
b. Users obtain supervisor approval to order software or hardware.

   c. An e-mail or fax showing approval is sent to the software/hardware purchase coordinator.

   d. The hardware/software purchase coordinator compares the request to the current list of standard, approved software.

   e. If the cost for an individual order exceeds $1,500 and the item(s) are not considered expense items, a capital spend form (CSF) must be completed and signed by the requestor and immediate supervisor or department head. The request is sent to the IT purchase coordinator, who reviews and forwards to the CIO of Operations (alternatively the VP and CIO). The CIO signs if it meets standards for IT software and is otherwise appropriate. The form is then sent to accounting for a CSF number, which serves to chargeback the business unit. After assignment of a CSF number, the document is sent back to the IT hardware/software purchase coordinator for actual ordering (an e-mail may be used to expedite ordering).

   f. If the request matches the approved list and does not exceed $1,000, the purchase coordinator orders the software from the approved vendor(s) and sends an e-mail to the original requestor.

   g. Purchases for IT equipment, software, and services up to $150,000 may be approved by the Director of Operations. Larger amounts must be approved by the CIO.

   h. For "one off" items not on the approved software list, the purchase coordinator maintains an inventory to demonstrate compliance with license agreements and legal restrictions.

   i. Annually, the purchase coordinator requests printouts or electronic records from vendors supplying software (e.g., CDW). Combined with the "one off" items mentioned above, these records constitute an informal software licensing database.

   j. Time sensitive requests: On an exception basis, software can be ordered prior to receipt of a CSF number for chargeback. Such exceptions must be approved by the CIO.

   k. Overall corporate purchase policy. All capital purchases must conform to the enterprise-wide capital procurement policy.

IT Budgeting and Cost Management

An annual budget is prepared by IT management and submitted to XYZ CORP's senior management for review. After approval, variances are tracked during the year and significant deviations from anticipated expenditures are explained.

Alternative providers (hardware, software, and human resources) are continually evaluated for cost effectiveness; existing providers are replaced if service and/or quality delivery is insufficient.

IT Human Resources Management

XYZ CORP IT human resources management conforms to XYZ CORP's general HR policies and procedures (see HR for a hard copy).

Highlights of relevant practices include

a. New IT employees go through orientation where training on general policies and procedures is provided. New employees are required to read and sign (a) code of business conduct and ethics, (b) acknowledgement of receipt of the employee policy manual, (c) disclosure and release of liability form, and (d) consent to substance abuse testing.

b. Both contractors and new employees are screened for illegal drug usage. Where contractors are provided through an agency, they are screened prior to presenting to XYZ CORP.

c. Statements made by employees and independent contractors are investigated by an independent agency. Court and law enforcement agency records are reviewed for potential felonies or serious misdemeanors.

d. Contractors working at the Seabrook location are required to swipe time cards to ensure accurate timekeeping.

e. Human Resources retains resumes for all employees.

f. Employees receive annual reviews of performance.

g. IT employees are hired by either promotion/transfer from within other XYZ CORP business units as well as recruitment from the outside.

Appendix H

Recommended Reading

Outside a dog, a book is your best friend. Inside a dog, it's too dark to read.

Groucho Marx

Broadbent, Marianne and Ellen S. Kitzis. *The New CIO Leader*. Boston: Harvard Business School Press, 2005.

Brown, Eric J., et al. *Achieving Success as a CIO*. New York: Aspatore Books, 2007.

Carr, Nicholas. *The Big Switch, Rewiring the World, from Edison to Google*. New York: W. W. Norton & Company, 2008.

Cohen, Linda and Allie Young. *Multisourcing: Moving Beyond Outsourcing to Achieve Growth and Agility*. Boston: Harvard Business School Press, 2005.

Davenport, Thomas H. and Jeanne G. Harris. *Competing on Analytics, The New Science of Winning*. Boston: Harvard Business School Press, 2007.

Friedman, Thomas L. *The World is Flat*. New York: Picador, 2007.

Howson, Cindi. *Successful Business Intelligence, Secrets to Making BI a Killer App*. New York: McGraw-Hill, 2008.

Ittelson, Thomas. *Financial Statements: A Step-by-Step Guide to Understanding and Creating Financial Reports*. Boston: Career Press, 1998.

Jaquith, Andres. *Security Metrics*. Reading, MA: Addison-Wesley, 2007.

Kao, John. *Innovation Nation, How America Is Losing Its Innovation Edge, Why It Matters, and What We Can Do to Get It Back*. New York: Free Press, 2007.

Kruchten, Philippe. *The Rational Unified Process: An Introduction*, 3rd ed. Reading, MA: Addison-Wesley, 2003.

Medina, John J. *Brain Rules, 12 Principles for Surviving and Thriving at Work, Home, and School*. Seattle, WA: Pear Press, 2008.

Pyzdek, Thomas. *The Six Sigma Handbook: The Complete Guide for Greenbelts, Blackbelts, and Managers at All Levels, Revised and Expanded Edition*. New York: McGraw-Hill, 2003.

Rachlin, Robert and Allen Sweeny. *Accounting and Financial Fundamentals for Nonfinancial Executives.* New York: Amacon, 1996.

Ross, Jeanne W., Peter Weill, and David C. Robertson. *Enterprise Architecture as Strategy, Creating a Foundation for Business Execution.* Boston: Harvard Business School Press, 2006.

Sangwan, Raghvinder. *Global Software Development Handbook.* Boston, MA: Auerbach, 2006.

Smith, Gregory S. *Straight to the Top, Becoming a World-Class CIO.* Hoboken, NJ: John Wiley & Sons, 2006.

Taleb, Nassim Nicholas. *The Black Swan, The Impact of the Highly Improbable.* New York: Random House, 2007.

Taleb, Nicholas Nassim. *Fooled by Randomness.* New York: Random House Trade Paperbacks, 2005.

Taylor, James and Neil Raden. *Smart (Enough) Systems, How to Deliver Competitive Advantage by Automating Hidden Decisions.* New York: Prentice Hall, 2007.

Thrasher, Harwell. *Boiling the IT Frog, How to Make Your Business Information Technology Wildly Successful without Having to Learn Anything Technical.* Duluth, GA: MakingITclear, 2007.

Tzu, Sun. *The Art of War.* New York: Shambhala, 2005.

Weill, Peter and Jeanne W. Ross. *IT Governance.* Boston: Harvard Business School Press, 2004.

Westerman, George and Richard Hunter. *IT Risk, Turning Business Threats into Competitive Advantage.* Boston: Harvard Business School Press, 2007.

Yarberry, Jr., William A. *Computer Telephony Integration,* 2nd ed. Boston, MA: Auerbach, 2002.

Index

A

ABC, *see* Activity-based costs
*Accounting and Financial Fundamentals for
          Nonfinancial Executives*, 62
Activity-based costs (ABCs), 155
Agile development, 69, 70, 78
American Institute of Certified Professional
          Accountants (AICPA), 29, 50
Anchoring effect, 187, 188
Application Services Library (ASL), 194

B

Backup encryption, 164
BCP, *see* Business continuity planning
BI, *see* Business intelligence
Big Switch, 198, 203
BISL, *see* Business Information Services
          Library
Black Swan, 164
BMC Configuration Management package,
          165
Boiling the IT Frog, 43, 129
Botnets (zombie networks), 162
BPML, *see* Business process markup language
Business continuity planning (BCP), 168
Business Information Services Library
          (BISL), 194
Business intelligence (BI), 140
Business intelligence and analytics, 139–159
     activity-based costs, 155
     analytical skills, 154
     bad data, 152
     bottom line, 158–159

business capability ratings, 153
business intelligence, selling, 140–145
business uses, survey of, 151–153
core components, 145
culture, 140
data quality, 151–153
data warehouse, 145–148
data warehouse alternative, 147
decision support systems, 147
democratic strategy, 140
descriptive statistics, 150
drivers for BI, 152
effective implementation, 153–158
     actual users, 158
     distribution of intelligence, 155–156
     organizational structure, 156
     roadblocks, 156–158
extract and transform process, 146
financial presentation, 142, 143, 144
fuzzy logic, 148
getting started, 140–145
hierarchy of activities, 149
in-line ETL processes, 145
intelligence distribution, 155
killer application, 157
known knowns, 139
predictive analytics and data mining,
          148–151
     data mining, 151
     predictive analytics, 150–151
routine decisions, 141
search-based BI, 148
security, 151–153
speed of delivery, 141
spreadmart, 157

317

system components, 146
unknown unknowns, 139
value proposition, 141
Business model
    development, 98–100
    enterprise architecture, 98–100
Business Objects, 154
Business process markup language (BPML),
        104
Business strategy exist, 16–19

C

CA Plex, 91
CAA, *see* Clean Air Act
Capital budget, example, 44–45
Capital spend form (CSF), 312
Career development, *see* Core skills and
        career development
CCA, *see* Clinger-Cohen Act
CCIE, *see* Cisco Certified Internetworking
        Expert
CEMEX, 121
Central office (CO), 300
Central processing unit (CPU), 110, 196, 204
CEO, *see* Chief executive officer
CERCLA, *see* Comprehensive Environmental
        Response, Compensation and
        Liability Act
Certified public accountants (CPAs), 181
CFO, *see* Chief financial officer
Change management, 32
    governance and, 32
    incident management and, 33
    operations framework, 195
    policy and direction, 288–289
    release management, 195
Chargeback, allure of, 56
Chief executive officer (CEO), 37, 101, 120
Chief financial officer (CFO), 101, 120
Chief information officer (CIO), 1, 37, *see also*
        CIO interviews
    considerations in using consultants, 186
    roles, 2–3
    success, information technology
        governance and, 15–16
    viruses, 11–12
        information cocooning, 11
        technology isolation, 12
        zealotry temptations, 12
Chief technology officer (CTO), 37

CICS, *see* Customer information control
        system
CIO interviews, 207–223
    anonymous CIO (West Coast utility),
        221–223
    David Finn (Texas Children's Hospital),
        208–211
    Dennis M. Klinger (Florida Power & Light
        Company), 211–215
    George Conklin (CHRISTUS Health),
        215–219
    Harold D. Bates (Community Resource
        Credit Union), 219–221
Cisco
    Certified Internetworking Expert (CCIE),
        282
    NAC appliance, 165
Citizen Soldier, 83
Clean Air Act (CAA), 271
Clean Water Act (CWA), 271
Clinger-Cohen Act (CCA), 55
Cloud computing, 198, 203
Cloudmark, 162
CO, *see* Central office
CobIT, *see* Control Objectives for IT
COBRA, *see* Consolidated Omnibus Budget
        Reconciliation Act
Code, *see* Good enough code, creation of
Cognos, 154
Cold standby, 304
Comprehensive Environmental Response,
        Compensation and Liability Act
        (CERCLA), 268, 269
Computer resource units (CRUs), 110
Consolidated Omnibus Budget Reconciliation
        Act (COBRA), 261
Consultants, effective use of, 185–191
    anchoring effect, 187, 188
    becoming skilled buyer of professional
        services, 185–187
    CIO's objective, 186–187
    consultant's objective, 186
    comments about consultants, 191
    defense tactics, 189–191
    defined schedule, 187
    emotional intelligence, 185
    knowledge transfer, 191
    matching interests, 187–189
    one-way surprises, 190
    scope limitation, 186

Control Objectives for IT (CobIT), 25, 46, 116, 132, 194
Core skills and career development, 1–13
  business orientation, 10
  career jumps, 3
  CIO roles, 2–3
  CIO viruses, 11–12
    information cocooning, 11
    technology isolation, 12
    zealotry temptations, 12
  education, 3, 10
  generations, 8–9
  likeability and income, 10
  magic "AND", 12
  no one is planning your career, 3–6
  order-taking mindset, 2
  profit margins, 10
  senior leadership club, 2
  strategic planning, 6–7
  technical expertise, 8
  weak ties, 11
  what affects compensation, 9–11
COSO criteria, 30
CPAs, *see* Certified public accountants
CPU, *see* Central processing unit
CRM, *see* Customer relationship management
CRUs, *see* Computer resource units
CSF, *see* Capital spend form
CTO, *see* Chief technology officer
Culture, business intelligence and, 140
Customer information control system (CICS), 16
Customer relationship management (CRM)
  software, 133
  system, 99
CWA, *see* Clean Water Act
Cybercrimes, 162

D

Data
  bad, 152
  encryption, mobile device, 165
  loss prevention systems, 164
  management, governance, 32–33
  mining, 109
    infrastructure for, 123
    predictive modeling and, 151
  quality, security and, 151
  warehouse, design of, 147

Data Warehousing Institute, 145
Database(s)
  administrators (DBAs), 90, 130
  design, 102
  snapshots of, 305
DataCenter administration, 197
DBAs, *see* Database administrators
Decision support systems (DSSs), 147
Demilitarized zone (DMZ), 167
Digital Deflation, 202
Disaster recovery (DR), 303
  application to be recovered, 304
  budget, 40, 43
  documentation, 282
  effect of downtime, 303
  4A model, 78, 79–80
  governance, 33
  offsite facility, 102
  outsourced, 130
  policy and direction, 302
Discharge monitoring reports (DMRs), 271
DMRs, *see* Discharge monitoring reports
DMZ, *see* Demilitarized zone
DoC, *see* U.S. Department of Commerce
DR, *see* Disaster recovery
DR Data Center, 304
DSSs, *see* Decision support systems

E

EA, *see* Enterprise architecture
Ebase Platform, 91
EDP, *see* Electronic data processing
Electronic data processing (EDP), 2
E-mail
  acceptable uses of, 302
  being careful with, 5–6
  blocking of, 164
  developer, 11
  MS Outlook/MS Exchange Server, 301
  rule, 170
  system, 301–302
Emergency Planning and Community Right to Know Act (EPCRA), 268, 272
Emotional intelligence
  consultant selection and, 185
  information technology governance and, 21
Endeca Technologies, 147
Enron
  mainframe systems, 110
  outsourcing deal, 54, 132

stock, 24
Telecom Director, 31
Enterprise architecture (EA), 95–118
  alignment, 98
  architectural maturity, 114–116
  business benefits, 102
  business drivers and selling of enterprise
      architecture, 100–101
  business model development, 98–100
  communicating with management and
      employees, 109–114
    enforcement and governance of EA,
      111–114
    outsourcing alternative, 110–111
    tools, 111
  compliance, 115
  consensus building, 99
  content management, 103
  database design, 102
  effective architecture, road map to,
      107–109
    business architecture, 107–108
    IT architecture, 108–109
  example concept, 117
  governance strategy, 113
  information architecture and process
      modeling perspective, 101–105
  ISO certification, 104
  MBWA, 99
  metrics, 102
  putting it all together, 116
  selling points, 100–110
  Six Sigma, 104
  starting points for development, 97
  team objectives, 107–108
  technical arhcitecture example contents,
      106
  technology architecture perspective,
      105–107
  telco billing debacle, 96
  toolkit features, 112–113
  top-down integration, 99
  transition from mainframe technology, 110
Enterprise Architecture as Strategy, 121
Enterprise Computing Institute, 194
Enterprise resource planning (ERP), 104
  business units on common platform, 7
  control, 228
  databases, 104
  full system restore, 310

security system, 29
staff skills levels, 282
EPCRA, *see* Emergency Planning and
      Community Right to Know Act
ERP, *see* Enterprise resource planning

F

FASB, *see* Financial Accounting Standards
      Board
Federal Enterprise Architecture Framework
      (FEAF), 111
Federal Insecticide, Fungicide and
      Rodenticide Act (FIFRA), 268
Fiberlink Communications, 165
FIFRA, *see* Federal Insecticide, Fungicide and
      Rodenticide
File wrapper, 276
Finance, *see* Information technology finance
Finance/accounting, due diligence checklist
      for, 258–259
Financial Accounting Standards Board
      (FASB), 51
Fooled by Randomness, 22
Foreign culture differences, 5
Futures, 201–206
  atomization of outsourcing, 203
  cloud computing, 203
  dependence of society on software, 202
  embedded systems, 205
  event-driven architecture, 205
  green mandate, 203
  mashups, 205
  nonlinear growth, 201
  retirement, 202
  smartphones, 204
  social networks, 203
  society and demographics, 202–203
  technology, 203–205
  virtualization, 204
  Web applications, 204
Fuzzy logic, 148
Fuzzy meter, 50

G

General Managers, The, 24
Generally accepted accounting principles
      (GAAP), 29, 275
Good enough code, creation of, 89–93

code reviews, 90
coding standards, importance of, 90
example guidelines, 91
factors influencing developer's
    productivity, 90
hiring good developers, 93
mentoring, 90
porting, 92–93
prima donnas, 90
prototypes, 91
release philosophy, 91–92
toolboxes, 91
value of good developer, 91
Governance, *see* Information technology
    governance
Governance grinder, 209
Graham Leachy, 97
Green mandate, 203

H

Health Insurance Portability and Account-
    ability Act (HIPAA), 97, 208
Help desk, 195
HIPAA, *see* Health Insurance Portability and
    Accountability Act
Homeland Security, creation of, 110
Hot standby, 305
HP's Opsware Server Automation System,
    165
Human resources, due diligence checklist for,
    260–263
Hyperion, 154

I

IBM, 104
    Rational Business Developer Extension, 91
    Rational Unified Process package, 73
IDS, *see* Intrusion detection system
IDS Scheer, 104
iGrafx, 104
IM, *see* Instant messaging
Incident management
    governance, 33
    structure, 195
Information cocooning, 11
Information technology (IT), 2, 119
    annual expense budget, example, 39–42
    controls testing, 26

integration, CIO responsibility for,
    124–127
investment, management of, 46–49
outsourcing, *see* Sourcing
outsourcing agreement, Enron's, 54
procurement
    detailed procedures, 48
    policies, 47
projects, general methodology for
    prioritizing, 21
staff training, governance, 34
vendor-specific training for, 182
Information technology application controls,
    key, examples of, 231–235
    accounts payable, 231, 232
    fixed assets, 232
    general accounting, 232
    inventory, 233
    payroll, 233
    purchasing, 233, 234
    revenue, 234, 235
Information technology finance, 37–62
    basic financial ratios, 58
    bloated costs, 52
    budget construction, 40–43
    budgeting, 38–40
    chargeback, 56–57
    contract management, 59–61
        contract repository system, 59
        contract review, 61
        copyright registrations, 61
        entity names, 59
        maintenance charges, 60
        quarter-end deals, 60
        self-audit, 60
        software contracts, 59
        vendor audit clauses, 60
        vendor contracts, 59
    cost management, 52–54
    example capital budget, 44–45
    example financial metrics for projects
        using Microsoft Excel, 49
    example IT annual expense budget, 39–42
    example telecom bill with recurring but
        unnecessary changes, 53
    fuzzy meter, 50
    gray areas and tilt, 54–56
    infrastructure investments, 43
    IT investment, management of, 46–49
    looking financially smart, 57–59

Microsoft Share Point, 59
off balance sheet hiring, 57
program management office, 40
quarter-end deals, 60
rate stability, 60
rational buying, 43–46
secret handshake, 59
smoothing the numbers, 38
SOP 98-1, 50–52
summary, 61–62
vendor contracts, 59
vendor invoices, 38
Information technology general controls, key,
    examples of, 225–229
acceptable use policy, 225
backup/operations, 225
change control, 226
information security, 227, 228
operations controls, 228
physical security, 228
segregation of duties, 228
systems development, 228, 229
Information technology governance, 15–35
actionable strategy, 16
alignment, 16
alignment tools, 19–24
    IT risk management, 23–24
    value delivery, 22–23
business strategy exist, 16–19
CIO success pills, 15–16
compliance, 24–31
demagoguery, 23
emotional intelligence, 21
example committee structure, 18
example techniques to improve alignment,
    17
Google search, 15
managing department with governance,
    32–34
    capacity management and planning,
        33–34
    change management, 32
    data management, 32–33
    disaster recovery and business
        continuity, 33
    incident management, 33
    infrastructure for analytics, 34
    merger and acquisitions methodology,
        33
    network management, 34

operational dashboards, 33
policies and procedures, 33
security, 32
systems development life cycle, 33
user training/IT staff training, 34
vendor management, 33
performance management, 31–32
prioritization, 19
resource management, 31
Sarbanes-Oxley compliance, steps to, 25–31
accounting system policies, 26
auditor opinion, 30
business interruptions, 26
CobIT, 25
COCO criteria, 30
computer program changes, 26
control breakdown, 28
environmental practices, 25
external auditor, 25
404 failure, 29
framework, 25
incompatible responsibilities, 26
Internal Audit tests, 27
IT controls testing, 26
key control categories, 25
key control failure, 27
material weakness, 29
physical security over IT assets, 26
significant deficiency, 29
systematic restore testing, 27
three way match, 28
Information Technology Infrastructure
    Library (ITIL), 165, 193
Information technology mergers and
    acquisitions, due diligence checklist
    for, 281–283
application architecture, 281
governance capabilities, 282
operational components, 282
platforms, 281–282
security, 282–283
skill levels of staff, 282
Information technology policies and direction,
    example, 285–313
backup of data, programs, and operating
    systems, 309
change management, 288–289
cold standby, 304
core code, 293

database security and administration,
   292–293
data retention and management, 306–308
   policy, 306–307
   procedures and description, 307–308
   purpose, 306
disaster recovery and business continuity,
   302–306
   application recovery process, 304
   disaster recovery planning and
      capability, 303–306
   policy and direction, 302–304
firewalls, 294–295
hardware and software purchase policy,
   311–312
   policy and direction, 311
   software, 311–312
help desk, 296
hot standby, 305
infrastructure standards, 298
   documentation and standards, 298
   high-level policies, 298
insurance, 310–311
intrusion detection, 294–295
IT architecture, 285–287
   infrastructure, 286–287
   policy and direction, 285
   technological direction, 286
IT budgeting and cost management, 312
IT governance, 310
IT human resources management, 313
messaging, 300–302
   e-mail system, 301–302
   policy and direction, 300–301
network operating system parameters,
   293–294
password monitoring, 290
performance and capacity, management of,
   297
physical security, 295
problem management, 296–297
project management, 295–296
   direction and goals, 296
   tools and methodologies, 296
restore testing, 309–310
   annual, 310
   quarterly, 309
routers, 294–295
security administration, 289–292
segregation of duties, 292

systems development life cycle, 297
telecommunications, management of,
   298–300
   connectivity standards, 300
   network management, 299
   network performance reporting, 300
   network reliability, 299
   telecommunications service levels,
      298
third-party services, management of, 297
uninterruptible power source, 308
warm standby, 304
Information technology risk assessment
      checklist, 247–255
   complexity of existing system, 248–249
   documentation of existing system, 249–250
   necessary resources, 253–254
   project definition, 250–251
   project management structure,
      effectiveness of, 252
   project size, 253–254
   sponsor support of system, 254–255
   structural impact, 247
   vulnerability of organization to system
      failure, 255
Instant messaging (IM), 9
Intellectual property, 121, 276–280
Intelligent grid, 222
Internal Audit, governance and, 214
Internal rate of return (IRR), 46
Internet protocol (IP) sharing, 61
Interviews, *see* CIO interviews
Intrusion detection system (IDS), 198
IP sharing, *see* Internet protocol sharing
IRR, *see* Internal rate of return
ISO certification, 104
IT Governance, 15
IT Governance Institute, 116
*IT Risk, Turning Business Threats into
      Competitive Advantage*, 23
ITIL, *see* Information Technology
      Infrastructure Library

J

Job
   scheduling, 196
   shadowing, 179

K

Key controls, *see* Information technology
      application controls, key, examples
      of; Information technology general
      controls, key, examples of
Key performance indicators (KPIs), 123
Knowledge management, training and,
      183–184
KPIs, *see* Key performance indicators

L

LANSA RDML language, 91
Legal, due diligence checklist for, 263–277
      corporate, 263–265
      environmental, 266–272
      litigation, 266
      real estate, 266
Light map, 9
Linux, 92

M

M&A, *see* Mergers and acquisitions
MACRS, *see* Modified Accelerated Cost
      Recovery System
Material safety data sheets (MSDSs), 268
Material weakness, 29
MBWA, 99, 223
Mega, 104
Mergers and acquisitions (M&A), 119–128
      alpha male, 128
      best-of-breed systems, 126
      CEMEX, 121
      Chainsaw Al approach, 124
      CIO's golden opportunity, 120
      CIO's responsibilities, 120–127
            due diligence, 120–124
            IT integration, 124–127
      culture change, 125
      due diligence checklist, 122
      governance, 122
      intellectual property, 121
      key performance indicators, 123
      methodology, governance, 33
      success factors, 128
      USSR, 119
Mergers and acquisitions (business), due
      diligence checklist for, 257–280
      finance/accounting, 258–259

      human resources, 260–263
      intellectual property, 276–280
      legal/corporate, 263–265
      legal/environmental, 266–272
      legal/litigation, 266
      legal/real estate, 266
      operations, 257–258
      risk management/insurance, 259–260
      tax, 272–276
Mergers and acquisitions (IT), due diligence
      checklist for, 281–283
      application architecture, 281
      governance capabilities, 282
      operational components, 282
      platforms, 281–282
      security, 282–283
      skill levels of staff, 282
Microsoft, 12, 104
      COM+ runtime services for APIs, 109
      Excel, 49
      Exchange Server, 301
      Operations Framework, 194
      Outlook, 181, 301
      Project, 75, 76
      Share Point, 59, 156
      SQL Server, 157
      Visual Studio, 91
Model
      business
            development, 98–100
            enterprise architecture, 98–100
      DoC, 114
      predictive analytics, 150
      project management
            agile methodologies, 68–70
            informal approach, 65–67
            out of scope/embedded project, 73
            rapid prototyping/rapid application
                  development, 68
            rational unified process, 71–73
            traditional approach, 67–68
      project risk assessment, 76–78
      rational unified process, 72
      Zachman, 104, 111
Modified Accelerated Cost Recovery System
      (MACRS), 55
MSDSs, *see* Material safety data sheets
Mythical Man-Month, The, 63

N

NAC, *see* Network Access Control
National Pollutant Discharge Elimination
      System (NPDES) permits, 271
National Security Agency (NSA), 166
NCC, *see* Network Control Center
NCI Building Systems, 30, 57, 121, 126, 127,
      141, 174
NDAs, *see* Nondisclosure agreements
Net present value (NPV), 46
NetBeans, 91
Network
    administration, 197
    management, governance, 34
    operating system parameters, 293–294
    performance reporting and, 300
    zombie, 162
Network Access Control (NAC), 167
Network Control Center (NCC), 299
New CIO Leader, The, 19
Nondisclosure agreements (NDAs), 61
NPDES permits, *see* National Pollutant
      Discharge Elimination System
      permits
NPV, *see* Net present value
NSA, *see* National Security Agency

O

Occupational Safety and Health
      Administration (OSHA), 261, 271
Off balance sheet hiring, 57
On-boarding process, 196
Oops factor, 47, 68
OpenROAD, 91
Operating system (OS), 293
Operations, 193–199
    capacity management, service levels,
      availability, job scheduling,
      195–196
    change management, 195
    configuration management, 194–195
    cloud computing, 198–199
    common-sense approaches, 197–198
    day-to-day management, 197
    discipline, 199
    expression of creativity, 193
    first step, 193
    help desk, incident and problem
      management, 195

    job scheduling, 196
    management frameworks, 193–194
    on-boarding process, 196
    release management, 195
    resource usage, 197
    utility computing, 198
    VAL IT, 194
    workload management, 196
Oracle, 92
    Applications development, 85
    On-Demand ERP software, 109
OS, *see* Operating system
OSHA, *see* Occupational Safety and Health
      Administration
Outsourcing, *see also* Sourcing
    agreement, Enron's, 54
    alternative, 110
    atomization of, 203
    culture, 131
    decision factors, 212
    pendulum of opinion on, 129
    pros and cons, 130
    rifle shot philosophy, 213

P

PA, *see* Predictive analytics
Password monitoring, 290
Payment card industry (PCI), 106
PCI, *see* Payment card industry
Phishing scams, 162
Plain old telephone service (POTS), 300
PMI, *see* Project Management Institute
PMO, *see* Program management office
Porting, risk profile, 92
POTS, *see* Plain old telephone service
Predictive analytics (PA), 149
Predictive modeling, data mining and, 151
Problem management, 195
Proforma, 104
Program management office (PMO), 40, 63, 64
    dilemma of, 81–83
    function, 84
    mergers and acquisitions, 125
    strategy, 83
Project management, 63–87
    agile methodology, 69, 70, 78
    brain cycles, 86
    connections, 75
    consultants and, 190
    core features of successful projects, 73–74

eCommerce application development
 project, 64
flexibility, 85
4A model, 78, 79–80
future of project management, 86
job scope, 81–83
late project, vicious circles of, 74
life-cycle steps, 77
metrics, 82
practitioner's perspective, 83–86
program management office, 63, 64
 dilemma, 81–83
 function, 84
 operational tasks, 77
 strategy, 83
project dynamics, 73–81
 project risk assessment, 76–81
 reasons for project failure, 73–74
 work planning, 75–76
project organization, 64
public programs, 67
rapid application development, 68
rational unified process, 71, 72
risk analysis output, 82
scope creep, 83
Scrum project flow, 69, 71
Standish Group CHAOS report, 63
systems development methodologies,
 65–73
 agile methodologies, 68–70
 informal approach, 65–67
 out of scope/embedded project, 73
 rapid prototyping/rapid application
 development, 68
 rational unified process, 71–73
 traditional approach, 67–68
 waterfall method, 67–68
Project management artifact examples,
 237–245
 business requirements overview, 243–244
 acceptance criteria, 244
 business process, 244
 constraints and assumptions, 244
 definitions and acronyms, 244
 documentation requirements, 244
 examples, 244
 existing processes, 243
 functional detail, 244
 functional requirements, 244
 introduction/business case, 243
 required processes, 243

 usability requirements, 244
 user community, 244
 contents, 238, 243
 document control, 242
 change record, 242
 distribution, 242
 open and closed issues for deliverable, 245
 closed issues, 245
 open issues, 245
 project charter, 237
 purpose, 238–241
 constraints and assumptions, 240–241
 deliverables, 239
 project objectives, 238
 project organization, 239–240
 project overview, 238
 project scope, 238
 summary schedule, 240
 requirements document, 242
 technical detail, 244–245
 data requirements, 244
 performance requirements, 245
 scalability requirements, 245
 security requirements, 245
 technical requirements, 244
Project Management Institute (PMI), 295
Public Switched Telecommunication Network
 (PSTN), 299

Q

Quarter-end deals, 60

R

RAD, *see* Rapid application development
Radiofrequency identification (RFID), 177,
 205
Rapid application development (RAD), 68
Rational unified process (RUP), 71, 72
RCRA, *see* Resource Conservation and
 Recovery Act
Release management, 195
Request for proposal (RFP)
 information technology finance, 46
 telecommunications delivery and, 287
Resource Conservation and Recovery Act
 (RCRA), 268, 269
Restore testing, 309–310
 annual, 310
 quarterly, 309

Retail
  management, 109
  outlet, 123
  system, Web-based, 68
Return on investment (ROI), 2, 18, 38, 212
RFID, *see* Radiofrequency identification
RFP, *see* Request for proposal
Risk management/insurance, due diligence
      checklist for, 259–260
Robertson Ceco Corporation, 121
ROI, *see* Return on investment
RUP, *see* Rational unified process
Russian mafia, 169

S

SANs, *see* Storage area networks
Sarbanes-Oxley (SOX), 25, 97, 174, 214
Sarbanes-Oxley compliance, steps to, 25–31
  accounting system policies, 26
  auditor opinion, 30
  business interruptions, 26
  CobIT, 25
  COCO criteria, 30
  computer program changes, 26
  control breakdown, 28
  entity-level questions, 26
  environmental practices, 25
  example remediation work-paper entry, 28
  external auditor, 25
  404 failure, 29
  framework, 25
  incompatible responsibilities, 26
  Internal Audit tests, 27
  IT controls testing, 26
  key control categories, 25
  key control failure, 27
  material weakness, 29
  physical security over IT assets, 26
  restore testing, 27
  significant deficiency, 29
  systematic restore testing, 27
  three way match, 28
School for Scandal, The, 47
Script kiddies, 169
Scrum project flow, 69, 71
SDLC, *see* Systems development life cycle
Secure Logix, 166
Security, 161–177
  air layer isolation, 172
  authentication, 173

  backup encryption, 164
  benchmarking, 167–168
  biometrics, 173
  botnets, 162
  budget, 163
  checklist for building security, 167–168
  comments from security practitioners,
      168–176
  cybercrimes, 162
  data quality and, 151
  defense in depth, 162–163
  e-mail rule, 170
  firewalls, 164
  money, 162
  phishing scams, 162
  privacy and, 210
  script kiddies, 162
  social issues, 173
  sources of risk, 162
  telephone security, 166–167
  theft of assets, 169
  tools and automation processes, 164–165
  tools and defense automation, 163–166
  viruses with planned obsolescence, 169
  zombie network, 162
Segregation of duties (SOD), 174, 175, 228, 289
Service-level agreement (SLA), 287
  allocated resources and, 196
  network performance reporting and, 300
  telecommunications delivery and, 287
  vendor management and, 33
Service-oriented architecture (SOA), 105, 106,
      131, 205, 223
Shadow knowledge, 183
Siebel CRM OnDemand, 113
Silo knowledge, 182–183
Six Sigma, 104, 212
SLA, *see* Service-level agreement
Smart Enough Systems, 141
Smartphones, 204
SOA, *see* Service-oriented architecture
SOD, *see* Segregation of duties
Solaris, 282
SOP 98-1, 50–52
SOP-98 standard, 4, 50
Sourcing, 129–137
  ADP, 133
  con (customer's perspective), 131–133
  Control Objectives for IT, 132
  customer relationship management
      software, 133

Enron outsourcing deal, 132
manufacturing system, 134–135
maturity meter, 135
outsourcing, 133–134
pendulum of opinion, 129–130
pro (provider's perspective), 130
pros and cons, traditional, 130–133
rifle shot philosophy, 213
Xshoring, 134–137
    keeping Xshoring and sourcing in
        perspective, 136–137
    proximity factor, 135–136
    sourcing is more than IT services, 137
SOX, *see* Sarbanes-Oxley
Spill Prevention Control and Countermeasure
    (SPCC) plans, 267
Storage area networks (SANs), 295
Systems development life cycle (SDLC)
    enterprise architecture, 114
    governance, 33, 122
    guidelines, 171
    process, documentation, 282
    production deployments, 287
    XYZ Corp, 297
Systems development methodology, example,
    66

T

Tax, due diligence checklist for, 272–276
TCO, *see* Total cost of ownership
Technology isolation, 12
Telecommunications, management of,
    298–300
    connectivity standards, 300
    network management, 299
    network performance reporting, 300
    network reliability, 299
    telecommunications service levels, 298
Telecommunications Act of 1996, 96
Telelogic, 104
Thirty Methods of Influence, 63
Time-sharing operation (TSO), 54, 110, 132
Total cost of ownership (TCO), 287
Toxic Substance Control Act (TSCA), 268, 270
Training, 179–184
    amount of training needed, 181–182
    e-learning, 181
    institutionalized, 180

job shadowing, 179
knowledge management, 183–184
learning process,179
payback, 181
risks of informal training, 179–180
seminars or vendor-specific training for IT,
    182
shadow knowledge, 183
silo knowledge, harsh punishment of,
    182–183
tools, 180–181
user needs, 181
TSCA, *see* Toxic Substance Control Act
TSO, *see* Time-sharing operation

U

UAT, *see* User acceptance testing
UML, *see* Unified Modeling Language
Unified Modeling Language (UML), 71
Uninterruptible power source, 308
Unity Project, 218
Unix, 92, 282
U.S. Department of Commerce (DoC), 114
User acceptance testing (UAT), 32, 289
Utility computing, 198

V

VAL IT, 194
Value delivery, 22
VBA, *see* Visual basic for applications
Vendor(s)
    audit clauses, 60
    contracts, 59
    invoices, 38
    management, governance, 33
    -specific training, IT, 182
    treatment of, 5
Virtualization, 204
Visual basic for applications (VBA), 157
Voice over IP/IP telephony, 166

W

Wal-Mart infrastructure hardware purchases,
    287
Warm standby, 304

Weak ties, 11
Web
    applications, as desktop applications, 204
    -based retail system, 68
    browsers, HTML enabled, 156
Wikkis, 203
Windows, 282
Windows XP, guide for securing, 166
Workday HR software, 109
Workload management, 196
World Is Flat, The, 134

X

Xshoring, 134–137
    keeping in perspective, 136–137
    more than IT services, 137
    proximity factor, 135–136

Z

Zachman model, 104, 111
Zealotry temptations, 12
Zombie network, 162

T - #0099 - 101024 - C0 - 234/156/19 [21] - CB - 9781420064605 - Gloss Lamination